How to Buy and Build a House in Thailand

Philip Bryce

PAIBOON

PP

PUBLISHING

Paiboon Publishing
582 Nawamin 90 (Sukha 1)
Bungkum, Bangkok 10230
THAILAND
Tel 662-509-8632
Fax 662-519-5437

Paiboon Publishing
PMB 256, 1442A Walnut Street
Berkeley, California 94709
USA
Tel 1-510-848-7086
Fax 1-510-666-8862

สำนักพิมพ์ไพบูลย์

582 ถ. นวมินทร์ 90 (สุขาภิบาล 1)

เขตบึงกุ่ม ก.ท.ม. 10230

โทรศัพท์ 662-509-8632

โทรสาร 662-519-5437

info@paiboonpublishing.com
www.paiboonpublishing.com

Cover and graphic design by Gordon Morton

ISBN 1-887521-71-2

Table of Contents

Introduction

Who is this book for and how will it help?

This book is for foreigners (and Thai people too!) who are contemplating or are currently buying land and/or building a house in Thailand. It may also be of interest to current home owners or people buying a condo or other real estate. I use the word "house" to mean any small structure, whether house, bungalow, restaurant, etc. This book does not address large commercial buildings.

This book will help you understand the intricacies of Thailand land titles, purchase contracts, and other foreign ownership options. It will help you navigate your way through the building process ensuring that you get the best value for your baht, protect your investment and remain sane!

The book is targeted at a would-be home owner with a modest knowledge of building techniques. It will also be helpful to anyone, from experienced builder to anyone who has never held a hammer before. The success of your house building project will depend largely on the amount of effort you put into it. Like the saying goes, "if you want something done right, do it yourself".

Thai builders are often very skillful and quite ingenious at doing things with very primitive tools. They are use to doing things the Thai way, which is usually not to the standard we are used to in Europe and America. This book is designed to help you get the best house for your baht; a place that is structurally sound and you will be happy with.

Each chapter includes useful English/Thai words and phrases specific to land deals, legal issues, contracts, building techniques, materials and tools, etc. This book also includes checklists to take the guess work out of building project management.

Some things in this book are so important you would be crazy to ignore them. That's why they are written in bold typeface.

This book is organized in roughly the same sequence you would build a house in. However, I suggest you read the whole book prior to buying land and starting the building process to get the benefit of all the information.

What is and isn't this book about?

This book is a collection of information and opinion about the legalities of buying and leasing land, land titles and the techniques, materials and tools commonly used to build houses in Thailand. If is not a legal reference book, or a construction reference book.

This book aims to educate the reader about must know information and how things are done differently in Thailand to the way they are done back home, and what you can do about it! "Building is building" you may say, why do I need to have a book about building in Thailand? Materials, tools and techniques are different here from what you are used to back home. Your land and house in Thailand may be the last big investment of your life; you owe it to yourself to protect your investment.

I am not saying that Thai people do not know how to build houses or that the farang (western) way is always better. This book offers advice and proposes a better way to do some things. I find Thai builders very eager to learn new techniques provided they understand what the benefits are and how to do it. For a little extra effort, it is possible to get a far better house; this book aims to show you and your builder how. However, please be aware that once you commit to doing things differently, it's up to you to follow through. If you plan to follow the building advice in this book, you or your project manager will need to help your builder understand what you want and how to do it. This book will help, but it will take effort and diligence on your part to see it through.

For a comprehensive book on building techniques, I recommend "Building Construction Illustrated" by Francis D. K. Chiang and Cassandra Adams, which is also available in Thai at Se-Ed bookstores (usually found in Tesco Lotus).

Romanization of Thai language

This book is not primarily intended as a Thai language teaching book but it will help in your overall Thai speaking and will definitely help in your knowledge of building related words and phrases and in communications with your builders and suppliers.

Since few people know how to pronounce the phonetic alphabet, I have opted not to use it. I use a format similar to that used in http://thai-language.com/ for English-Thai translations and transliteration of words and phrases. thai-language.com is a wonderful, free resource for the Thai language. It has a very extensive English/Thai dictionary and phrase book. I also like search feature; enter an English keyword and you will not only get its translation, but many example sentences based around the word.

Thai is a tonal language; there are 5 tones in Thai which are indicated in this book using the superscripted letters 'L', 'H', 'F' and 'R':

	No mark, mid tone
New ใหม่ mai^L	Low tone
Wood ไม้ maai^H	High tone
Burn ไหม้ mai^F	Falling tone (start high, then lower the pitch)
A question ไหม mai^R	Rising tone (start low, then raise the pitch like asking a question)

Tones are probably the hardest thing about the Thai language for English speakers. Where bad use of tone will be extra confusing for Thais to understand, for example, "lek^L" low tone is steel and "lek^H" high tone is small, I will include translations of similar sounding words. You can listen to proper pronunciations on the buildingthailand.com website.

Thai language, classifiers and containers

In English, we would say "5 sheets of plywood". "Sheets" is called a classifier, and unlike in English where it is used occasionally, every Thai proper noun has a classifier. The classifier should be used when talking about the number of, or size of things, etc. It would be very bad English to say "I would like 3 plywoods", you would say "I would like 5 sheets of plywood". In Thai, "dtaawng gaan 3 maai at" would not be understood at all, you would have to say "dtaawng gaan maai at 3 phaaen". Often, the noun is dropped completely and only the classifier is used, so it is essential you get used to the classifiers for common nouns.

Classifiers are based on the shape, size and composition of the object; here are the common ones you will need for building materials:

อัน an   small objects: sanding belts, paint brushes.

ตัว dtuaa   misc wood, 2x4, 2x6, etc, screws, nuts, bolts, drill bits,

                                electric receptacles (plugs), pipe connectors (but not
                                pipes), chairs, tables (but not sets), tools, stair treads,
                                fans, door handles, hinges. If in doubt, use dtuaa.

เส้น sen[F]   pipes or tubes: water pipe, etc.

บาน baan   doors, windows, mirrors

หลอด loort[L]   light bulbs, tubes of glue

ต้น dtohn[F]   vertical post: trees, columns

แผ่น phaaen[L]   sheets, flat, thin objects: plywood, sandpaper sheets,

                                tiles, sheets of glass, floor mats

ห้อง hong[F]   rooms

ชั้น chan   floors (levels)

หลัง lang[R]   houses

หลัง khon   people

ท่อน thaawn[F]   logs

กระป๋อง gra[L]-bpong[R] cans: of paint, of glue, etc

ชุด chut[H]   sets of things: fan with lights, toilets, sinks, shower units,

                                table and chair set, etc

ก้อน goorn[F]   bricks

หลุม lum[R]   big holes: hole for footing, swimming pool, etc

รู ruu   small holes: hole for screw, bolt, etc

ถุง tung[R]   bags: bags of cement, etc

ใบ bai   round objects and thin sheets: saw blades, paper (not sandpaper)

One thing that continues to confuse and annoy me about Thai transliteration, and this is also true of Thai writing, is that most Thais, with the possible exception of news readers, almost always pronounce 'r' like 'l' or not at all. "a-rai" is almost always pronounced, "a-lai", "thao-rai" is almost always pronounced, "thao-lai". I often think it would be more helpful to transliterate the way it sounds in real life, not the way it sounds on language teaching tapes. However, I'm going with convention and transliterating with an 'r', not an 'l'.

To speak Thai politely, you should always end a request and optionally any sentence with khrap (male speaker), but more commonly and less embarrassingly pronounced khap, or ka (female speaker). I don't add khap and ka in this book; that is up to you.

Just as some building terminology is different between British English and American English, so is it sometimes different between Thai Thai and Lao Thai. The source of some of the Thai translations in this book speaks Lao Thai and my builder is from the south so you may find the origin of some of the Thai building terms in this book are a bit schizophrenic!

Also, since builders in much of Thailand are from Esaan (or maybe Burma), it's not a bad idea to learn a little Esaan men bor.

Research and accuracy of information

This book was compiled from numerous sources, including my experience, my lawyer, my builder, land and building professionals in Thailand, other farang land/home owners and information from the internet. This book represents a collection of information and opinion. **This book has been researched well BUT IT MAY BE WRONG!!!** Consider this food for thought, not the definitive reference book!

Please check the Thailand Land and Building Forum at www.buildingthailand.com/forums for important corrections and updates.

I have no legal training of any kind at all, so all of the legal opinion in this book is only that, opinion. I strongly urge you to check everything regarding land titles, purchase options, contracts, etc. with your own lawyer.

The author, publisher and buildingthailand.com do not under any circumstance warrant or guarantee the accuracy of information or opinion in this book. The author, publisher, and buildingthailand.com do not assume any responsibility or liability resulting from information or opinion expressed in this book. Like everything else in Thailand, **double check everything**!

Thai friend

Maybe others would disagree, but I think it would be almost impossible to build a house in Thailand without the assistance of a close Thai friend who is totally committed to the project. Even if you speak Thai very well, there are going to be occasions, probably every day, where only a Thai person can deal with a situation.

Even though I speak some Thai and my builder speaks some English, I could not have built my house without my girlfriend's help. She dealt with the land office, the water and electricity people; helped in countless ways ordering doors and windows, custom steel work, tile, etc; much of it on the telephone where I am useless at Thai.

Why buy land and build a house in Thailand and what are the risks?

Thailand is a beautiful country with wonderful people, a pleasant climate (except for April, phew!); has a stable government and economy and is reasonably foreigner friendly as far as buying/leasing land and setting up home is concerned.

In most parts of the country, it is inexpensive for Americans and Europeans to buy land, build a house and live here compared to a typical retirement destination such as Florida or France. Also, many people build to rent or as an investment.

However, there are numerous potential pitfalls that the prospective land/house buyer must be aware of; the biggest is that foreigners can not directly own land in Thailand in their own name.

Thailand is still largely a rural based economy and country. The richer Thai's with nice houses tend to live in Bangkok or other big cities and the people in the countryside are often poor farmers and hand craft workers (or these days builders or connected to the tourist industry). With the exception of already heavily developed areas like Bangkok, Phuket, Pattaya, Ko Samui, etc. it is likely you would not be able to find a Thai house in the countryside to meet your needs. However, in rural areas, there is usually plenty of land available at very reasonable prices, with spectacular views, which makes buying land and building a house in Thailand so attractive and exciting to farangs.

"It's so cheap to rent here, why buy?" That's a good question and maybe after reading this book you will think buying sounds like lot of trouble, renting is fine! I chose to build because I could not find a house that I wanted to rent long term in Ko Phangan, and even if I did, I am sure it would be very expensive. I hope that my investment will appreciate in value and I plan to rent out the house.

But there are significant risks to buying and leasing land and investing in Thailand, and any prospective buyer must be aware of the risk and be willing to take a chance that in the worst case, you may loose everything! The Thai legal system does not exist for the benefit or foreigners, land disputes and fake documents are common, relationships, even long term ones, often end in dispute.

About the author

Philip Bryce is a computer software engineer by trade but has owned and renovated old houses in America for the last 20 years and has personally designed and built numerous structures and additions including attic, kitchen and bathroom conversions, garage, deck, re-roof, re-wire, re-plumb, foundation upgrade, etc, etc, etc.

I have lived in Thailand since 2004 and personally supervised the building of my house. I purchased the land through my company but recently changed ownership to my wife.

My wife and has no building background, but has learned about building very quickly and has been of invaluable help in this project. She has translated the Thai language portions of this book.

In much of the text of this book I assume you are male and you have a Thai mate. I apologize to any reader that does not fit the profile.

Since most of my building experience is from America, I primarily talk about American building techniques and use American building terminology in this book. If there are differences, I will often add the English word in parentheses.

Section 1: Land, laws and preparing to build

Chapter 1

Buying and leasing land and house

Can foreigners own land in Thailand?

The first question everyone asks when thinking about buying land and building a house in this paradise we call the Land of Smiles is "can foreigners own land in Thailand"? The direct answer, unfortunately, is no, but there are ways we can legally secure the right to use land and build a house.

There are two preferred ways to "own" land in Thailand, 1) buy the land in the name of a Thai person, usually your mate or someone you think you can trust, then lease it back for 30 years with an option to extend; 2) start a Thai company in which you can own up to 49% of the shares and buy and own land through the company.

30 year lease with option to extend

The simplest way to "own " land in Thailand is to buy the land in the name of a Thai citizen and lease it back from them for 30 years with option to renew. By simplest, I mean cheapest and quickest. The Thai citizen has their name on the title deed for the land, which means THEY OWN THE LAND, NOT YOU. However, at the time of the purchase you enter into a separate agreement with the new land owner to lease back the land for 30 years with an option to extend for another 30.

Many real estate companies will attempt to convince you land can be leased with up to 3 continuous 30 years leases, a guaranteed total lease of 90 years. There is no provision in the Civil and Commercial Code for continuous leases. The least MUST be renewed after each 30 year period. Section 540 Civil and Commercial

Code: *'The duration of a hire of immovable property cannot exceed thirty years. If it is made for a longer period, such period shall be reduced to thirty years. The aforesaid period may be renewed, but it must not exceed thirty years from the time of renewal'*.

Any lease over 3 years must be registered at the Amphur (district office) and there will be a 1.5% fee for registration and stamp duty. Also the lease value will be considered taxable income of the Thai owner.

The lease agreement can specify any terms you want such as the lease amount, what happens in the event of your death or the death of the real owner, what happens if you want to sell the property, etc. Your lawyer should also add that if the laws change to allow foreign ownership of land, the land title will be transferred to you.

If your relationship with the land owner becomes uncooperative, you may have problems with the lease extension. Thai courts have found lease extensions to be a legally binding, contractual matter between the parties involved, but you may have to go to court to enforce the contract and Thai courts are not known for their sympathy towards farangs. The conditions of the lease extension, such as price, taxes, registrations fees etc, should be specified in the lease contract but the option to extend the lease cannot be registered at the land office.

The lease will survives the death of the land owner and transfer to their heirs, or transfer of the land ownership to another party, but you may find the new owners uncooperative and unwilling to extend the lease.

Supreme Court Judgment 6763/ 1998; *'In case the lessor promises in the lease agreement to extent or renew the lease term, but has sold the leased land before the lessee was entitled to accept, the 'contractual rights' are not binding upon the new owner and only lease rights that are 'real rights' will transfer to the new owner'*.

Your lease should allow for sub leasing. If in the future, you want to sell, and you don't have the support of the land owner, you can sell a sub lease on the land, plus the house. However, you will probably not get the same price as if it was freehold land and house.

If your Thai wife is buying the land, you have to sign a document stating that the money did not come from abroad and that the property is the separate property of your wife and that you acknowledge that you have absolutely no rights or interest in the property. This is significant in case of divorce.

One additional protection for the leaseholder is to hold physical possession of the title deed (Nor Sor 3 or Chanoht). Without the original title document, the land owner would be unable to transfer the land to another party, borrow against it or make other agreements using the land as collateral.

Here is an example of a lease agreement. **This example is for information only and should not be used as an actual lease agreement**. Please have your lawyer draft your lease agreement.

LEASE   AGREEMENT
AGREEMENT   MADE   AT_____
DATE_____

This Lease Agreement is between_____ hereafter known as the Lessor and
_____ hereafter known as the lessee.

It is hereby agreed as follows.

1. The Lessor agrees to lease and the Lessee agrees to rent land located at _____ in accordance to Land Title Deed No. _____ Land Number _____

Book   number   _____   Page   number   _____
Tambon   _____   Total   Land   Size   _____Sq   Wah
hereinafter known as the "Said Premises" for a rent period of 30 years.

2. The Lessee agrees to a one time advance payment for the entire rent period in the amount of _____ Baht (_____) to the Lessor on the date of this Agreement. The Lessor and the Lessee agree to register the leasing terms and conditions at the District Land Office within 7 days after making this agreement. The rent begins on the date of registration at the District Land Office.

3. Both parties agree that the Lessee shall have an option to renew this lease for an additional 30 years, for rental terms and conditions as mutually agreed by both parties.

4. After the date of this agreement the Lessee shall have the right to live in and conduct legal and socially acceptable businesses in the Said Premises during the term of this Lease Agreement.

5. The Lessee agrees to take care of and to preserve the Said Premises as one would do to his/her own and maintain the upkeep of and also attend to repairs of the Said Premises which may be caused by accidental or intentional actions of the Lessee or the Lessee,s subordinates.

6. The Lessee may assign or sublet the Said Premises to other Parties. Should there be the need to make official registration or other legal proceedings, the Lessor agrees to give consent and to assist the Lessee in providing proper documentation and shall not ask for any returns from the Lessee. The Lessee agrees to pay for any fee and other expenses that may arise from such proceedings.

7. The Lessee agrees not to damage or deface the Said Premises or make structural alterations or additions thereto without the written consent in writing of the Lessor and all structural alterations shall be in accordance with government and municipal guidelines. The Lessee agrees to pay any costs involved while the Lessor agrees to provide necessary documentation in obtaining such official permits.

8. Should the Lessor wish to sell the Said Premises, the Lessee shall have the first option to purchase from the Lessor or the option to find another party to purchase from the Lessor. Should the Lessee be unable to find such party to purchase from the Lessor the Lessor may sell Said Premises as he/she so wishes. The Said Premises shall not be sold or Title transferred during the Lease period. Debts accrued by the Lessor to outside parties shall not effect the lease terms.

9. Should Thai laws allow non-Thai citizens to purchase properties, the Lessor shall give the first right to purchase the Said Properties to the Lessee as a special condition.

10. The terms and conditions of this Lease Agreement obligate the heirs of both parties to fulfill to the letter and shall not be altered without mutual consent.

11. The Lessee shall be responsible for paying Building Tax (Rong Ruen Tax) and Land Tax for the duration of the lease period.

12. Should the Lessor be unable to carry out the terms and conditions stated above the Lessee has the right to ask for compensation five times the rent amount and the special condition amount that the Lessee has prepaid.

13 In the event of the Lessee's untimely death while the Lease Agreement is still in effect, the rights and obligations of the Lessor shall be transferred to_____

Both parties having read and fully understanding its contents, agree to comply with all the terms and conditions. Therefore both parties have hereunder affixed their signatures in presence of two witnesses on the date at the place first written   above.

_____The Lessor

_____The Lessee

_____Witness

_____Witness

Create a majority Thai owned company

The following information was originally written before May 15th, 2006. On that date the Thai government issued a directive to all land offices that effectively made the "company method" of buying land significantly more complicated, if not impossible. The information is for reference but should no longer be considered a viable method for buying land.

A more complicated and expensive way to buy land, but one in which you have your name as a registered owner, is to start a majority Thai owned company, in which you can own up to 49% of the shares (but the majority of the voting rights), and 6 or more people own the remaining 51% or more shares. There must be more Thai shareholders than foreign shareholders and a minimum of 7 shareholders who must be at least 18 years old. The company is legally able to buy and sell land and hold a mortgage, same as a Thai individual.

Several years ago, if a company was more than 40% foreign owned, the Central Land Office in Bangkok would investigate to check that is was not created for the sole purpose of circumventing the law against foreign ownership of land. For that reason, most lawyers recommended your company had only 39% foreign ownership to 61% Thai ownership. That law was repealed in 2003 but you may still consider it wise to limit foreign ownership as an extra safeguard.

The Thai shareholders must own a minimum of 51% of the shares jointly but the amount that each share holder owns is at the discretion of the company. If one or more of the shareholders are trusted family or friends, the company can allocated the majority of the 51% Thai owned shares to them and as little as 1 share each to the other shareholders. This may be a useful protection should your company ever be liquidated, declare a dividend or be forced to close down and dispose of the assets (see below). However, if your spouse is one of the shareholders and has the last name as you, the land department may consider the sum of yours and your spouses shares as community assets of the marriage and therefore, foreign controlled, and refuse to register land transfers to the company. Apparently, there is no problem transferring shares to your spouse after land transfers are complete.

To set up a Thai company usually costs about 10-30,000 baht plus an annual tax and accounting fee of about 15,000 baht. Typically your lawyer will have the names of several Thai citizens who will provide their names on share certificates, photocopy of their id cards and pre-signed share transfer documents.

If a company is liquidated, the assets will be divided amongst the share solders in proportion to the number of shares held. However, the split ratio will be more complicated if there is a preference/ordinary share structure, so please check with your lawyer how assets will be split if the company in liquidated.

If you build a house on land purchased by a company, officially the house will be your office or place of business. On any official document referring to buildings on land purchased by a company, it should use the word "office" or some other word indicating business premises, not house.

Another benefit of the company method is you can get a work permit through your own company which is necessary if you intend to work for your own company and run the company as an active business. By active business, I mean one that has real cash flow, makes a profit and pays taxes. Inactive companies, ones that simply own land but have not significant ongoing financial transactions, are not advisable because they may be considered illegal by the government.

When your lawyer sets up your company, you will get about 15 pages of official documentation in Thai. You may also want to get the English equivalent of each page. You will also get a company stamp. You will likely need copies of every Thai page plus the stamp for any action involving the company including setting up a bank account, buying land, getting a visa, tabien baan, electricity, water, etc. so save yourself a lot of time and make several copies of the company documents and keep the originals in a safe place.

For additional information about companies in Thailand, please see http://www.dbd.go.th/eng/law/fba_e1999.phtml

Note however that all shareholders, including Thai shareholders, are required to be real investors in the business, not simply nominees, i.e. people who supply their names and ID cards for the purpose of assisting the setup of a company. Until recently, this rule was rarely enforced and many companies were formed using nominee shareholders who in reality paid nothing for their shares and had no knowledge of the business activities. On May 15, 2006[1], the Thai government issued a directive to all land offices that they must scrutinize all shareholders of any company attempting to register land to verify the shareholders have paid their share of the capital investment and that they are "qualified" to be investors. Following this directive, many companies attempting to buy land where refused by local land offices throughout Thailand, effectively closing a loop hole that many foreigners had used to effectively buy land.

In response to the government crackdown on companies with any foreign ownership, owning land in Thailand, lawyers and real estate companies have invented more complex and devious schemes to attempt to circumvent the law. One such scheme is to create two companies, the first company is 100% Thai owned (including real Thai shareholders and Thai company shareholders) and therefore in principal can buy land without being scrutinized by the land office. The second company is 49% foreign owned and majority controlled as described above. The second company owns controlling interest in the first (land holding) company therefore effectively controlling the land ownership. This method is a fairly transparent attempt to circumvent the law and also expensive to set up and maintain (two sets of company setup, accounting and taxes).

Another method I have read about is to have the company 100% real Thai shareholders at the time of land purchase, and then transfer majority control to a foreigner after the transfer paperwork is complete. The land office has announced they will check that companies owning land are still 100% Thai owned so this is not a particularly safe method either. Also, the foreign investor would need to trust that the Thai shareholders will give up controlling interest.

Since it is the obvious intent of the Thai government to prohibit foreigners from owning land, it seems unwise to me to go to extreme measures like those described above. •

---

[1] http://www.bangkokpost.com/breaking_news/breakingnews.php?id=100007

Other land ownership and right or use methods

Sit thi gap gin ta lord shee vit

There is a legal mechanism that may allow a foreigner to secure guaranteed access and use to a piece of land for his or her lifetime.

The Thai legal term "Sit thi gap gin ta lord shee vit" is a translation from Roman Law of the term "Usufruct". (u·su·fruct n. The right to use and enjoy the profits and advantages of something belonging to another as long as the property is not damaged or altered in any way). It is similar to a lifetime lease. However, please note that some Usufruct agreements have been appealed by the land owner and in some cases the period of the Usufruct has been reduced to 30 years in line with French Law.

The Usufruct or "Sit thi gap gin ta lord shee vit" in Thai, is a notation that is added to the land title document together with your name. It costs 75 baht to add this to the land deed/title and must be done at the time of purchase/title transfer. I believe there is a limit of 1 Rai on the size of the land this can apply to and there may be other restrictions. This method has the advantage over a lease because it is not limited to 30 years. However, unlike a lease, it cannot be willed or transferred to another party, the benefit dies with you.

Very few people, including Thai lawyers and real estate professional have heard of "Sit thi gap gin ta lord shee vit". I suspect lawyers don't want to know about it because there is no way for them to make money out of it. Check with your lawyer and if your lawyer hasn't heard of it, ask him to research it. It may be a very useful way to secure a lifetime lease without the limits and expense of a lease agreement. This method may have advantages over a lease if you plan to live longer than 30 years, plan to keep the land until you die and are happy to leave everything to your Thai partner and their heirs when you die.

I have heard that not all land offices will register a "Sit thi gap gin ta lord shee vit". You should check with your local land office before you purchase the land.

Here is an excerpt from the Civil and Commercial code of Thailand:

Title VII

USUFRUCT

Section 1417. An immovable property may be subjected to a usufruct by virtue of which the usufunctuary is entitled to the possession, use and enjoyment of the property.

He has the right of management of the property.

The usufruct of a forest, mine or quarry entitles the usufrutuary to the exploitation of the forest, mine or quarry.

Section 1418. A usufruct may be created either for a period of time or for the life of the usufructuary.

If no time has been fixed, it is presumed that the usufruct is for the life of the usufructuary. If it is created for a period of time, the provisions of Section 1403 paragraph 3 shall apply *mutates mutandis.*

In any case the usufruct comes to an end on the death of the usufrutuary.

Section 1419. If property is destroyed without compensation being paid, the owner is not bound to restore it; but, if he does so to any extent, the usufruct revives to that extent.

If any compensation is paid, the owner or the usufrutuary must restore the property so far as it is possible to do so, having regard to the amount of the compensation received, and the usufruct revives to that extent; but, if restoration is impossible, the usufruct comes to an end and the compensation must be divided between the owner and the usufructuary in proportion to the damages suffered by them respectively.

The same rules apply *mutais mutandis* in case of expropriation as well as in case of partial destruction of the property or of partial impossibility to restore the property.

Section 1420. When usufruct comes to an end, the usufructuary must return the property to the owner.

The usufructuary is liable for the destruction or depreciation in value of the property, unless he proves that the damage was not caused by his fault. He must replace anything which he has wrongfully consumed.

He is not bound to give compensation for depreciation in value caused by reasonable use.

Section 1421. The usufructuary must, in the exercise of his rights, take as much care of the property as a person of ordinary prudence would take of his own property.

Section 1422. Unless otherwise provided in the act creating the usufruct, the usufructuary may transfer the exercise of his right to a third person. In such case the owner of the property may sue the transferee direct.

Section 1423. The owner may object to any unlawful or unreasonable use of the property.

If the owner proves that his rights are in peril, he may demand security from the usufructuary, except in the case of a donor who has reserved to himself the usufruct of the property given.

If the usufructuary fails to give security within a reasonable time fixed for the purpose, or if, in spite of the owner's objection, he continues to make use of the property unlawfully or unreasonably, the Court may appoint a Receiver to manage the property in his stead. Upon security being given the Court may release the Receiver so appointed.

Section 1424. The usufructuary is bound to keep the substance of the property unaltered, and is responsible for ordinary maintenance and petty repairs.

If important repairs or measures are necessary for the preservation of the property, the usufructuary must forthwith inform the owner thereof and permit them to be carried out. In case of default by the owner, the usufructuary may have the work carried out at the owner's expense.

Section 1425. All extraordinary expenses must be borne by the owner, but in order to meet these expenses coming under the foregoing section he may realize part of the property unless the usufructuary is willing to advance the necessary funds without charging interest.

Section 1426. The usufructuary shall, for the duration of the usufruct, bear expenses for the management of the property, pay taxes and duties, and be responsible for interests payable on debts charged upon it.

Section 1427. If require by the owner, the usufructuary is bound to insure the property against loss for the benefit of the owner; and if the property is already insured he is bound to renew such insurance when due.

He must pay the premiums of the insurance for the duration of his usufruct.

Section 1428. No action by the owner against the usufructuary or his transferee in connection with the usufruct or vice versa may be entered later than one year after the usufruct comes to an end. But in an action by the owner who could not have known of the end of the usufruct, the prescription of the year shall run from the time when he knew or ought to have known of it.

It is possible for the usufructuary (the holder of right of use) to lease out the land.

Supreme court judgment 2297/1998; *'the lessor does not have to be the owner of the property. Therefore the usufructuary can rent out the land. Although in the event of death of the usufructuary within the lease term, only the usufruct will be terminated but not also the lease'.*

Amity Treaty

You may hear the term "Amity Treaty". An Amity Treaty company allows Americans to own a majority share in a Thai company. But that company cannot own land in Thailand. To own land, the company must have at least 51% Thai share ownership and at least 7 shareholders as noted above.

1 Rai, 40 million baht

You may be allowed to own up to 1 Rai of land in your own name if you invest 40 million baht in Thailand and receive Board of Investment approval, provided the land is used for residential use, and other conditions apply.

Long term lease from current owner

Many properties are offered on a long term or "never ending" lease by the current owner. You would agree upon a price, payable at 1, 3 or 5 year intervals or for the duration of the contract or any other interval. The terms and conditions of the lease are generally open to negotiation with the owner. If you are not paying the full lease amount up front, the contract should specify the periodic payment schedule and amount and if the amount is allowed to change, there should be a formula describing how the change is calculated, i.e. inflation rate plus 2% per year for example.

This method has the advantage that you may not have to commit a large amount of money up front. Also the transaction is relatively simple, however, any lease over three years must be registered with the Oar-Bor-Tor's office and tax must be paid on the lease amount. For your protection, you should register the lease with the land office. The land must have a title that allows leasing, i.e. Nor Sor 3 or Chanoht.

This may be a good method if you do not want to commit too much money up front or if you prefer a lease to the company method but you do not want to buy the land in the name of a Thai person such as your wife, girlfriend, etc. But be careful however, building a house can cost 2 or 3 times the cost of buying land, so do your homework before you commit. Also, you may never be able to liquidate (sell up) your investment. You should have the option to sub-lease written into the contract, so if you do want to move on, you can sub-lease the land and sell the house or rent the land/house out as described above.

If you lease land thought a broker or real estate company, they may already have a standard lease contract. You should have your own lawyer check over the contract to be sure your rights are protected.

Talk to your lawyer about what would happen if you die or the land owner dies and any other risks associated with this method and write a will coupled with the lease.

Which is the best method and how safe is my investment?

Please talk to your lawyer for this advice. All I can give is my opinion.

Since in my opinion, buying land through a company is no longer a viable option, the choice is limited to a 30 year lease or a Sit thi gap gin ta lord shee vit.

The lease has the disadvantage that it may be hard or impossible to extend in 30 years but you can sell or will a lease to another person. The Sit thi gap gin ta lord shee vit dies with the holder and could potentially be contested by the land owner after 30 years, so nether option is fool proof.

Only invest an amount in Thailand that you are willing to walk away from. If life with your Thai partner turns sour or the government becomes very anti-farang, you may loose everything, so always have a backup plan.

Can my Thai spouse own land?

Yes. There was a law prohibiting Thai people married to foreigners from owning land but that law was revoked in 1999; now there is no limitation on Thai spouse owning land.

If you are already married to a Thai national, and you wish to buy land in the name of your Thai spouse, there is one small detail you should be aware of. Since assets acquired while married are considered the community property of the two of you, and since foreigners are not allowed to own land, then technically speaking, the married couple cannot own land in Thailand because it would be partly foreign owned.

However, if you sign a document stating that the money to pay for the land came from your Thai spouse exclusively and you make no claim on the land, then the Thai spouse can legally own the land. However, this does mean that in the event of a divorce, you will have no claim to the value of the land when determining community assets.

This link provides more detailed information about legal issues involving Thai spouses and Thai children:

http://www.tillekeandgibbins.com/Publications/thailand_legal_basics/index.html

Some land offices will not allow a company to transfer land directly to the spouse of the company director. If you want to transfer land from your company to your Thai spouse, you may need to go through a third person, such as a Thai friend. Unfortunately this means you will have to pay transfer tax two times. Also, the land office may not let you do two title transfers in one day. They may require a few days waiting period.

Can my spouse or I buy and sell land when not in Thailand?

Yes, if you give your lawyer the appropriate power of attorney, copies of ID card, passport and all relevant documents.

Thai citizens can have documents notarized by the Thai consulate in most countries.

If your spouse is buying land, she will have to sign a declaration stating that the funds used for the purchase belong to the Thai spouse from before the marriage, and therefore the land is not considered a joint asset in the event of a divorce. See Chapter 2 for more information about divorce.

Taxes and fees

When transferring land, there will be a 2% transfer fee, 1% withholding tax and 0.5% stamp duty. If the land is being sold by a company or and individual that has owned it for less than 5 years, there will be business tax of 3.3%. Also, company income tax or capital gain tax for individuals must be paid on the profit.

Taxable value for calculating transfer fees is based on the higher of the purchase price or the government valuation. Often the government valuation can be significantly higher than the purchase price and be quite a surprise to the new buyer and seller.

You should negotiate with the seller to pay some or all of the costs.

If there is back tax owed on the land, it will have to be paid up prior to transfer.

Real estate agents and fees

In parts of Thailand with a well developed farang infrastructure, such as Bangkok, Chiang Mai, Pattaya, Ko Samui/Phangan, Phuket etc. you should have no problem finding many English speaking real estate agents offering land, legal and building services.

Like in America, the seller usually pays the agents commission, so the buyer should not be asked to pay agent fees. The usual agent commission is 5%, although sellers may have room to negotiate if there is a lot of realtor competition in your area.

Many Thai land owners selling land through an agent for the first time may not fully understand the 5% commission idea until they have a buyer. When the agent tells the seller how many baht the agent fee is, the seller may want to increase the price to cover the 5% or try to do a deal with you directly, outside the agent. I would advise against going around the agent, since they probably have more experience buying and selling land in their corner of the world than you do and may provide you with valuable protections. It's up to you if you want to accept the price increase of course, but you may want to offer to cover some of the sellers cost as a gesture of good will.

In off the beaten track places, you may find that the lady selling hammocks in the corner shop, who speaks a little English, knows some people selling land, or some such thing. Be extremely careful in these situations. Have your lawyer check everything before you give any deposits or commit to anything.

Renting a house, condominium or apartment

In Bangkok, Pattaya, Phuket and other major cities with large farang populations, you will find many condominiums and apartments for sale, lease and rent. Condominiums and apartments offer the convenience of a modern building in close proximity to shopping and services, usually with a nice swimming pool and maintained grounds. Maid services may often be provided.

Condos in Bangkok, Jomtien Beach, Pattaya, Phuket etc. typically rent for about 10 to 40,000 baht/month, or about 300 to 600 baht/m^2.

If you need more private space, or you live outside a city, you can buy or lease a house. Costs vary dramatically based on the size, condition and location of the house and land. A simple 1 bedroom house, up to about 500m^2 with basic Thai style bathroom and kitchen would typically start at about 4000 baht/month in a countryside, village or small town location.

A slightly larger house, up to about 100m^2 with western (but simple) bathroom and kitchen, starts at about 10,000 baht/month. If you have a nice view, expect to pay about 2000/month more.

For a larger, modern house with 2-3 bedrooms and bathrooms and nicely finished, expect to pay 16,000 baht/month or as much as 40-60,000/month in popular locations and big cities such as Bangkok, Pattaya and Phuket.

Buying a house, condominium or villa

Villas close to Jomtien Beach in Pattaya sell for around 6 to 20 million baht, or about 15-20,000 baht/m2.

Condos in Bangkok, Jomtien Beach, Pattaya, Phuket etc. typically sell for about 1 to 10 million baht, or about 30,000 to 80,000 baht/m2.

Be EXTREMELY careful about buying into projects still under construction. In Thailand, construction projects are almost never completed on time, if at all and countless people have lost deposits and more.

English/Thai words and phrases

Land	ที่ดิน thee^F din
Buy	ซื้อ seuu^H
Sell	ขาย khaay^R
Rent or lease	เช่า chao^F
To take on a lease	เช่าเอาไว้ chao^F ao wai^H
To rent to someone	ให้เช่า hai^F chao^F
30 year lease	สัญญาเช่าสามสิบปี san^R yaa chao^F saam^R sip^L bpee
Company	บริษัท baw^L ri^H sat^L
Company Limited; Co.; Ltd.	บริษัท... จำกัด baw^L ri^H sat^L .... jahm gat^L
Director or president	ผู้อำนวยการใหญ่ phuu^F ahm^M nuay gaan yai^L
Owner	เจ้าของ jao^F khaawng^R
Share (in a company)	หุ้น hoon^F
Share holder	หุ้นส่วน hoon^F suaan^L
Certificate of share ownership	ใบหุ้น bai hoon^F
Preferred shares	หุ้นบุริมสิทธิ์ hoon^F boo^L rim sit
Ordinary shares	หุ้นสามัญ hoon^F saa^R man
Investment	การลงทุน gaan lohng thoon
Problem	ปัญหา bpan haa^R
No problem	ไม่มีปัญหา mai^F mee bpan haa^R
Serious problem	ปัญหาหนัก bpan haa^R nak^L
Suppose	สมมุติ sohm^R moot^H

Chapter 2

Lawyers and contracts

Choosing a lawyer

The first lawyer I talked to in Thailand gave me some interesting advice, "never trust a lawyer, never trust Thai people and especially, never trust local people"! Personally I thought the warning was perhaps a little over stated but it's good to keep it in mind. It is certainly true that Murphy's Law, "what can go wrong, will go wrong", works overtime in Thailand.

First and foremost, I would say that your lawyer should speak English well (I'm assuming that you speak English well). I find the single biggest cause of problems with living in Thailand in general, not just building, is misunderstanding. Accurate communication is critical to the success of your house building project, which is the primary reason I wrote this book.

Secondly, the lawyer should have extensive experience setting up land deals for farangs, both company set-up and lease methods.

Have a good long conversation with a prospective lawyer and try to throw in a few subtle tests to see if he/she is paying attention to your needs. Mention something early in the conversation and see if he/she remembers it later in conversation or another day.

Asian cultures tend to value making people temporarily happy higher than providing accurate information which may be disturbing. This is unfortunately true even for Thai lawyers. In America, it's a lawyer's duty to paint the bleakest possible picture for any scenario; in Thailand, you will find its all, "Mai pben rai", no problem! Thais tend to say what they think you want to hear, not what you need to know, so it's good to get a sense for how your lawyer is going to discuss possible problems.

Written English skills are also a good thing to check. Does your lawyer use email regularly? If you are non resident in Thailand, you will need to email a lot. Try sending a few test emails to see how timely and understandable the replies are.

Many popular areas of the country, have well established real estate companies, selling land and offering related services. Often these companies will have a close relationship with a law firm and a building project management firm. Be very wary of accepting legal advice from a lawyer that works for the real estate agent or the seller. The concept of "conflict of interest" doesn't seem to count for much here and you may find that even through you are paying the bills, your lawyer may be helping the seller or the seller's agent.

Depending on which part of Thailand you live in, you may have limited access to legal services. I lost a reasonable amount of money when I tried to buy land in Pai, a rural town between Chiang Mai and Mai Hong Son. I saw some land I liked but it had problems with road access. There are no lawyers in town, and I foolishly gave a deposit to the land owner based on a hand written "contract", in Thai, written by the local real estate agent. The contract stated that if the land owner cannot provide guaranteed road access to the land by a specific date, I would get my money back. The date came and went, and the land owner's idea of guaranteed road access was, "my family has used that dirt track for generations, "mai bpen rai,   mai mee bpan-haa!". I didn't buy the land without access and I never saw the deposit again and because the "contract" was so badly written, it was not worth the effort to enforce it.

I should have gone to Chiang Mai, consulted a lawyer and got a real contract with some security for my deposit money. I would probably have found that the land owner would not have agreed to a real legal contract anyway since it turned out that there was no way he could ever secure a guarantee of road access. So I would probably never have got to give the deposit anyhow and I would have saved that money and 3 months of wasted time for the cost of a bus ride to Chiang Mai and a few hours of lawyer time.

The moral of the story is, make the time to find a good lawyer before you hand over the money, or else!

Another check is to check references from farang customers your lawyer had previously done similar deals for. An even better check is to find customers that your lawyer doesn't want you to talk to, maybe a bad experience. Ask around, get names, buy a few beers and seek out information.

As a property owner in Thailand, you will likely have ongoing need for legal services. Evaluate your lawyer's performance constantly and talk to other people about their legal experiences. Once you have some experience in Thailand, you may find your interests can be better served by a different lawyer.

If you are uncertain about your lawyer's advice, ask another lawyer. A second or even third opinion is a good safety mechanism on important information and is usually free if you tell the other lawyer you are evaluating his services.

Get to know your local area, lawyers and other building services

The longer you live in your prospective area, the better prepared you will be. Drive around looking at local building projects. Keep coming back to building sites day after day, looking for a farang who looks like the owner. Get his advice, (it's always a guy), about lawyers, builders, where to buy materials, anything you can, and if you are anything like me WRITE IT DOWN! kee-leum!

In the more popular, farang centric parts of the country, such as Bangkok, Pattaya, Phuket, Ko Samui, you should have no problem finding a host of lawyers and law firms with experience working with farang land deals.

In off the beaten track areas, you can still use the big law firms or you may choose to find someone closer to home. Legal fees are very low in Thailand compared to America and Europe so it makes no sense to skimp on legal services. A typical land deal may cost around 15-25,000 baht, a company setup, maybe 10-30,000 baht and the cost of a mistake could be millions of baht.

Guarantee of work

A lawyer should guarantee their work in case they make a mistake. In America, a title company checks the land title to verify its true ownership and if there are any liens or other encumbrances (problems) against the property. You typically pay title insurance incase the title company makes a mistake and later find out that the land has a problem.

In Thailand, your lawyer must do the title search and check for things like the real owners, loans against land, rights or way through your land, special considerations. Ask your lawyer what they plan to do if they make a mistake in the title search.

The names of owners, loans against the land and other factors affecting the land are written on the back of the title deed and stamped at the land office therefore, the title information should be easy to find and accurate. Having said that; I discovered a problem several months after buying my land, which was not documented on the land title. Three years ago, the previous owner of my land had cleared and terraced the land and bulldozed some trees and dirt into the sea. Apparently there was a black mark lodged against the title somewhere in the land office but no one knew about it until I started building the house. The problem was cleared up but like I said, check everything.

Lawyers do make mistakes and omissions. Check everything yourself.

Contracts

Is a contract worth the paper it's written on in Thailand? I'm kee song-sai, skeptical! The best way to ensure compliance with contracts is to have it backed up by something that is tangible and truly legally binding, like your name on a transferable title like a Chanoht or Nor Sor 3, or your deposit money in an escrow account.

In theory, contracts, if written correctly, are legally binding. But to enforce a contract, you would have to go in front of a judge, with your lawyer and hope the judge is going to favor the words in the contract and some rich farang over a dirt poor Thai family. Many farangs who have had dealings with the Thai justice system will tell you that in any case of Thai versus farang, the Thai will win regardless of the evidence, contracts, agreements, etc. Search on google for "Adventures in Thai justice" by Jeffrey Rice for more info.

Contracts will usually be written in Thai (unless you are buying from another farang in which case English is OK). But you should also ask that every part of the contract be translated to English, paragraph by paragraph. You should also add the words, in English and Thai. "In case of any discrepancy between the English and Thai versions of this contract, the English version takes precedence". This may not be legally binding, but it's good to have.

Many Thais don't want to enter into a real legally binding contract. Maybe they are afraid of having to pay tax, but more likely, they have something they don't want to you know about the land/house and don't want to be held accountable if something goes wrong with the deal. Usually they will not tell you right away that they have a problem with a contract. They will wait until you've negotiated all the terms and paid the lawyers bill, then they will say they don't want to sign the contract, they just want the money. At that point, you should find another place.

If one party violates the terms of the contract, for example, does not return a deposit as specified by the conditions of the contract, the other party will likely have to go to court to seek compensation. Even if the court awards the plaintiff compensation, that doesn't mean the defendant is simply going to pay up. If the defendant refuses to pay, the plaintiff must go to the police, with the court judgment and ask them to seize assets from the defendant. The police will likely charge a significant fee for this service.

Contract to buy land

A contract to buy land will include the basic information; title identification information, name and address of buyer and seller, purchase price, deposit amount, etc.

If you are purchasing a subdivided part of a larger land, it should specify the exact details of the subdivided (small) land. The terms "large land" or "big land" and "small land" are commonly used in such contracts.

Since there are often contingencies that delay an outright purchase, such dividing land into smaller lots, securing rights of way etc., you should clearly state the conditions that must be met for the purchase to proceed. Specify the date by which such conditions must be met and the consequences of not meeting the conditions (i.e. refund of deposit).

The contract should specify who is responsible for paying transfer tax.

If the seller has made other commitments, such as providing landscaping, a paved road, electricity, water, etc. check that is in the contract too.

Land prices are currently going up quite quickly in Ko Phangan, so I added a clause that if the seller pulls out of the deal and it is subsequently discovered that the seller sold the land to someone else, the seller would have to compensate me for 3 times my deposit amount.

Last Will and Testament

Since you will be investing a large amount of money in Thailand, you should have your lawyer write a Last Will and Testament, detailing what should happen to your money and property if you die.

I wrote a will in Thailand, in English and Thai, specifying what would happen to my assets (company, land, house, cash) in Thailand only. I have another will for my assets in my home country. I am not sure how two wills would be interpreted. Since in my case, the assets they refer to do not overlap, I assume there is problem, but you should check with your lawyer.

If you will your assets in Thailand to someone living outside of Thailand, I am not sure they would easily be able to take the funds out of the country. I suggest you get a Foreign Exchange Transaction Form (formerly called a Thor Tor 3 form) when you transfer money to Thailand. This form may help your heirs repatriate any money you will them.

Divorce

Under Thai law, any property that either party had at the start of the marriage remains 100% property of that party after divorce. Any property that either party acquires during the course of the marriage is split 50:50 on divorce (Note that land may not be included in the 50/50 split as described below). If the land was bought in your wife's name and lease agreement was entered into while married, the lease it self will be considered joint property.

If buying land under the name of your Thai wife, you have to sign to say it is her property alone and you have no claim to it after divorce which means you will not get your 50% of the value of the land.

If you bought land in your wife's name and have a 30+30 year lease, the first 30 years of the lease are registered at the land office and will survive the divorce. The lease extension may be a problem however, since it's unlikely your ex-wife will want to do you any favors, not without a large amount of money changing hands anyway.

Also, if your land/house is in your ex-wife's home village, you may not want to stay there (possibly with a new girlfriend) after the split. You should carefully consider your exit strategy before marriage and write a prenuptial agreement with a lawyer.

The photos are shoe prints in the sand, how cute!

English/Thai words and phrases

Lawyer — ทนาย tha^H naay

Contract — สัญญา san^R yaa

Company — บริษัท baw^L ri^H sat^L

Company documents — เอกสารบริษัท aehk^L saan^R baw^L ri^H sat^L

Balance sheet — บัญชีงบดุล ban chee ngohp^H doon

Report — รายงาน raay ngaan

Financial account — งบการเงิน ngohp^H gaan ngern

Budget — งบประมาณ ngohp^H bpra^L maan

Purchase-sale agreement or contract — สัญญาซื้อขาย san^R yaa seuu^H khaay^R

Mutual parties to a legal contract — คู่สัญญา khuu^F san^R yaa

Document — เอกสาร aehk^L saan^R

Official document — ตราสาร dtraa saan^R

Genuine or original — ตัวจริง dtuaa jing

To forge a document — ทำหนังสือปลอม thahm nang^R seuu^R bplaawm

Copy of a document — ฉบับสำเนา cha^L bap^L sahm^R nao

Faxed document — บันทึกโทรสาร ban theuk^H thoh ra^H saan^R

Date stamp — ตราประทับวันที่ dtraa bpra^L thap^H wan thee^F

Land — ที่ดิน thee^F din

Buy land — ซื้อที่ดิน seuu^H thee^F din

Deposit — ฝาก ngern faak^L

Immovable property — อสังหาริมทรัพย์ a^L sang^R haa^R rim ma sap^H

Percent	เปอร์เซ็นต์ bper-sen
Guarantee	รับประกัน rap[H] bpra[L] gan
Guarantee	รับรอง rap[H] raawng
Last will and testament	พินัยกรรม phi[H] nai gam
Married	แต่งงานแล้ว dtaaeng[L] ngaan laaeo[H]
Divorce	หย่าแล้ว yaa[L] laaeo[H]

Chapter

Land types and titles

Thai law recognizes two types of land holding: the right of possession (Possessory Right) says that land can be used by an individual for its benefit (agricultural use etc.) under the Civil and Commercial Code; and the right of ownership, where an individual or company holds title deeds and ownership documentation to a piece of land.

Sor Kor 1

Sor Kor 1 is the form required to notify the government of a possessory claim to a piece of land. This was introduced in December 1954 and was used by the government to verify claims upon the land with the eventual issuance of Nor. Sor 3 or Nor. Sor. 3 Gor certification (see below) The government plans to eliminate this title and upgrade all Sor Kor 1 land to Nor Sor 3, but TIT (This is Thailand), things take a long time!

Sor Kor 1 entitles the holder to occupy and farm the land. The land can not be sold; it may only be transferred to direct heirs of the person who holds it. Only the long term land owner can apply to have the title upgraded. You cannot.

Por Bor Tor 6

Por. Bor. Tor 6 is documentation that all land must have in order for a tax number to be issued and tax to be paid upon the benefits of the land. It does not in anyway infer title, ownership or possessory right of the land, only that it has been assessed as taxable.

Por Bor Tor 5

Por Bor Tor 5 is agricultural land or forestry land not recognized as having ownership by the local land office. The local village headsman will be classed as the sole Administrator and he should know ownership by possessory rights title, and also the boundaries of the land. When sold, money changes hands with the knowledge of the village headsman. Strictly speaking no development can take place, but in many areas Guest Houses, Restaurants and homes have been built with full knowledge of local Planning officials. This is particularly common on islands such as Koh Chang. However there have also been cases where restaurants have been bulldozed.

Sor Por Kor 4-01

Sor. Por. Kor 4-01 refers to land allotted by the Land Reform Committee. Land with this documentation cannot be bought or sold, and may only be transferred to the direct heirs of the person who holds it.

Buying and leasing land with lesser grade documentation

Sometimes you may find a deal on a piece of land of one of the above types at a fraction of the price of similar Nor Sor 3 or Chanoht land. Thai law does not allow for the sale, title transfer or lease of these types of land. The best you can do is to enter into a contract with the "owner" to secure the right to purchase the land when a transferable title such as Nor Sor 3 or Chanoht (see below) becomes available. This is a very risky proposition.

The biggest problem you will likely face is that the upgrade to a transferable title never happens. You may want an expiration date on the contract such that if the upgraded title does not become available by a given date, you get your deposit back. However, in my experience, you never get your deposit back. Even if the upgrade does come through, the seller may increase the price to reflect the true value of the land or back out of the deal. In such a case you could sue but even if you win, collecting damages is almost impossible in Thailand.

If you decide to build and live on land of the above types you will face several problems. You will not be able to get a building permit so if the orbator sees a building; you may be required to remove it. I have read that it may be possible to build a "farm house" on some of the above land types but you may find that the land owner claims the house as his own since you cannot have any claim to the land. Since the boundaries of the above land types are very loosely defined, you may accidentally build on someone else's land. If you are determined to build and live on land of the above types, I recommend you build either a very cheap house that you are willing to walk away from or a house that could be dismantled and moved on a big truck.

Moving a whole house is not as crazy as it sounds. It actually happens quite often in Thailand. If you think you may want to move a house, build light, using mostly wood and make the floor high enough to back a flat bed truck under, then cut the support legs out from under the house to load it on to the truck. Obviously, road access must be good enough to get a large truck to the house.

If you are determined to "invest" in land and building on the above land types, consider it gambling, not an investment. Would you stake hundreds of thousands of baht on a cock fight? Probably not, yet a cock probably has about a 50/50 chance of winning, a deal to buy land of the above types probably has a single digit chance of working out!

Nor Sor 3. น. ส. ๓.

Nor Sor 3 (Nor Sor saam) certifies that the land has been issued to the proprietor by the government and the land can be used for its benefits by the holder of this documentation. However, this is not a clear title, and is relevant only to the individual holding the land and the land use.

No parcel points are marked and it is issued upon a specific plot with no frame of reference to connecting plots. Problems can occur when attempting to verify the actual land area of such plots covered by this documentation. For this reason whenever purchasing Nor.Sor.3 land which lacks clearly defined physical boundaries (such as a river, road, etc) it is a wise precaution to ask the owner to stake out the boundaries and then ask neighboring land owners to confirm the vendors interpretation of the boundary. Don't rely solely on the drawing on the deed. Legal acts in connection to the land must be publicized for 30 days prior to their enactment.

In plain English, Nor Sor 3 can be bought and sold, but the boundaries are only recorded in relation to the neighboring plots and survey errors are common. If you are building on Nor Sor 3 land, I suggest you stay well within the boundaries so you are absolutely sure the house is actually on your land, not your next door neighbors.

Nor Sor 3 Ghaw. น. ส. ๓. ก.

Nor Sor 3 Ghaw (often spelt Nor Sor 3 Kor or Nor Sor 3 Gor) has similar legal basis as Nor Sor 3, however, with this documentation the land area is defined with parcel points and is accurately mapped showing adjoining plots on a map using a standard scale of 1:5000.

Nor Sor 3 and Nor Sor 3 Ghaw are legal certificates allowing the person named upon them the right to use the land, including building a house or running a business. This documentation may be used to confirm the rights of the land user in legal disputes with individuals or the government.

It is usually safe for farangs to buy Nor Sor 3 Ghaw land. Nor Sor 3 Ghaw is a documented right of use, forever, and can be bought and sold and the boundaries are well defined. However, it is not a certificate of ownership; only Chanoht (below) specifies actual ownership.

Survey errors can apparently happen even in Nor Sor 3 Ghaw land; it happened to me. The real estate company I bought the land from did there own survey and found the land was a little smaller than the Nor Sor 3 Ghaw indicated. The seller did not want to sell land with uncertain boundaries so they applied for a new official survey. If a new survey is required, it will require notification of neighboring land owners.

Nor Sor 3 Ghaw may be sub-divided but sub-dividing or upgrading title to Chanoht requires you to get permission from all the neighboring land owners. The land office will help you find them. They will have to sign a document agreeing to the current land boundaries and asking them to be present when the government surveyors come to survey the new boundaries. If your neighbors cannot be contacted within 30 days, their permission is assumed. If your neighbors do not agree to the land split, you can ask for a court order. Beware, many texts will incorrectly tell you that legal acts need not be publicized for Nor Sor 3 Ghaw land.

Nor Sor 3 Ghaw translation and explanation

Book guaranteeing acts of use (lit. book guarantee action use)

หนังสือรับรองการทำประโยชน์ nang^R seuu^R rap^H raawng gaan thahm bpra^L yoht

Position of land   ตำแหน่งที่ดิน dtahm^M naaeng^L thee^F din

Sub-district   ตำบล dtahm bohn

District   อำเภอ ahm phuuhr

Province   จังหวัด jang wat^L

Name of location aerial photograph (lit. location photograph way air name)

ระวางรูปภาพทาง อากาศชื่อ ra^H waang ruup^F phaap^F thaang aa gaat^L cheuu^F

Registration	ทะเบียน tha^H biian
Ordinal number (first, second, etc)	เลขที่ laehk^F thee^F
Volume (as in book volume)	เล่ม lehm^F
Page	หน้า naa^F
Land number	เลขที่ดิน laehk^F thee^F din
Number (maybe aerial photo?)	เลขที่ maai laehk^F
Sheet	แผ่น phaaen^L

This book is issued for the purpose of guaranteeing acts of use (lit. book guarantee action use issue this out give for the purpose of to show that)

หนังสือรับรองการทำประโยชน์ฉบับนี้ออกให้เพื่อ

แสดงว่า nang^R seuu^R rap^H raawng gaan thahm bpra^L yoht cha^L bap^L nee^H aawk^L hai^F pheuua^F sa^L daaeng^R waa^F

Name	ชื่อ cheuu^F
Nationality (usually Thai)	สัญชาติ san^R chaat^F
House number (of owner)	บ้านเลขที่ baan^F laehk^F thee^F
Village	หมู่ muu^L

Get possession and use of this plot of land
(lit. get possession and get do use in this plot of land at say on the side of supporting part already)

ได้ครอบครองและได้ทำประโยชน์ ในที่ดินแปลง

ที่กล่าวข้างต้นแล้ว

dai^F khraawp^F khraawng^M lae^H thahm bpra^L yoht nai^M thee^F din bplaaeng thee^F glaao^L khaang^F dtohn^F laaeo^H

Amount of area	จำนวนเนื้อที่ jahm^M nuaan^M neuua^H thee^F
Rai (1600m^2)	ไร่ rai^F

Ngaan (400m^2)   งาน ngaan

Square Waa (4m^2)   ตารางวา dtaa raang waa

Scale for this portion   มาตราส่วน maat^F dtraa suaan^L

Shape or land and boundary connections รูปที่ดินและเขตติดต่อ ruup^F thee^F din lae^H khaeht^L dtit^L dtaaw^L

Nor Sor Saam Ghaw
(น.ส. ๓ ก.)

แยกจาก น.ส.3ก. 3 เล่ม 1 ก.หน้า 3

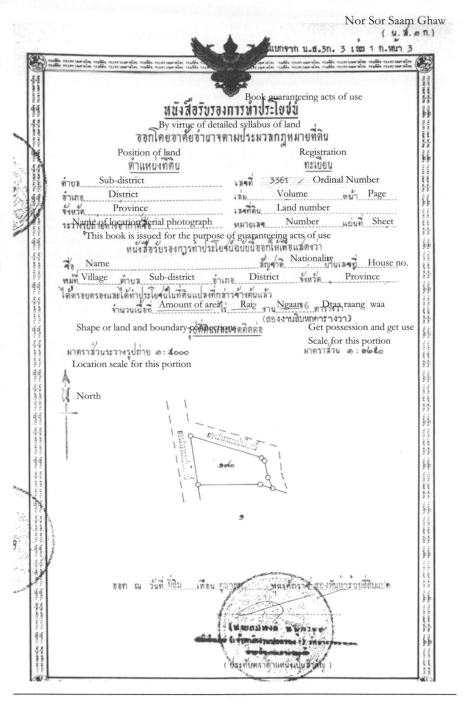

Book guaranteeing acts of use

หนังสือรับรองการทำประโยชน์
By virtue of detailed syllabus of land
ออกโดยอาศัยอำนาจตามประมวลกฎหมายที่ดิน

Position of land ตำแหน่งที่ดิน	Registration ทะเบียน

ตำบล ___ Sub-district ___ เลขที่ 3361 Ordinal Number

อำเภอ ___ District ___ เล่ม ___ Volume ___ หน้า ___ Page

จังหวัด ___ Province ___ เลขที่ดิน ___ Land number

ระวางรูปถ่ายทางอากาศ Name of location aerial photograph หมายเลข ___ Number ___ แผ่นที่ ___ Sheet

This book is issued for the purpose of guaranteeing acts of use
หนังสือรับรองการทำประโยชน์ฉบับนี้ออกให้เพื่อแสดงว่า

ชื่อ ___ Name ___ สัญชาติ ___ Nationality ___ บ้านเลขที่ ___ House no.

หมู่ที่ Village ตำบล Sub-district อำเภอ District จังหวัด Province

ได้ครอบครองและได้ทำประโยชน์ในที่ดินแปลงที่กล่าวข้างต้นแล้ว

จำนวนเนื้อที่ Amount of area ___ ไร่ Rai ___ งาน Ngaan 6 ตารางวา Dtaa raang waa
(สองงานสิบหกตารางวา)

Shape or land and boundary connections รูปแผนที่และการติดต่อ Get possession and get use

Scale for this portion
มาตราส่วนระหว่างรูปถ่าย ๑ : ๕๐๐๐ มาตราส่วน ๑ : ๐๖๕๐
Location scale for this portion

North

ออก ณ วันที่ ยี่สิบ เดือน กุมภาพันธ์ พุทธศักราช สองพันห้าร้อยสิบแปด

(นายธมพงษ์ ...)
... (เจ้าพนักงานที่ดิน ...)
...
(ประทับตราตำแหน่งเป็นสำคัญ)

Nor Sor 4 Jor น. ส. ๔ จ. (Chanoht)

Nor Sor 4 Jor, or Chanoht (often spelt Chanote or Chanoot) as it is more commonly called, is the preferred title dead for land purchase in Thailand.

A Chanoht is a certificate of land ownership. "Chanoht thee-din", โฉนดที่ดิน, literally translates to "land title". The title deed indicates the GPS-verified area and boundaries to the land, although the GPS coordinated do not appear anywhere on the document! The owner named upon a title deed, may use the title as proof of ownership in all legal undertakings. Banks are usually willing to load money with a Chanoht as collateral.

Chanoht land can be sub-divided but more than nine sub-plots must follow the Land Allotment Law, Section 286 and sub-dividing requires you to get permission from all the neighboring land owners as described previously for Nor Sor 3.

Chanoht land will normally have a uniquely numbered government pegs (concrete posts) at the corner points and possibly other places as well. This will be drawn on the Chanoht document (see following picture). A government peg is a concrete post, about 10 cm in diameter, buried in the ground with the top poking out (if you are lucky!). Have the land owner show you the government posts, if they exist.

It is usually very safe for farangs to buy Chanoht land and you will often pay a small premium over Nor Sor 3 Ghaw because it is so desirable.

Chanoht translation and explanation

Official name of Chanoht	น. ส. ๔ จ. Nor Sor See Jor
Land title	โฉนดที่ดิน cha^L n<u>o</u>ht^L thee^F din
Position of land	ตำแหน่งที่ดิน dtahm^M naaeng^L thee^F din
Location	ระวาง ra^H waang
Land number	เลขที่ดิน laehk^F thee^F din
Survey map page number	หน้าสำรวจ naa^F sahm^R ruaat^L
Sub-district	ตำบล dtahm bohn
Land title	โฉนดที่ดิน cha^L n<u>o</u>ht^L thee^F din
Volume (as in book volume)	เล่ม lehm^F
Page	หน้า naa^F
District	อำเภอ ahm phuuhr
Province	จังหวัด jang wat^L
Important book showing right of ownership	เป็นหนังสือสำคัญแสดง กรรมสิทธิ์ bpen nang^R seuu^R sahm^R khan sa^L daaeng^R gam sit^L
Give (Name of owner)	ให้ hai^F
Nationality (usually Thai)	สัญชาติ san^R chaat^F
This plot of land of approximate area	ที่ดินแปลงนี้เนื้อที่ ประมาณ thee^F din bplaaeng nee^H neuua^H thee^F bpra^L maan
Rai (1600m^2)	ไร่ rai^F
Ngaan (400m^2)	งาน ngaan

Square Waa (4m²)   ตารางวา dtaa raang waa

Scale for this portion   มาตราส่วน maat[F] raa suaan[L]

Map of shape   รูปแผนที่   ruup[F] phaaen[R] thee[F]

Nor Sor See Jor

(น.ส. ๔ จ)

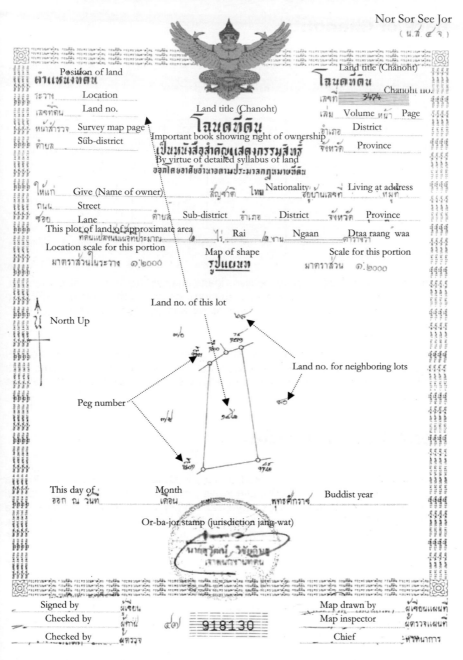

Position of land
ตำแหน่งที่ดิน

Land title (Chanoht)
โฉนดที่ดิน

ระวาง _____ Location

เลขที่ดิน _____ Land no.

Land title (Chanoht)
โฉนดที่ดิน

Chanoht no.
เลขที่ _____ 3474

เล่ม _____ Volume หน้า _____ Page

หน้าสำรวจ _____ Survey map page

Important book showing right of ownership
เป็นหนังสือสำคัญแสดงกรรมสิทธิ์

อำเภอ _____ District

ตำบล _____ Sub-district

By virtue of detailed syllabus of land
ออกโดยอาศัยอำนาจตามประมวลกฎหมายที่ดิน

จังหวัด _____ Province

ให้แก่ _____ Give (Name of owner) _____ สัญชาติ ไทย Nationality _____ อยู่บ้านเลขที่ _____ Living at address _____ หมู่ที่

ถนน _____ Street

ซอย _____ Lane ตำบล _____ Sub-district อำเภอ _____ District จังหวัด _____ Province

This plot of land of approximate area
ที่ดินแปลงนี้เนื้อที่ประมาณ _____ ๒ ไร่ _____ Rai _____ ๒ งาน _____ Ngaan _____ Dtaa raang waa

Location scale for this portion
มาตราส่วนในระวาง ๑:๒๐๐๐

Map of shape
รูปแผนที่

Scale for this portion
มาตราส่วน ๑:๒๐๐๐

North Up

Land no. of this lot

Land no. for neighboring lots

Peg number

This day of
ออก ณ วันที่ _____ Month
เดือน _____ พุทธศักราช _____ Buddist year

Or-ba-jor stamp (jurisdiction jang-wat)

Signed by ผู้เขียน

Checked by ผู้ทาน

Checked by ผู้ตรวจ

๙๗ 918130

Map drawn by ผู้เขียนแผนที่

Map inspector ผู้ตรวจแผนที่

Chief หัวหน้าการ

Back of Chanoht

In this space, information about leases, loans against the land, joint ownership, easements (right of way permitted though) or any other factors affecting ownership and use of the land will be noted and stamped by the Or-ba-tor's office.

These certificates are issued in duplicate and one copy is kept at the land office, the other kept by the owner or mortgage holder. All acts affecting the land, such as transfer of ownership, liens, rights of way, etc. will be noted and stamped on both copies.

Condominium title

A condominium title (first established under the condominium act of 1979) is a title to a part of a building or buildings with multiple owners, and a fractional interest in the land (always a Chanoht) and other common assets, such as a swimming pool and common parts of the building, such as the stair well or lobby. The title will state the floor area of the private apartment, the ground area of the common land and the percentage interest which that apartment has in the common property. This percentage also represents the value of the voting interest in the condominium company or owners association.

For foreigners to be eligible to purchase a condominium in Thailand they must present proof to the Land Department that the funds have been remitted from overseas in foreign currency.

The condominium title has recently been updated so check with your lawyer for current information.

As with any other major purchase, be very care and do your home work when buying a condo, especially one that is not built yet. Many developers go bankrupt before completing the project and it is virtually impossible to get deposits back. Have your lawyer check the developer's financial background, assets, loans, debts, etc. before handing over money.

Squatters rights

If Por. Bor. Tor, Nor Sor 3 or Nor Sor 3 Ghaw land is left unoccupied, anyone can legally occupy (squat) on the land. If they occupy the land for one year, they can actually claim possession rights! Ownership can even be contested if the owner does not occupy the land or at least put a fence around it to keep intruders out.

Even on Chanoht land a squatter can claim possessory rights but only of they have occupied the land for 10 years.

Dividing land and land surveys

Outside of the big cities in Thailand, you will mostly find rural areas which have typically been used for farming. The lot sizes are usually quite large, usually several Rai. If you are only planning to build a house you may only want to buy a small portion of the big land. The terms "big land" and "small land" are used often in contracts regarding land splitting.

Nor Sor 3 and Chanoht land may be sub-divided but sub-dividing or upgrading title to Chanoht requires you to get permission from all the neighboring land owners as described previously. The newly split land will require a survey. It is advisable to be present for the survey to check the borders of your land.

Land splits can take from a few weeks to many months depending on how busy the land office is. Also note that Chanoht land may be split in the district office but Nor Sor 3 land may be split in the sub-district office. There may be a difference in how long these two offices take.

I have heard it said that a little money can help your application get to the top of the pile quicker.

A lot cannot be divided if money is owed on it. The loan must be paid off before the owner can apply to split the land. Since it is likely the reason the land is for sale in the first place is that the owners have no money, it usually means you will have to pay off their loan. This may be more that the deposit you planned on putting down so you should check the loan amount before entering into a contract and giving a deposit.

You should always find a way to secure any money you give to the land owner. In Chapter 5, I suggest you put deposit money in an escrow account, controlled by your lawyer or another third party you think you can trust. However, if the owner needs the money of pay off the loan, that is not possible.

It is a good idea to hand over the deposit money at the bank where the loan is to be paid; just to be sure it doesn't get spent on something else on the way to the bank!

Another way to secure your deposit is to have your name (company name, Thai friend) written on the back of the original (large) land title deed as a co-owner of a part of the large land. There is no problem dividing land with multiple owners. The resulting new (split) title documents will show each respective owner only. However, you may be required to pay transfer tax twice using this method, once when the co owner is added to the original title and again when the split title is transferred to the new owner. Also, check that the original owner cannot borrow money using the land as collateral or perform other acts on the land which would impede your purchase of the land or even leave you liable for a debt.

I built most of my house before the land split was finalized; I expected the split to take a few months but I was wrong. I had my company name added to the large (original) land title indicating was joint owner of a small piece of the large land. In retrospect this was a VERY risky move. If the owner of the land had used the land as collateral for a loan or had incurred large debts, the land and perhaps even the property on it, i.e. my house, could have been seized by the courts! When I realized this, I had many sleepless nights worrying about when the title split would come through. Fortunately everything worked out OK for me.

Many people buy a few Rai of land with the expectation of keeping part of the land to build on and selling the rest later when the land appreciates in value. **If you plan to do this, tell the seller you want to buy the land already divided up into several lots. Smaller lots sell faster than big lots, so I recommend you spit your land into several ½ Ria or smaller lots.** It takes very little extra time and money to split land in more than two titles and will save you time and trouble down the road.

A survey is required when dividing land. You may want to get a survey done when buying any land to verify where the boundaries are, especially for Nor Sor 3 land where the boundaries are not well specified. Official government surveys can take many months and usually cost about 3-5000 baht for lot size of 1 or 2 Rai. If you want to know the boundaries for your own peace of mind before the government survey is done, you can hire your own surveyor or ask the government surveyor to do it privately, outside of office hours.

When you request a land split, you will be given a date to meet the land officer and look at the land. This will likely not be the survey; that will usually happen later. However at the first meeting you will be required to give the land officer the original title document. You will not get a title document back until the split is complete. This can be a problem if you are selling the land since you will not have an original title in your possession for many months. If a prospective buyer wants to see the original title (I know I would), you will have to go to the land office and hope they can produce the title for inspection.

Regardless of the title type, it is vitally important that you personally verify your boundaries with the land office, the seller and the neighbors. Mistakes are common and potentially VERY expensive if you accidentally build a house on someone else's land!

Land areas measurement and survey methods

Land area for Chanoht and Nor Sor 3 Ghaw land is measured by the land's footprint size, i.e. the size of the land is calculated based on the view from space. If the land is on a slope this will be a smaller area than the actual surface area of the land. For lesser title types, land area is calculated by measuring the distance between boundaries and calculating the surface area inside. So one Rai of Chanoht or Nor Sor 3 Ghaw land on a 45 degree slope will measure 1.41 Rai, if it was Nor Sor 3 title, FOR THE SAME LAND!

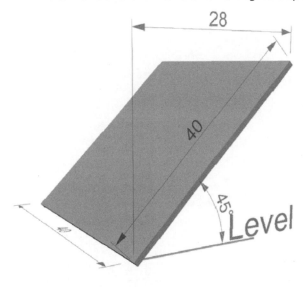

This may be a little hard to visualize so lay this book flat on a table and look at it from above. Now tilt the book 45 degrees from the surface of the table and you will see that from above, it makes a smaller footprint.

In the drawing (left), if the land area was calculated using the Nor Sor 3 method, it would measure 40m*40m = 1600m2 = 1 Rai. However, if the land is Chanoht or Nor Sor 3 Ghaw, the measurement would be from above, which is 40m*28m = 1120m2 = 0.7 Rai. In surveyor lingo, this has been "reduced".

This distinction may be important if you are paying for land by the Rai. If the land is sloping, you will actually get more land for your money with a Chanoht or Nor Sor 3 Ghaw title than another title!

Also, if you upgrade from a lesser title to Chanoht or Nor Sor 3 Ghaw, you may loose land which may affect your possible selling price!

Upgrading titles

Upgrading Nor Sor 3 and Nor Sor 3 Ghaw to Chanoht is only possible when your village (moo) is surveyed and Chanoht upgrades approved by the district land office. You will have to ask the village chief, phuu^F yai^L baan^F when the next scheduled visit by the government officer to survey to your village is. I believe the cost is quite small, low thousands of baht but it may take a long time, potentially many years.

I have no information about upgrading lesser titles to Nor Sor 3 or Chanoht.

Neighboring Land

If your neighbors are splitting land or upgrading titles, they will ask you to sign a form at the Amphur approving the split. The form will ask you to agree to boundaries on the current title documents and be present to witness the survey. I suggest you take this form to your lawyer and check the neighbors' title document to make sure there are no discrepancies with your title document or your knowledge of your boundaries.

Land sizes

All land documents refer to lot sizes in rai, ngaan and data-raang waa and the numbers will be written in Thai.

- Waa and dtaa-raang waa. A waa is 2 meters, a square waa (dtaa-raang waa) is 4 square meters.

- Ngaan. A Ngaan is 100 dtaa-raang waa or 400 square meters.

- Rai. A Rai is 1600 square meters. 1 acre is 2.53 Rai and 1 hectare is 6.25 Rai.

Reading and organizing Thai documents

If you cannot not read or write Thai, I recommend that at the very least you learn to read the name of your company or your Thai partner whose name is on the land title and other legal documents. Being able to recognize that often comes in useful.

If you own land, either via a company or a lease, you will likely have a significant amount of paperwork to maintain, in Thai! Add to that, house contracts and receipts, bank account information, a Will, maybe a work permit and you end up with a lot of Thai documentation, which I find is hard to keep track of. I find it useful to make a filing system, labeled in English and Thai. The filing system should be easily transportable so you can take it to your lawyer or the land office or wherever and put everything back in its correct place when finished.

English/Thai words and phrases

Land	ที่ดิน thee^F din
Title for a plot of land or property	กรรมสิทธิ์ gam sit^L
Plot of land	แปลง bplaaeng
Land boundary	แดน daaen
Land boundary	เขต khaeht^L
Land title	โฉนดที่ดิน cha^L noht^L thee^F din
Nor Sor see^L Jor	น. ส. ๔ จ.
Chanoht	โฉนด cha^L noht^L
Nor Sor saam^R (3)	น. ส. ๓
Nor Sor saam^R (3) Ghaw	น. ส. ๓ ก.
Government	รัฐบาล rat^H baan
Government official	ข้าราชการ khaa^F raat^F cha^H gaan
Or-bor-jor (Provincial Administration Organization) Or-bor-tor (Sub-district Administration)	
Amphur (District)	อำเภอ ahm phuuhr
Tambon (Sub-district)	ตำบล dtahm bohn
To survey or measure a piece of land	รังวัด rang wat^H
Rai (1600m^2)	ไร่ rai^F
Ngaan (400m^2)	งาน ngaan
Square Waa (4m^2)	ตารางวา dtaa raang waa
Meters	เมตร maeht^F
Square meter	รางเมตร dtaa raang maeht^F

M (Abbreviation for meter)	ม.
0	๐ suun^{R}
1	๑ neung^{L}
2	๒ saawng^{R}
3	๓ saam^{R}
4	๔ see^{L}
5	๕ haa^{F}
6	๖ hohk^{L}
7	๗ jet^{L}
8	๘ bpaet^{L}
9	๙ gao^{F}
1.2	neung^{L} jòot saawng^{R}
2 by 4	saawng^{R} khuun see^{L}
300 meters by 400 meters	saam^{R} raawy^{H} khuun see^{L} raawy^{H} maeht^{F}
5 Rai, 2 ngaan and 7 Talang Wahhaa^{F} rai^{F} saawng^{R} ngaan jet^{L} dtaa raang waa	
How many rai is this land?	ที่ดินแปลงนี้ เนื้อที่กี่ไร่ thee^{F} din bplaaeng nee^{H} gee^{L} rai^{F}
Where is the land boundary?	แดนที่ไหน daaen thee^{F} nai^{R}
Chanoht post	หลักโฉนด lak^{L} cha^{L} n̲o̲ht^{L}
Boundary post	หลักเขต / เสาเขต lak^{L} khaeht^{L}, sao^{R} khaeht^{L}
Government peg (concrete post)	หมุด moot^{L}
Where are the boundary posts?	หลักเขตที่ไหน lak^{L} khaeht^{L} thee^{F} nai^{R}
Land used for farming	เรือกสวนไร่นา reuuak^{F} suaan^{R} rai^{F} naa
Owner	เจ้าของ jao^{F} khaawng^{R}
Who is the owner?	ใครเป็นเจ้าของ khrai bpen jao^{F} khaawng^{R}
How many owners are there?	มีเจ้าของกี่คน mee jao^{F} khaawng^{R} gee^{L} khohn

Can I buy only 1 Rai?	ขอแบ่งซื้อหนึ่งไร่ได้ไหม khaaw^R baaeng^L seuu^H neung^L rai^F dai^F mai^R
How much for 2.5 Rai?	สองจุดห้าไร่เท่าไร saawng^R joot^L haa^F rai^F thao^F rai
How much per Rai?	ไร่ละเท่าไร rai^F la^H thao^F rai
I want to buy 1 Rai	ต้องการซื้อหนึ่งไร่ dtaawng^F gaan^M seuu^H neung^L rai^F

Chapter 4

Access and services

Access road, right of way

Many farangs find themselves buying/leasing undeveloped land in rural areas with a plan to build a house. Undeveloped land is likely to be larger lot size than developed land. Thais like to live close together (gluaa phee!) so Thai houses tend to be in towns and on small lots. Rural houses are usually very basic. If you buy/lease land with a house already on it, it may be useful for recyclable wood or a place for the workers to live while building your house.

Government roads

In Thailand, a government road may be little more than a dirt or sand track. Regardless of the condition for the road, buying land on a government road is the safest bet because you will be guaranteed access forever for free (I hope!). A government road should be on the government map at the land office unless it has recently become a government road. In either case, you must have your lawyer check if the road you are on is actually a government road.

If the government road is in poor condition, and you want to spend some money to develop it, most local governments will be happy to take your money.

Private tracks

Many lots will not be on government roads. They will be accessed via a dirt track though a farmers field or a sand road through someone else's land. There is a general rule in Thailand that if a track has been used by the public for more that 10 years, it becomes quasi-public property. The public should, in theory, be able to use that track forever.

However, that certainly does not give you the right to develop it into a real road (i.e. put concrete down) and does not preclude the owner of the road from making it difficult or impossible for you to access your land through it.

I strongly advise against buying land unless you have a guaranteed, documented, right of way.

There are several ways to guarantee right of way. The ideal situation is to buy a strip or land, that connects your prospective land to a government road. Do this before you buy land otherwise you will find the prices goes up 10x. Also, before you buy the main land, you can get the current land owner to negotiate a favorable deal with the neighbors for the right to buy a strip. Buying a strip of land should be treated in the same way you buy the main land. Your lawyer should do a full title search etc. Also, because the strip will need to be separated from the big land, this is likely to take some time, maybe 6 months or more. Do not be tempted to go ahead and buy the main land until the access issue is fully resolved, remember Murphy 's Law, "what can go wrong, will go wrong".

If you do buy a strip of land for access only, consider donating it to the government. Once the government owns it they may develop it for you (concrete it). In any case, it may add value to your and your neighbors land to be on a government road.

Another way to secure access is to buy or in some other way acquire the right to access through a neighbor's land, an "easement" as is it called in America. Any such deal should be documented on the back of the neighbor's land title deed at the land office and you should get a copy. Check with your lawyer!

Be careful, there may be more than one land owner between you and the government road. Your lawyer should be able to show you a map of how you will access your prospective land and that he/she has secured right of way all the way from the government road.

Water

Government (public) water

Ideally your prospective land will already have a water supply from government water. If not, you will probably want to run one. This may be a problem because, like access roads, it may have to run through a neighbors land to reach the main water supply. Your lawyer should check before you buy.

Do not assume that because you have road access that you can easily get a water pipe to your land. The main water pipeline may not necessarily be at the point where you access the land.

Protect the water pipe from the meter to your house. If it is above ground, it could easily be broken. Even if underground, it could be damaged by digging. I prefer to leave my water off at the meter and only turn it on when I need to fill the tank. Many of my neighbors leave the water on at the meter all the time. One neighbor got a 10,000 baht water bill because the pipe was broken under ground and leaking water for a month.

Well water

Is there a well on the land? Is there water in it? Is there water in the dry season? Of course the land owner is going to say yes, but you should ask around if you can.

If there is no well, it may be a good idea to put one in. Government water in rural areas often stops for days or weeks at a time, maybe longer. See if the neighbors have wells and ask if they have water all year.

A well is typically a 1-2 meter diameter hole in the ground, lined with concrete rings. Well digging in Thailand is usually done by hand. Digging a well may cost about 1000-2000 baht/meter plus another 3,000-20,000 baht for the pump depending on the depth. Better quality water and more reliable supplies are usually found at greater depths, sometimes 50 meters or more.

A cheaper and simpler way to make a well is to use 2″ galvanized steel pipe. Have your local steel shop fabricate a sharp pointed end on a section of steel pipe. Drill many holes along the length of the pipe to allow water to percolate into the pipe. Protect the threads on the pipe end and with a very big hammer, force the pipe into the ground. This is probably best done at the end of the rainy season when the ground should be quite soft.

As the pipe sinks into the ground, attach more lengths of pipe until you get to the desired depth. Put a 1″ PVC pipe down the well pipe and a suction pump at the top to get the water out.

You may need a permit to drill a well, especially if it's deeper than 30 meters, check with the land office or Amphur.

You should test the water quality from other wells in the area before spending money on a well. Sometimes the ground water may contain large amounts of impurities such as iron which will add a brownish color to the water.

Many homes in the north of Thailand use a slow sand filter. To build a slow sand filter, construct a tower about 3 meters high using 70cm or 1m concrete pipe rings. Cement the joins for water tightness. The bottom 30cm is filled with gravel and a perforated drain pipe is inserted to collect the filtered water. The next 1m to 1.5m is filed, with fine sand and the upper portion has a water reservoir, typically .5 to 1.5m deep. The water reservoir is necessary to push the water through the filter and can be kept full with a pump on a float switch.

These sizes could be scaled down to fit in a 2-3000 liter plastic or fiberglass water tank if the water source is fairly clean.

The water passes through the sand from top to bottom. Any larger suspended particles are left behind in the top layers of sand. Smaller particles of organic sediment left in the sand filter are eaten by microscopic organisms including bacteria and protozoans which stick in the layers of slime that form around the sand particles. Provided that the grain size is around 0.1mm in diameter, a sand filter can remove all fecal coliforms (bacteria that originate from feces) and virtually all viruses. The microscopic organisms develop naturally after about 1 week of use.

http://www.agr.gc.ca/pfra/water/slowsnd_e.htm

http://www.oasisdesign.net/water/treatment/slowsandfilter.htm

If you want to make water that is clean enough to drink, look into a UV ozone filter. UV ozone filters are used by most water bottling companies in Thailand. Ask your local water bottler where they buy their equipment. A UV ozone filter is a simple device that produces ozone gas using an ultraviolet light. Ozone gas cleans impurities from water without the use of any chemical additives.

http://www.freepatentsonline.com/5935431.html

http://www.cyber-nook.com/water/index.html

http://www.healthunit.org/water/infosheet/system.htm

Run your own pipe

Sometimes you may run a pipe directly from a reservoir, lake, river or stream. You will need to secure access rights to run a pipe. Needless to say, the pipe will have to run mostly down hill, although a small uphill incline will probably be ok depending on the water pressure at that point. Many people run the thin blue plastic pipe which is mainly designed for use inside the house. The blue plastic pipe will only last 2 to 3 years maximum if exposed to the sun and will crack if driven over by a car of hit by a falling coconut. Black polypropylene pipe, which costs about twice as much as the blue pipe, will last for 10 years or more, can be driven over and will survive coconut hits. Also, you can buy the black pipe in large rolls of 50 meters or more which means less joints to go wrong.

Depending on how far down hill you are running the pipe, you may find you have too much water pressure for the pipe. This could be a problem because it may cause your faucets/taps to leak or even bust a valve or the pipe. You can put pressure reducers in the pipe at regular intervals if this is a problem.

Electricity

Concrete poles and transformers

Does the land have power supplied on government concrete electricity poles already or close by? This is the ideal situation since government electricity is quite cheap. Check how you will get from the pole to your land. Your lawyer needs to check the right of way.

If the land has never had electricity before, you will need to apply for temporary electricity while building. You will need to buy the meter also (usually about 7000 baht). When you have a tabien baan (house registration), you can apply for permanent electricity.

If you need to extend the concrete poles to your land, you will need to check the right of way. Concrete electricity posts cost from 3000 to 7000 baht each (including cable) and can be spaced 50 meters apart. So budget 6,000 to 14,000 baht per 100 meters.

You will need a transformer if connecting to high voltage lines. Transformers cost from 50,000 baht for single phase to 200,000 baht or more for 3 phases. Check your options with the power company and tell them how many kilowatts you want. This will largely be based on how much air conditioning you plan to use since AC is usually the biggest user of electricity in Thailand. Since electric clothes dryers and stoves (cookers) are rare in Thailand, a typical house without air conditioning should be fine with 5 to 10kW of power (about 20 to 40 amps). If planning to use air conditioning, check the wattage of the units you plan to install. If you plan to use central air conditioning, you may need 3 phase power supply which is not commonly available to homes in rural areas.

You should research the electricity and water supply situation before you buy the land, it may be more expensive than you think.

If there are neighbors close by, they may be interested in sharing the cost of the power installation.

Bamboo/wood poles

If electricity is running to the land on bamboo poles, the poles probably belong to a private person and you would have to pay them to run wire on their poles. I have also been told that the electricity is more expensive on bamboo poles but I'm not sure how that works.

Bamboo pole electricity may be sufficient for temporary use during building but you should research getting the government to put concrete poles to your land. You will have to pay as discussed above.

Generators

If electricity is not available at your site, you will likely have to buy a generator. You may also want a backup generator if your electricity supply is unreliable. You should locate the generator away from the house if possible to minimize the noise. Put it in a well ventilated shed so it will not overheat and produce dangerous gasses, and locate it above possible flood level.

Generators can be gasoline (petrol) or diesel powered. Small ones tend to be gasoline, larger ones diesel. For emergency backup of critical systems, like water pumps, a small gasoline generator may be fine, but be careful of storing gasoline. If the gasoline leaks, it can produce explosive gasses. Diesel generators are safer and last longer, and are cheaper to run, important factors if it is your main source of electricity supply. I have seen many home brew generators in use in Thailand. Talk to your local engineering shop, maybe they can put something together far cheaper than a commercial unit.

Renewable (green) energy

With all the sun in Thailand it is tempting to think about free electricity from the sun. I researched solar electric panels for my house and quickly came to the same conclusion as everyone else; it's very expensive to produce a small amount of power from solar panels. The purchase price is high and the life expectancy is not very long. Add to that, the government adds a very high import duty when bringing panels into the country.

When pricing up a solar system, remember that solar panels produce direct current DC electricity. All your appliances use AC so you will need an inverter to convert DC to AC, adding to the cost and complexity. Also, the panels only produce power when the sun shines (obviously!) so they are no use for lighting at night. If you want to use solar power for lighting, refrigeration or just about anything useful, you will need batteries to store the power through the night. Batteries will add a lot of expense and complexity to the system and have a limited life.

There always seems to be a breakthrough just around the corner that will provide cheap electricity from the sun; here is one such http://www.greenandgoldenergy.com.au/

Unfortunately, these promising technologies rarely see commercial production.

Wind generators may be a more cost effective way to generate electricity if you live in a suitable location, i.e. consistent wind, day and night of at least 10 MPH. However, wind generators will need an inverter and probably battery storage.

In some cities in America, it is possible to generate your own electricity and put it back into the power grid. If you are producing more power than you are using, your meter will run backwards! So you total bill at the end on the month will be lower. I do not know if Thai electric meters offer this facility, check with your electric company.

If you are fortunate to have access to a free water supply with a head of at least 20 meters, you may be able to build a small hydro electric power generator. This would be the perfect situation because you could produce AC power directly and consistently.

English/Thai words and phrases

Boundary of land   เขตแดน khaehtᴸ daaen

Land survey   รังวัดที่ดิน rang watᴴ theeᶠ din

Divide land   แบ่งส่วนที่ดิน baaengᴸ suaanᴸ theeᶠ din

Right of way, access   ทางเข้า thaang khaoᶠ (Lit. way enter)

Road   ถนน thaᴸ nohnᴿ

Abbreviation for road   ถ.

Main road   ถนนใหญ่ thaᴸ nohnᴿ yaiᴸ

Soi, Lane   ซอย saawy

Alley   ตรอก dtraawkᴸ

Government road   ถนนหลวง thaᴸ nohnᴿ luangᴿ

Private road   ถนนส่วนบุคคล thaᴸ nohnᴿ suaanᴸ bookᴸ khohn

Dirt road   ถนนเลน thaᴸ nohnᴿ laehn

Junction, fork in the road   ทางแยก thaang yaaekᶠ

Neighbor   เพื่อนบ้าน pheuuanᶠ baanᶠ

Does this land have a guaranteed legal access (right of way) ที่ดินมีสัญญาทางเข้า ไหม theeᶠ din mee sanᴿ yaaᴹ thaang khaoᶠ maiᴿ

Where is the guaranteed legal access (right of way) สัญญาทางเข้าอยู่ที่ไหน sanᴿ yaaᴹ thaang khaoᶠ yuuᴸ theeᶠ naiᴿ

Water   น้ำ naahmᴴ

Public water supply, government water   ประปา bpraᴸ bpaa

Water well   บ่อน้ำ baawᴸ naahmᴴ

Well water   น้ำบ่อ naahmᴴ baawᴸ

Pipe	ท่อ thaaw^F
Water main, water supply pipe	ท่อประปา thaaw^F bpra^L bpaa
Is there a water pipe coming to this land?	ที่ดินมีน้ำประปาไหม thee^F din mee^M naahm^H bpra^L bpaa mai^R
Where is the pipe?	ท่อน้ำที่ไหน thaaw^F naahm^H thee^F nai^R
Where is the well?	บ่อน้ำที่ไหน baaw^L naahm^H thee^F nai^R
Does the well have water all year?	บ่อน้ำนี้มีน้ำตลอดปีไหม baaw^L naahm^H nee^H mee^M naahm^H dta^L laawt^L bpee^M mai^R
Do your neighbors have a well?	เพื่อนบ้านของคุณมีบ่อน้ำไหม pheuuan^F baan^F khaawng^R khoon^M mee^M baaw^L naahm^H mai^R
Electricity	ไฟฟ้า fai faa^H
Cable	เคเบิ้ล khaeh^M beern^F
Transformer	หม้อแปลงไฟ maaw^F bplaaeng fai
Is there electricity coming to this land?	ที่ดินมีไฟฟ้าไหม thee^F din mee^M fai faa^H mai^R
Where is the electric cable?	ไฟฟ้าที่ไหน fai faa^H thee^F nai^R
Where is the closest electricity pole?	เสาไฟฟ้าใกล้ที่สุดที่ไหน sao^R fai faa^H glai^F thee^F soot^L thee^F nai^R

Chapter  5

Money matters

Deposits

I am personally convinced that many Thai land owners and builders make a good living from collecting deposits from unsuspecting farangs, with dreams of buying land and living in paradise or making a quick baht by buying and selling cheap land.

Because much of the land for sale in Thailand is in large lots that require subdividing, or because there are right of access issues, or for a host of other reasons, you will often find that you cannot simply buy plots of land in Thailand without having to wait a significant amount of time for something to happen.

Usually the land owner will ask you for a deposit prior to splitting the land, securing access rights, or whatever. This can range for 10-20,000 baht to 50% of the value of the property, or more. You must decide how much you are comfortable giving, based largely on how likely it is you will get that money back if something goes wrong with the deal and how likely it is the seller may find someone willing to pay more than you.

When paying a deposit, you can be almost 100% certain that you will never see that money again. Even if you have an iron clad contract and are successful in wining a judgment against the deposit holder for breech of contract, there is little chance you will ever see your money again.

Where possible, you should get some kind of security for your deposit money.

Securing deposit

Often, the reason Thai people are selling land is because they are in debt and need the money. This means that if something goes wrong with the deal, you basically have no chance of getting the deposit money back because it's already been spent.

You should try protecting yourself against loosing your deposit where possible. Here are a few options, there are probably more:

1) Have your name (Thai owner or your company name) added to the land title document to indicate that you are a part owner of the large land, prior to the split to small land.

2) If the land owner owns other, more easily transferable land, add your name to the title of that land.

3) Open a bank account (escrow or trust account) in the name of your lawyer or some other independent party that both buyer and seller can trust to interpret the contract fairly. The deposits will be paid into that account and the funds released to the seller on successful conclusion of the deal.

4) Have the land title document held by your lawyer so the seller cannot borrow against it or sell it to someone else. Your lawyer may be able to hold it "hostage" unless you get your money back if something goes wrong, but I have no idea how legal that is! This method is also good protection against the seller selling to someone else.

Mortgages

Foreigners generally cannot mortgage properties in Thailand, however, many financial institutions in Thailand provide loans for real estate purchasing to Thais and Thai companies. It is common for real estate developers to arrange for customer financing.

Transferring money to Thailand

Bank wire transfer

Bank transfer is probably the safest and most cost effective way to transfer large amounts of money to Thailand. You will need to set up a Thai bank account first. This can be a private or a business account.

If you are starting a business account you will need to show all your company papers and stamp. Siam Commercial Bank does not give ATM cards on business accounts which can be quite inconvenient, so you should check with your bank.

Business accounts have the advantage that multiple people can have access to the account.

When transferring money to Thailand you will get a much better rate if you transfer the money in your home country's currency. Your bank in Thailand will convert it to baht and will give you a much better rate than a bank outside Thailand.

The first time I transferred a large amount of money, I didn't know about this. I sent baht to my Thai bank account and my bank in America gave me 40.25 baht to the dollar at a time when the rate was 41.7 baht to the dollar. I lost over $1500 compared to if I had sent the money in dollars.

This tip may save you many times the cost of this book!

Most banks require you to set up a wire transfer in person at the bank's branch which means you will have to transfer the money before you move to Thailand. I have recently discovered it is very hard to get money from my American bank now that I am living full time in Thailand.

If you are applying for a retirement visa or non immigrant visa in Thailand, you need to show proof that you have brought money to Thailand. So keep a record of the transfer and get a Foreign Exchange Transaction Form (formerly called a Thor Tor 3 form) at the bank in case you decide to transfer the money back out (see below).

Some banks, such as Citibank, Bank of America or a federal credit union may allow you to set up a monthly wire transfer to your Thai bank account.

ATM, cash, travelers checks, VISA/MasterCard advance.

It is unlikely you can carry enough cash into Thailand to pay for a whole house, but if you plan to, larger bills get better rates.

ATM is very convenient and gets as good a rate as wire transfer using the transfer as described above. There is usually a flat fee charged by the ATM machine and another flat fee charge by your bank so it is best to transfer the maximum amount your card allows.

I have heard that Nationwide Building Society (UK) does not charge an ATM withdrawal fee. If you have a Paypal account, Paypal ATM withdrawal fees is currently $2, far below most other American banks.

Traveler's checks get a better rate than cash and are safer to carry around.

VISA/MC advances are quite expensive, 2.5% I think, so should only be used in an emergency.

Transferring money from Thailand

You may decide to sell up and move on in future. When you transfer money to your Thai bank account, get a Foreign Exchange Transaction Form (formerly called a Thor Tor 3 form) at the bank. This will help you move that money back out of Thailand in the future should the need arise.

To get a Foreign Exchange Transaction Form, you must transfer a minimum amount $20,000US.

Importing personal effects into Thailand

Household items may be imported into Thailand, without paying the normal import duty; however, you must provide proof of residency in Thailand, such as a work permit. Items must be imported not earlier than one month prior to arrival and not later than six months after arrival. Only one electrical item is allowed for an individual or two items for a family.

Other conditions apply, please see:

http://www.lawyer.th.com/QR-household-items.asp for more information.

English/Thai words and phrases

Money	เงิน ngern
Bank	ธนาคาร tha^H naa khaan
Account	บัญชี ban chee
Bank Account	บัญชีเงินฝากธนาคาร ban chee ngern faak^L tha^H naa khaan
Bank book	สมุดฝากเงินธนาคาร sa^L moot^L faak^L ngern tha^H naa khaan
Bank account number	หมายเลขบัญชีเงินฝากธนาคาร maay^R laehk^F ban chee ngern faak^L tha^H naa khaan
Baht	บาท baat^L
ATM	เอ ที เอ็ม aeh thee em
ATM card	บัตร เอ ที เอ็ม bat^L aeh thee em
Telegraphic money order (wire transfer)	โทรเลขธนาณัติ tho-ra laehk^F tha^H naa nat^H
International wire transfer	ธนาณัติต่างประเทศ tha^H naa nat^H dtaang^L bpra^L thaeht^F
Exchange money	แลกเปลี่ยนเงิน laaek^F bpliian^L ngern
Exchange rate for money	อัตราแลกเปลี่ยนเงินตรา at^L raa laaek^F bpliian^L ngern dtraa
Receipt for money	ใบเสร็จรับเงิน bai set^L rap^H ngern
To withdraw (money)	เบิก beerk^L
Borrow money with interest	กู้ guuF
Owe money	มีหนี้สิน mee nee^F sin^R
To pay off or settle debts	ชำระหนี้ chahm ra^H nee^F

Chapter 6

Annual taxes and accounting

Taxes

For information on taxes in Thailand, see http://www.rd.go.th. Information is available in Thai and English.

There are two different taxes levied on property in Thailand:

- Land tax

- Structures Usage Tax

Land Tax is levied on land ownership and is a very small amount, in the order of a few hundred baht per Rai per year. The local land (Or-ba-tors) office should inform you when tax is due or you can check for notices at the Or-ba-tors office. If you fail to pay tax, you may be charged back tax and a fine at some point.

If a property is being used as a private residence, there is no property tax. If the property is being used for a commercial business, a Structures Usage Tax of 12.5% of the actual or assessed rentable value will be levied. Often, the actual or assessed rentable value will be far below the realistic market rate. Structures on land owned by a company may be considered commercial property and may be liable for Structure Usage Tax.

For information on company tax, see:

http://www.asiatradingonline.com/taxcompany.htm

Company Reporting and Accounting

Company accounts must be reported and taxes paid annually for a company to remain a legal entity. Yearly report, accounting and taxes usually costs abut 15,000 baht unless the company is very active. Your lawyer and/or accountant must prepare the company report and balance sheet at the end of the financial year.

It is critical you follow the law on reporting, accounting and taxes every year or the company will be closed down. However, the Thai Supreme Court has ruled that property cannot be confiscated when a business is closed down, but the company will be forced to sell its assets within 1 year or the government will auction the assets. Proceeds will be split among the shareholders.

English/Thai words and phrases

Tax　　　　　　　　　　　　ภาษี phaa see^R

Account　　　　　　　　　　งบ ngohp^H

Real estate tax　　　　　　　ภาษีที่ดิน phaa see^R thee^F din

Business tax　　　　　　　　ภาษีการค้า phaa see^R gaan khaa^H

Income tax　　　　　　　　　ภาษีเงินได้ phaa see^R ngern dai^F

Inheritance, estate tax　　　ภาษีมรดก phaa^M see^R maaw ra^H dohk^L

Pay tax　　　　　　　　　　　เสียภาษี siia^R phaa see^R

Government Tax Office　　　กรมสรรพากร grohm san^L phaa gaawn

Tax receipt　　　　　　　　　ปี๋ bpee^F

Duty (tax)　　　　　　　　　อากร aa gaawn

Accounting　　　　　　　　　การบัญชี gaan^M ban^M chee^M

Chapter 7

Architects, design and permits

Architects

When choosing an architect, you should take the same care and follow the same advice as I gave about choosing a lawyer. One common complaint I hear about architects in Thailand is that they are too busy and/or unwilling to complete the design or properly support the customer or the builder.

How much a design is likely to change during the building process is up to you. In my case it was almost every day! Bpian-jai eek laew. If this is the case for you, you should choose an architect close to home.

However, depending on the complexity of your design, your builder may be quite capable of building a house with just a basic sketch, so perhaps you can skip the architect altogether once the building permit (a-noo-yaat gaan gaaw saang) is approved. Depending on how flexible your local land office is, you may or may not need very detailed plans. I totally changed the design of my house after the architect finished the design and re-designed it myself, all in English, and had no problem getting the building permit.

Architectural design services can be quite expensive in Thailand so the better prepared you are to talk to an architect the faster and cheaper the process will be.

Some architects may have a problem finishing the design, so it's a good idea to hold on to most of the payments until you are satisfied with the work, and as an encouragement for the architect to finish.

A low cost alternative to hiring your own architect is to look at house plans at the local district land office. They may provide you with copies of plans at little or no cost, which you could modify to suit your own needs.

My experience with Thai architects is that if asked to do the design from scratch, they will over design the structure making it unnecessarily expensive to build. I think this is especially true for farang clients because they are afraid of under-designing and having problems later.

Since Thai buildings are typically based on the post and beam concept (i.e. walls are not structural, loads are supported by concrete, wood or steel posts and beams), then plan your floor layout based on a simple, regular grid of posts and beams. Each beam span should be 3 to 4 meters (4.5 as a maximum). Try to place walls over beams between posts. If you place walls that do not connect to posts you will usually need to add an intermediate under floor beam to support the weight of the wall. This adds cost and time. (I say usually because you may be able to avoid adding a beam if the wall is very light weight, such as steel studs and gypsum board).

Also, ask your architect to design all the beams the same size. For a 3-4m span, a 35-40cm high, 15-20cm wide beam with 6-8x16mm steel rods should be sufficient. The advantage of having all the beams the same size is that the builders can build them very quickly, like a mass production factory. Also, there is less chance of mistakes if one size fits all. I have seen plans that use 12 different beam sizes. This takes a long time to build the formwork and bend the reinforcing steel because the builders spend more time looking at the plans than building.

Architectural design software, 3D-CAD (Computer Aided Design)

For my house, I did the conceptual design myself on my computer using a 3D-CAD design tool, Rhino3D. I was able to visualize the whole house in photorealistic detail before talking to an architect, hiring a builder or digging a hole. I was even able to create detailed designs for complex items like spiral stairs, post/floor connections and plumbing systems in 3D, which was very useful for explaining what I wanted to the builder. This saved money, time and frustration in the long run because of less mistakes and re-builds.

I used Rhino3D, http://rhino3d.com/, which I believe is the best, most powerful, easy to use software tool for any 3D design project. There are many home design software packages available and I have tried most of them, but they are all very limited as soon as you want to do anything even slightly different from a basic American house (try creating this spiral staircase with a home architect software package!).

Rhino3D is a general purpose 3D modeling package, so you will have to create models for things like windows, doors, toilets, etc. yourself (you may be able to find models on the web and import them into Rhino). However, in my humble opinion, using Rhino3D is well worth the trouble to get a photorealist model of the end result and be able to walk around the virtual structure before you commit time and money to the real thing.

Autocad is the standard tool for architectural modeling of course, but again in my humble opinion, I think Autocad is the worst designed and hardest to use software package in the history of computer science. (I'm probably never going to be offered a job with Autocad after that!)

I get nothing for recommending Rhino3D by the way, I just think it's really good software. Like most software, it does crash occasionally so save your work often.

Since my plans were so well developed before I talked to an architect I was able to get a very good deal on the design work.

A useful tool for checking how the house will look before it is finished is Photoshop software.

I took this photo of the house after the main roof frame was started. I wanted to see how the roof angles would look on the finished roof and how the upper roof would look. I nailed a piece of wood where the upper roof line would be as a guide.

I downloaded an image of some roof tiles, of different styles and colors from the internet. Then in Photoshop, I created a complete roof.

Using this technique I was able to fine tune the roof design and choose the tile style and color.

Estimating the cost

Your architect should provide you with a detailed list of materials and perhaps even building costs for your project once the design is complete. However, it is often useful to brain storm a few ideas yourself first to see what you can afford before you spend time with and pay the architect.

A very rough estimate for total building cost (material and labor) for 2006, is:

- Very basic construction (bungalow), concrete on grade or raised wood floor, single sided cheap wood walls, light weight grass or asbestos (yes they still use asbestos here) roof - 5,000 baht/m^2 or less.

- Mid level construction (house), concrete floors and walls, nice tile or wood floor covering, hardwood window frames and doors, heavy concrete roof tile, good quality fixtures – 10,000 baht/m^2.

- High end constriction (luxury villa), top of the line construction and fixtures, marble, granite or hardwood floors, glazed roof tile, all the bells and whistles - probably more than 15,000 baht/m^2.

For a detailed estimate visit http://buildingthailand.com where you will find a downloadable excel spreadsheet. In it, you can enter the material quantities for your project and you will get an up to date price estimate for the material cost of your project. On some items, you can specify low, medium or high end. Using this tool you can quickly brainstorm ideas, like how many square meters to build? How many bedrooms and bathrooms can you afford? What kind of quality and finishing to use? etc. This will save you time and money with your architect.

Check the plans

Like everything else, you should carefully check the plans to make sure they make sense. The text will probably be written in Thai, so unless you read Thai, you will need a Thai friend to translate.

You should take the time to read the text carefully. I told my architect many times I wanted wood on the second floor but it still said concrete floors on the final plans.

Check that your windows have adequate protection from the sun and rain. This is usually achieved by an overhanging roof. Since Thailand is well inside the tropics, the sun will be in both the north and south sky at different times of the year, so you will need shade all around, not just the south side as in America and Europe. Shading windows will also help keep the house cooler.

For a very hot country, Thai architects seem to give very little attention to designing houses to be cool. Insulation is almost unheard of. Most buildings have un-insulated open frame roofs or improperly vented attic spaces. "Building Construction Illustrated", available in English and Thai, has very good information on site planning, solar radiation and environmental design. I highly recommend you read the English one and buy the Thai one for your architect and builder.

Another item to check is staircase design. In America, the building code requires an 11" tread and a 7" rise for each stair in residential buildings. In Thailand there is no standard, so check that the staircase is not too steep and check the handrail has sufficient balusters (vertical posts holding up the handrail) so a child cannot fall through. 4" is the maximum space between balusters in America.

Section 2 of this book details many things about construction techniques and materials in common use in Thailand and how they can be improved upon. Check your plans against the information in this book and if you feel your architect could improve on the design, show him this book to explain how.

Check that important details, like raising the reinforcing steel clear of the floor and side walls of footings and forms, is drawn and documented in the design. If you plan to use steel connectors for joining concrete to wood and wood to wood, or rough door frames as recommended in this book, tell your architect before he draws the plans.

Structural engineering details will probably be checked by a certified structural engineer, and the drawings stamped to certify the structural design. Your architect and the structural engineer should give you a guarantee of their work.

If you have already chosen a builder, have him check the design and if you are using a project manager, he must check the design also.

Building Permit

When you have the plans complete, you can apply for a building permit, a-noo-yaat gaan gaaw-saang, at the orbator's office. In theory you should get this before starting to build but many people start building before getting a permit, which seems not to be a problem. However, things may change, especially in overbuilt areas where local governments are starting to clamp down on excessive building developments.

To get a building permit you will need 3 sets of the plans, 3 sets of the structural engineering calculations and a guarantee letter from the structural engineer with a photocopy of his ID card and his original signature, and a copy of the land title document. If the person applying for the permit is not the land owner, you will also need a power of attorney to give the permit applicant the right to build on the owner's land. Permits will only be issued to Thai people or Thai companies. If you wish to own the house personally, the holder of the building permit must "sell" the house to you when the house is complete, which unfortunately means you will have to pay tax on the sale. This information is based on my experience in Ko Phangan, it may be different where you live so check with the Orbator's office first. Also, in recent months, my friend at the Orbator's office said it is better for a farang not to be involved at all in the permit process. Have your Thai friend take care of the permit and do not visit the Orbator's office yourself or you may find yourself with a hefty "farang tax".

In America, in order to get a building permit, the plans will be checked by the city plan checker in great detail for compliance with national and local building codes, zone compliance and a host of other rules and regulations. You will also have to pay a significant amount of money, something like 1-5% of the cost of the project! In Ko Phangan, the permit cost is negligible, a couple of hundred baht.

In some areas of Thailand, the building permit seems to be largely a formality. The plans are given a quick glance over and no one checks to see if the house you are building bares any resemblance to the house on the plans. The Thai system has the obvious advantage of minimizing bureaucratic overhead and makes changing the design far easier but it does mean that you or your project manager must be responsible for checking important structural and safety items as the building work progresses.

I have recently heard rumors that in Ko Samui, the local government is considering limiting building in some heavily developed parts of the island. Limits my range from limiting floor area to a maximum of 25% of the land size to prohibiting any building at all!

Note that typically you will have to build the house is at least 3m from the borders of the land. Also, for beach front land (at least in Ko Phangan) you cannot build the main structure within 12m of the sea. Decks and pools can be built closer than 12m from the sea providing they do not have a roof.

The following is an example building permit:

แบบ อ.1

ใบอนุญาตก่อสร้างอาคาร ดัดแปลงอาคาร หรือรื้อถอนอาคาร

เลขที่.........../2548

อนุญาตให้......บริษัท...เฮค..พร็อพเพอตี้.................. เจ้าของอาคารอยู่บ้านเลขที่.........45/1........

ตรอก/ซอย....-.......ถนน.......-.......หมู่ที่........ ตำบล/แขวง...เกาะพะงัน......อำเภอ.....เกาะพะงัน.............

จังหวัด .....สุราษฎร์ธานี.......

ข้อ 1 ทำการ............ก่อสร้างอาคาร คสล. สองชั้น..................ที่บ้านเลขที่........-........

ตรอก/ซอย..........-.......ถนน.......-.......หมู่ที่...8...ตำบล/แขวง...เกาะพะงัน...... อำเภอ/เขต...เกาะพะงัน...

จังหวัด.......สุราษฎร์ธานี.........ในที่ดิน โฉนดที่ดิน เลขที่/น.ส.3 เลขที่/ส.ค.1 เลขที่.................

ซึ่งเป็นที่ดินของ......นายสตีเฟ่น...การี...เฮค.....

ข้อ 2 เป็นอาคาร

(1) ชนิด........... อาคาร คสล. สองชั้น...... จำนวน....1....หลัง เพื่อใช้เป็น........ที่พักอาศัย..........

พื้นที่/ความยาว......200.00...ตารางเมตร ที่จอดรถ ที่กลับรถ และทางเข้าออกของรถจำนวน.....-.........คัน

พื้นที่.........-...........ตารางเมตร

(2) ชนิด.............-.................จำนวน...........หลัง เพื่อใช้เป็น.......-.......

พื้นที่/ความยาว............-............ตารางเมตร......ที่จอดรถ ที่กลับรถ และทางเข้าออกของรถจำนวน.......-....คัน

พื้นที่.........-............ตารางเมตร

(3) ชนิด.............-.................จำนวน...-..........หลัง เพื่อใช้เป็น.......-.......

พื้นที่/ความยาว............-............ตารางเมตร ที่จอดรถ ที่กลับรถ และทางเข้าออกของรถจำนวน..-......

คัน. พื้นที่............-............ตารางเมตร

ตามแผนผังบริเวณแบบแปลน รายการประกอบแบบแปลน และรายการคำนวณ

เลขที่.......-.......ที่แนบท้ายใบอนุญาตนี้

ข้อ 3. โดยมี..นายสตีเฟ่น การี เฮค เป็นผู้ควบคุมงาน

ข้อ 4. ผู้ได้ใบรับอนุญาตต้องปฏิบัติตามเงื่อนไขดังต่อไปนี้

(1) ผู้ได้รับใบอนุญาตต้องปฏิบัติตามหลักเกณฑ์ วิธีการ และเงื่อนไขตามที่กำหนดในกฎกระทรวง

และหรือข้อบัญญัติท้องถิ่น ซึ่งออกตามความในมาตรา8 (11) มาตรา9 หรือมาตรา 10 แห่งพระราช

บัญญัติควบคุมอาคาร พ.ศ. 2522

(2) ผู้ได้รับอนุญาตต้องปฏิบัติตามกฎหมายอื่น ๆ ที่เกี่ยวข้องด้วย

ใบอนุญาตฉบับนี้ใช้ได้จนถึงวันที่...8...เดือน....เมษายน......พ.ศ.2549

ออกให้ ณ วันที่...8...เดือน....เมษายน......พ.ศ.2548.

เรียน..นายทะเบียนอำเภอเกาะพะงัน .
อบต. ได้ทำการตรวจสอบรายละเอียดผังเมือง
แบบแปลนตามที่ยื่นมาปรากฏว่าถูกต้องตาม -
แบบแปลนผังเมืองทุกประการ
ขอแสดงความนับถือ

ลายมือชื่อ.................
(นายพิพัฒน์   อินทร์ทรง)
นายกองค์การบริหารส่วนตำบลเกาะพะงัน
เจ้าพนักงานท้องถิ่นผู้อนุญาต

House occupant registration (tha-biian baan)

When your house is complete, or in some places when you have the building permit, you can apply for a house occupant registration book, the tha-biian baan, which means the house will get an address. The tha-biian baan book lists the occupants of the building, not the ownership. Thais and foreigners with permanent residence who reside at the address will be registered in the tha-biian baan book. If the land is owned by a company, the tha-biian baan book can list the business name or premises name (restaurant, guest house, etc) under the house name heading on the first page.

Foreigners who are not permanent residents can apply for a yellow registration book. I am not sure there is any point to registering yourself in the yellow book.

Apply for a tha-biian baan at the Amphur (District) office. You will need to provide the building permit and the addresses of the neighboring houses, so the Amphur can find the location on their map.

You will need to get the signature of the sub-district headsman, the Gam-nan, who in theory should check to see if a house actually exists at the location you are claiming. Once you have the signature of the Gam-nan on the form provided by the Amphur office, pay 10 baht, watch a round of cock fighting, and you will get a nice new book with the new address and the name of the occupants listed inside.

A tha-biian baan is necessary for services like permanent electricity, water and telephone.

Since the address is new and unknown to the post office, it's a good idea to tell the post office the names or everybody living there at the new address and show them a map to the house if it is hard to find. Also, periodically check the undelivered mail pile at your local post office; you can find some interesting stuff about your friends in there too!

House ownership registration

Buildings other than condominiums do not have any form of title document, but their sale or long lease can be registered at the Amphur (district) land office. Proof of ownership, must be established either from proof of construction or document showing previous sale-purchase.

Transfer of a building as distinct from its land requires the posting of 30 days public notice (to see if anyone wishes to contest the ownership). Foreigners may own a building (as distinct from its land) and may register such transfer of ownership into their names at the local district office.

Post the plans on the job site

Communications is critical to the success of your house building project. Post the most recent drawings in a prominent place where the buiders can refer to them easily.

This is particularly important, if like me, you like to change things as you get new ideas during building.

Make sure the most recent drawings are posted with the date, and destroy old drawings to avoid confusion.

Photocopy drawings and descriptions from this book and post them too if you think it will help.

Working on your own house

If you do not have a work permit, you cannot legally work on your own house, at least not manual work. Even with a work permit, construction work is listed as a restricted occupation. Do a google search on "Restricted Occupations Thai law" and you will find several references detailing what you cannot do, even with a work permit.

Technically speaking it is illegal to check up on the building progress your self without a permit since it can be considered work, so be careful and stay friendly with the neighbors to avoid visits by the police.

You will probably get many offers from farang friends who want to help out for a little beer money. This is a bad idea! If you get caught, both you and your friend will be in big trouble.

English/Thai words and phrases

Architect — สถาปนิก sa^L thaap^L bpa^L nik^H

Structural engineer — วิศวกรโครงสร้าง wit^H sa^L wa^H gaawn khrohng saang^F

Interior designer — สถาปนิกตบแต่งภายใน sa^L thaap^L bpa^L nik^H dtohp^L dtaaeng^L phaay nai

Architecture — สถาปัตยกรรม sa^L thaa^R bpat^L dta^L ya^H gam

Design/plan — ออกแบบ aawk^L baaep^L

Floor plan — แผนผังชั้นพื้นดิน phaaen^R phang^R chan^H pheuun^H din

Sketch, describe roughly — วาด waat^F

Floor area — พื้นที่ไหม pheuun^H thee^F

Building permit — อนุญาตการก่อสร้าง a^L noo^H yaat^F gaan gaaw^L saang^F

House registration — ทะเบียนบ้าน tha^H biian baan^F

Village chief — ผู้ใหญ่บ้าน phuu^F yai^L baan^F

Sub-district headsman — กำนัน gam nan

Construction — สิ่งก่อสร้าง sing^L gaaw^L saang^F

Floors/levels — ชั้น chan^H

First floor — ชั้นหนึ่ง chan^H neung^L

Second floor — ชั้นสอง chan^H saawng^R

Chapter 8

Preparing to build

Road access

During construction of your house you will no doubt receive many deliveries from large trucks. You will need to ensure that you have an accessible road before you can start construction. Remember that a road that may be fine in the dry season can become impassable in the rainy season.

A 100cm thick, 3 meter wide road may cost between 3000 and 5000 baht per meter depending on the slope and the condition of the ground.

A more attractive alternative to solid concrete is paving bricks with concrete outer retaining frame. This method has the advantage that water seeps through the surface so there is less rain runoff which creates less side erosion than a solid concrete road. Also, since the paving bricks can move independently, there is no cracking of the surface so the road lasts far longer.

If planning to use a cheaper road, suitable only for motorcycles or a small car, you may want to hold off building it until the heavy work is done and there will be no more big trucks visiting your site.

Temporary water and electricity

You will need water and electricity while building your house. This can take longer than you think to set up, so plan ahead.

I cannot speak for the whole of Thailand, but in Ko Phangan, the water company will not connect new customers in the dry season. I was fortunate that my next door neighbor let me connect to their water supply while building the house; otherwise it would have had to truck it in at 800 baht per 1000 liters! Or delay building by 5 months.

You should also buy a water tank(s) since the water supply may be unreliable.

You can also purchase water from a truck, but this can be quite expensive. In Ko Phangan, 2000 liters from a truck costs about 800 baht.

Drainage and storm water

Torrential rain and flooding is quite common in Thailand as in any tropical country. Find out where the natural drainage occurs on your land in heavy rain. If you plan to put your house in the path of natural drainage, you should create a way for the water to drain that bypasses the house.

If the soil under your house frequently becomes saturated, you will be prone to flooding or sinking of the footing which can cause serious structural damage.

Be very careful when buying land on a slope. As I write this book, in December 2005, many houses in the south of Thailand are being swept away by landslides. The problem is over development. Many hillsides are been stripped of trees, vegetation and large rocks which have stabilized the land for hundreds or thousands of years. As a result, heavy rains can easily erode the exposed soil, especially if it has been disturbed by building projects. This causes not only the land that has been built on to slide, but also the land above and below.

Slopes and retaining wall

If your land is sloping, you may need a retaining wall to stop the ground under your footing eroding away or the ground above you washing into your house and pushing your house down the hill. Consult with a soil engineer familiar with your area if you are on a slope.

Retaining walls will typically be built with reinforced concrete and have pilings deep into the subsoil or bedrock. The wall should have drainage holes to relieve the water pressure on the up hill side in heavy rain.

A simple, low cost, easy to build alternative for short retaining walls (up to about 1.5 meters tall), is to use concrete fence posts and concrete floor slabs. Place concrete fence posts about 50cm deep and about 50cm apart in a straight line. Tilt the fence posts towards the hill at about a 30-40 degree angle, DO NOT BUILD THE WALL VERTICALLY. Fence posts are usually not very strong and will break easily of the wall is build vertically. By tilting the wall towards the hill, the pressure of the soil behind the wall will tend to push down, not just out, and therefore will put less stress on the support post. Note that Thai builders will have a very difficult time not building it vertically, you must emphasize the tilt is needed and check they do it.

When the line of support posts are in place, lower concrete floor slabs in between the posts and the hill and back fill with soil as you build up the wall. Adding a little cement at the base of the posts will help stabilize the whole thing.

I built a 1.5m tall, 3m long wall in 1 hour with 5 chang at a cost of about 1000 baht. It's survived this rainy season without problems.

Mature trees also help stabilize the soil so avoid cutting trees on slopes and plant fast growing tress if possible.

Vertiver grass is a special, long rooted grass that is perfect for stabilizing hillsides. The King is encouraging the planting of Vertiver throughout Thailand for natural erosion control and pollution cleanup http://prvn.rdpb.go.th/. Vertiver grass is available free from district agricultural offices. See www.**vetiver**.com http://www.chaipat.or.th/chaipat/vetiver/vetiver_3/vetiver_e3.html for more information about this amazing grass.

When to build

If you have flexibility about when to build, I recommend starting construction about 1 to 2 months before the end of the rainy season in your area.

It is easier to dig the footings while the ground is wet and it will be easier to keep the concrete cooler and moist while curing if it rains often. After the concrete work is complete, you will probably be using more wood and/or steel. Since the roof will not be on yet, dryer weather is preferred.

However, be aware that you may have problems with access and deliveries via dirt and sand roads in the rainy season.

Site preparation

Mark out the desired location for your house with posts and string. Walk around, check the size, check the view, etc. I originally designed my house at 12m x 12m, which on paper didn't seem too big. Only after I did the basic design then paid an architect to do the detail design, did I mark out a 12 meter square on my land. I immediately realized that 12m x 12m was way too big and too close to the boundaries of the land!

Check that there are no problems with your choice of house locations, such as trees, big rocks, streams, etc.

If you have trees close to the house location, within about 5 meters, you should remove them before you start building. If you remove them later, they may crash into the house as they are being felled. Some kinds of trees cannot be cut down without a permit, or at all, so check with the local land office.

I forgot to deal with 6 big coconut trees (the tropical menace as I call them) within a few meters from my house until the roof was half finished. Removing them became much harder and more dangerous than if I

had done it before building.

However, since I didn't want the wood, I had them cut for free in return for the wood.

For trees in difficult positions, hire a tree expert. Note the anti-tailgating device (left)!

Sometimes, on land that was rice paddy, or low lying, the owner builds up the level by trucking in soil or sand. New, loose soil and sand must be heavily compacted before footings and foundations can be build into it otherwise you will get large amounts of settling, especially in the rainy season. Settling (uneven sinking of the footings and foundation) will cause cracks in floors and walls and possibly major structural damage. If you plan to raise the level of your lot, I suggest you hire a steam roller like the ones used to build roads, and let the land settle through one rainy season.

Storage and worker accommodation

Often the builders will live on your job site, usually because they are too poor to rent or they are migrant workers. This has the advantage that they can safeguard the building supplies and they will probably work 7 days a week.

Since building temporary accommodation will cost you money, look into options to save money. Is there a house or barn on the property they can use? Can they live somewhere else until the foundation/concrete work is finished then use the form wood to build a temporary house, or live under your house?

You will probably need a place out of the rain to store concrete and expensive items too. Typically the builder will make a simple storage shed with metal, asbestos or canvas roof and plastic sheet walls.

English/Thai words and phrases

Prepare	เตรียม dtriiam
Temporary	ชั่วคราว chuaa^F khraao
Permanent	ถาวร thaa^R waawn
Temporary water	น้ำชั่วคราว naahm^H chuaa^F khraao
Temporary electricity	ไฟชั่วคราว fai chuaa^F khraao
Water tank	ถังเก็บน้ำ thang^R gep^L naahm^H
Septic tank (simple hole in ground)	ส้วมซึม suaam^F seum
Septic tank (with separator/filter)	ถังบำบัด thang^R bahm bat^L
Slope	ลาด laat^F
Retaining wall	กำแพง gahm phaaeng
Clear land of weeds and rubbish	เคลียร์พื้นที่ clear pheuun^H thee^F
To cut down a tree	โค่นต้นไม้ khohn^F dtohn^F maai^H
To dig a hole, excavate	ขุด khoot^L
Tent, temporary outdoor shelter	ปะรำ bpa^L rahm
Shed	เพิงหมาแหงน pheerng maa^R ngaaen^R
To drain (water)	ระบาย ra^H baay
Drainage ditch	คูน้ำ khuu naahm^H
Landslide	ดินถล่ม din tha^L lohm^L
Back hoe (excavator)	แบ็คโฮ back hoe
Bulldozer/grader	รถไถ roht^H tai^R
Steam roller	รถบด roht^H bot^L

About how much will it cost to build a road to here? ทำถนนเข้ามาที่นี่

ประมาณ เท่าไร thahm tha^L nohn^R khao^F maa^M
thee^F nee^F bpra^L maan thao^F rai

About how long will it take to build a road to here? ทำถนนเข้ามาที่นี่นาน

ประมาณ เท่าไร thahm tha^L nohn^R khao^F maa^M
thee^F nee^F naan bpra^L maan thao^F rai

Do you think a retaining wall is necessary? คุณคิดว่าจำเป็นต้องทำกำแพง

ไหม khoon khit^H waa^F jahm bpen dtaawng^F
thahm gahm phaaeng mai^R

Will you cut down the trees and clear the land? คุณจะโค่นต้นไม้และเคลียร์พื้นที่

ไหม khoon ja^L khohn^F dtohn^F maai^H lae^H clear
pheuun^H thee^F mai^R

How much is the back hoe per hour? แบล็คโฮชั่วโมงละเท่าไร back hoe
chuaa^F mohng la^H thao^F rai

Chapter 9

Builders and project managers

Types of building arrangements

When I was shopping for a builder, I was offered 3 totally different arrangements, as described below. There may be more. (I use the arrangements rather than contracts because a contract implies something more concrete than what I was actually offered).

Pay as you go

With "pay as you go", you pay the wage bill for each worker that works that day, plus the wage for the boss. Typically, the men get paid around 130-300 baht/day, the women, 120-200 baht/day and the boss 300-500 baht/day or more depending on how experienced he is and how much you think he is worth.

You are usually responsible for ordering the materials and paying for them when they arrive. If your materials arrive late and the workers are idle, you still pay the wage bill of course.

There are many disadvantages to this arrangement. The biggest one is that you have no idea how much your house is going to cost until it's finished. The other major problems are you have to monitor how many people show up every day or you will likely be paying for no shows, and every time they take another 1 ½ hour lunch break you wonder where your money is going.

This arrangement may be suitable for a very small structure that only requires a few days of work, or you think you are going to change the design so often, you don't want to be tied to a contract.

You will probably actually pay the wage bill every week or so. You should randomly check the number of people on-site, to be sure the check-bin is accurate.

In the closing chapter of this book, I talk about how to get the highest possible quality house. The main suggestion is that you pay the builders as you go so that the builder is not under financial pressure to cut corners and get the job finished quickly.

Pay for labor, buy your own materials

In this type of arrangement, the builder will usually quote you a labor price for the whole job, which is typically based on the number of square meters and adjusted for the complexity of the design. His price should be fixed, but don't be too surprised if he needs to raise it to finish the job because of some change you made or some unforeseen circumstance. It would be safe to allow a 30% safety margin on top of the quote for what the final labor cost will be.

Often the builder will not include things like electrical, tile, wood finishing, kitchen cabinets, painting, etc. Everything required to get the house completely finished, riiap raawy laaeo, should be discussed and documented as to whether it's included in the price or not. There is a checklist at the end of this book for the things to ask about.

In this arrangement, as in "pay by the day", you are responsible for buying the materials, however your builder may order some basic materials such as concrete, steel, brick, structural wood, concrete form wood, plumbing, etc. You will typically order doors and windows, tile, bathroom and kitchen fixtures, wood floors, paint, etc. You should determine with your builder who orders what before you start, to avoid confusion and over buying.

In my humble opinion, this is the best way to build your house. You can make a reasonable estimate as to the cost at the start of the project. If you change your mind during the build and say change the size, you can easily agree on a new price based on the square meter rate. Also, since you are responsible for buying the materials, you can choose to the quality and supplier to suit your own taste. If the builder is buying as in the next case, you can be sure he will buy the cheapest regardless of quality.

In this arrangement, you may be asked to pay by the week, months, etc, or when a major milestone is reached, such as footing complete, floor complete, etc. Clearly the milestone method is better for you because if the builder suddenly disappears and never comes back (it happens) at least you have got something for your money.

My builder built about one third of the whole house before he asked me for a single baht! But I suspect that is unusual. You will probably need to pay something to get started and make frequent progress payments. Be clear about what the payment schedule is. It will probably be written in Thai so you will probably want to translate and re-write it in English.

A good "rule of thumb" is

- 25% - Footings, posts and slab/floor complete

- 25% - Walls and roof complete

- 25% - Doors, windows, floor/wall cover, stairs, plumbing, electrical complete

- 25% - House 100% complete and outside cleaned up.

Builder does everything

With "builder does everything" arrangement, the builder will provide labor and materials and will hand over a finished house. You will have to negotiate how finished the house actually is. Things like kitchen fixtures, electrical and plumbing fixtures, may be extra. You will need to sure you know exactly what is included and what is excluded from the contract.

Also, you will need to be specific about the quality and type of material, especially for things like floor tile, bathroom and kitchen fixtures, etc. You will probably want to select these items yourself even through the builder will be buying them, so you should work out how much is budgeted for those items in the contract. Your builder may say "all grade A, no problem" but your idea of grade A and his may be very different.

This may be your preferred way to build the house if you do not plan to be heavily involved in the building process, or if the house is from a standard plan and you can see a similar example already built.

This method has the advantage that you should know exactly how much it's going to cost at the start of the project, but jacking the price up is not un-heard of!

Hire your own team

In many "farang" parts of the country, builders may be expensive and so busy that they don't have time to work on your house (even through they claim they will). If you have contacts "up country"; outside of the rice season, you may be able to hire your own team to come on your site for a few months and build the house. You will typically have to pay transportation to and from the job site, provide housing on site and pay a monthly salary, rain or shine, but you will likely pay rates more comparable to rural Thailand and have the advantage that the worker are committed to your project alone. Also, you can hire and fire workers as needed and generally have more control than hiring through a boss.

Contracts and payments

Your builder may have a building contract which can be modified to fit your situation, or your lawyer can write a contract for you. Many builders prefer not to have any contract at all. You will likely get a better price quote without a contract.

A building contract should specify exactly what is and is not covered by the contract, material quality, approximate time schedule, payment schedule including bonuses or penalties, guarantees, etc. If the builder provides a contract, have your lawyer check it to make sure your rights are protected. The checklist at the end of this book lists several items you should verify who is responsible for.

Check that there is a provision for early termination of the contract. In the event that you are not satisfied with the quality or the work, you will want a way out of the contact without having to pay the full amount.

Be very careful about how much money you give before work is done and materials arrive. Ideally, you will not pay anything until a significant milestone is reached and the amount you pay is consistent with the value of the work and materials you have acquired. My builder quit before the house was finished (actually, it was by mutual agreement since I was not satisfied with the quality of the finish work). However, I feel I got a fair amount of work for what I paid, which was considerably less than the price had he finished the house. Builders quitting in the middle of a job is actually quite common it seems, especially during times where there is a high demand for builders.

Many builders, especially in busy housing markets, will demand a large deposit before any work begins. **Often, the builders will not start building your house for a long time, maybe never; they will just sit on your deposit.** Your building contract should specify the start and completion date of project, so if your builder misses the start data, in theory you can get your deposit back. You may have to go to court to get your deposit back which would incur legal bills. Even if you win the court case, that does not mean the builder will simply pay up. You will likely have to go to the police to seize the builder's assets. The police will charge 10-15% for this service. The builder will probably plead hardship; "Oh, you can't take my truck, I need that for work. You can't take my house, I need somewhere to live", etc. **The bottom line is, it may be cheaper to walk away from your deposit and hope for better luck next time!**

Do not pay for materials and services until you have received them and keep contact information of other builders incase you end up needing them to finish your house. Also, remember to get written receipts from the builder to prove you have paid.

The contract should include a warrantee. Often many problems will not become obvious until you have lived in the house for a while. Check that the length of the warrantee covers at least one rainy season as problems like doors and windows not fitting, roof leaks etc. will become far more noticeable in the rainy season.

Choosing a builder; shop around and estimate total cost

When you have the plans ready, you should ask several builders for quotes. You may get quotes in any or all three of the types mentioned above, or maybe something else.

If the quote seems reasonable, you will want to do "due diligence", the same as you would when choosing a lawyer. Look at other houses he has built or better yet, is currently building and if possible find out about the houses he doesn't want you to see.

You should also find out how many projects the head guy is currently working on, how many people at his disposal and how often he plans to show up at your site. If he has several ongoing projects, it's likely he will only visit your site for an hour of so per day, so you will also be heavily dependent on the quality of the on-site foreman. It's pretty unlikely you will get to check out the foreman ahead of time since your builder may not even know who he will use, so you basically have to trust your builder's judgment and team.

Ask if the same foreman is going to stay with your house until it is finished. Depending on your part of the country, the workers may be migrant workers. Often, when they have enough money saved up, they go home or back to the farm for growing season. If you have a foreman or a key worker you are happy with and you are well into the job, check that he will stay to the end of the job. Maybe offer him a little bonus to stay if necessary. It is quite frustrating to spend a lot of time helping the foreman understand how you want things done, only to find he is leaving and the new guy has no idea what is happening.

If your builder is managing several simultaneous building jobs, that is not necessarily a bad thing. It probably means he has access to a bigger work force of specialists. So you may get one team, for foundation and concrete and another for wood work, etc. Each team may be more skilled in their own field that the jack-of-all-trades that a smaller operation may have access to. I had different teams for foundation and concrete, walls, wood floor, roof, plumbing, electrical and finish work.

You should estimate the labor and materials cost for your house independently of the builder so you can check and compare the different quotes, "apples to apples". Also it's good to have and estimate so you can budget the total cost. Maybe you may want to change a few things based on the estimate and/or the quotes. It always best to change before you start building of course.

You should talk to as many builders as you can find in your local area. It's worth taking your time to find the right guy. In parts of the country with lots of farangs, you will probably find many builders used to dealing with farangs, contracts, etc. Don't get lazy because the builder speaks English and appears to know what he is doing, you should check everything. In rural areas, you may have no choice but to hire a foreman and hire the builders yourself. The builders will often be farmers with little or no building experience, at least not to the standard you would like. You will need to be very actively involved in managing the building and speak reasonably good Thai (or Burmese or Lao!).

Please read the summary Chapter 20, "When the rubber meats the road" for more information about how my building experience worked out. One very important point in this section is that your builder may be very proficient at general construction but may but totally incapable of certain "specialty" jobs such as plumbing, electrical, flooring, detail and finish carpentry. In addition to verifying your builders general construction skills, you should pay special attention to there specific areas. **If you are unsure about your builders ability to do a good job on these specialty items, take them off the list of jobs for your general contractor and hire a team with the necessary skills to do the jobs right.**

Project managers

If you are not living in Thailand full time or you are not supervising the building yourself, you should definitely consider hiring a local project manager.

A project manager is usually a native English (or your language) speaking person with a background in construction, who has lived in, and supervised the building of houses in your area and has some building experience from the West.

Project managers usually charge a 25% fee on top of the total cost of your project. For that they will help you hire a builder, supervise the building process and help with the purchase of materials. They will do project planning and scheduling of deliveries, and may do budgeting and handling of payments.

Since project managers are critical to your success and have control of your money, you should have a high level of trust in a project manager's work and honesty! Do your homework when choosing a project manager just as you would a lawyer, architect or builder.

You should check how many concurrent projects a project manager has on the go at any time. It is vital that the project manager spend significant "quality" time at your job site. If he is handling too many projects at the same time, he may miss a critical check point in the process and the consequences could be disastrous.

I noticed my builders would start concrete pours when they thought I was not going to be around, early in the morning or when I had to go pick up supplies! After I noticed this little trick, I would spend all day at the job site for the day of the concrete pour and the day before, checking the form work and everything that is mentioned in the checklists at the end of this book.

In America, the city building inspector will check everything before you move on to the next stage. He will sign it off, on the checklist on the back of the building permit, or if he is not satisfied with the work, your builders will have to fix it and the inspector will come back and check again. In Thailand, at least for residential buildings, there is no such check, YOU OR YOUR PROJECT MANAGER MUST CHECK EVERYTHING YOURSELF! If you or your project manager miss a critical check point, the consequences could be disastrous!

If you or your project manager is going to be away from the job site for a few days, I suggest you either have the builders do something that is virtually impossible to do wrong, like painting or digging, or stop work until you get back. Otherwise you may be quite surprised with what you find when you come back to the house. (Note: I wrote this paragraph early in the building work. I have subsequently discovered that the builders can actually paint and dig holes wrong, so it is probably best that they take a few days off while you are gone!)

Health and safety in the work place

Not applicable! But seriously, in Thailand, the complete disregard for dangerous situations is quite shocking. Workers will happily work on high roofs or climb coconut tress without any safety gear; mothers bring their toddlers to work and let them roam around freely, in bare feet, playing with power tools or whatever they can find; power saws always have the safety plate wired back before it hardly leaves the shop!

My builders did not want to put anything on the floor joists to make a safe temporary floor while they worked on the 2nd story and the roof.

Thai builders seem to have a sixth sense of survival. I guess they learn it while toddlers, walking around building sites in bare feet, playing with power tools!

I have no suggestions about how to improve workplace safety, Thai builders will do some things their way, and working style is one of them. Keep a first aid kid handy just in case.

Care and feeding of the workers

I have a "beer bust", as we call it in Silicon Valley high-tech companies, every week, usually Friday or Saturday. I bring beer, Thai whiskey, and drinks for the girls, etc. Also if we have reached a major milestone like the floor finished, we have a barbeque too. The workers love it and I love it too. It gives a chance to meet the workers socially and practice my Thai.

To the Thai builders we are rich beyond their wildest dreams. This can create a divide and possibly resentment. If you are like me and walk around the building site every day, checking everything and telling them to fix things, they can get a little ticked off. I have heard of many building teams getting up and leaving a job, never to return, because the farang owner was too demanding and not tactful.

The beer bust is a good team building exercise and helps you get things done your way.

I rented a bungalow next to my site so the workers have a bathroom. Normally the builder should supply a portable toilet, but for some reason I could never convince my builder to get one. The bungalow rental worked out very well for several uses, toilet, office, tool storage.

I also supplied a CD/radio and some Thai music CD's. The workers are usually quite poor and may not have even the basic luxuries that we take for granted.

I don't know if this is the same for everyone, but at my site, the workers worked seven days a week, every week (except Song-kran).

English/Thai words and phrases

Builder	ช่าง chang^F
Builder	ช่างก่อสร้าง chang^F gaaw^L saang^F
Elephant	ช้าง chaang^H
To build	สร้าง saang^F
Build a house	ปลูกบ้าน bpluuk^L baan^F
Project manager	ผู้จัดการโครงการ phuu^F jat^L gaan khr<u>o</u>hng gaan
Labor	แรงงาน raaeng ngaan
Materials	วัสดุ watsa^H doo^L
Contract to build house	สัญญาปลูกสร้างบ้าน san^R yaa bpluuk^L saang^F baan^F
Bricklayer, mason	ช่างก่ออิฐ chang^F gaaw^L it^L
Painter	ช่างทาสี chang^F thaa see^R
Plumber	ช่างประปา chang^F bpra^L bpaa
Welder	ช่างเชื่อมโลหะ chang^F cheuuam^F loh ha^L
Electrician	ช่างไฟ chang^F fai^M
Carpenter	ช่างไม้ chang^F maai^H
Guarantee	รับรอง rap^H raawng
How many builders do you have?	มีกี่ช่าง mee gee^L chang^F
When do I pay?	จ่ายเมื่อไร jaay^L meuua^F rai
Who will buy the materials?	ใครจะซื้อวัสดุ khrai^M ja^L seuu^H watsa^H doo^L

How long to build?	ปลูกสร้างบ้านนานเท่าไหร่ bpluuk^L saang^F baan^F naan thao^F rai^L
How many months?	กี่เดือน gee^L deuuan
Neat, ready, all in order	เรียบร้อยแล้ว riiap^F raawy^H laaeo^H
How long is the guarantee?	รับรองนานเท่าไหร่ rap^H raawng naan thao^F rai^L

Section 2: Building techniques, materials and tools

Thai houses come in many shapes, sizes and types. Here in Ko Phangan we have 50 or more building projects at the moment. My house is standing on concrete legs and has a concrete first floor, wood second floor and wood frame roof. Another project has a concrete slab floor, concrete walls on both levels and a steel frame roof. Many bungalows are built with concrete legs and wood floor, walls, roof, etc.

The style is up to you of course; all have pros and cons. Building up on legs provides you with storage under the house, gives easy access to sewer pipes and other utilities, is safer if your land is prone to flooding, maybe gives you a better view and adds privacy from the neighbors. Building on a slab at ground level is quicker, cheaper and better if you don't like stairs but may have problems with flooding and dampness. Wood looks nice and is strong if well cared for but concrete should last forever, needs no maintenance and is usually cheaper.

See http://www.orientalarchitecture.com/thaicountryside/thaihousesbindex.htm for some traditional Thai architecture ideas.

Ko Phangan does not have the grand luxury villas of Phuket and Ko Samui, but we do have some very beautiful homes, restaurants and resorts. Here are a few of the nicer buildings on Ko Phangan.

This restaurant uses a concrete

first (ground) floor with stones set in concrete for the siding and beautiful wood on the second (first) floor with Wat style roof details.

This all concrete house has a very interesting roof design and a nice blend of traditional and modern Thai styling. The owners have done a very nice, simple but elegant job with the landscaping too.

This spectacular resort shows traditional Thai style and Thai wood working skills at their best.

The details on the roof are:

กาแล ghar leah

หน้าบัน naa^F ban

หยดน้ำ yot^L naam^H

All buildings will start with a hole in the ground, some steel and concrete. This section will go into detail about building techniques, materials and tools commonly used in Thailand, and a few suggestions on ways to improve on them where necessary.

Chapter 10 Parts of a house

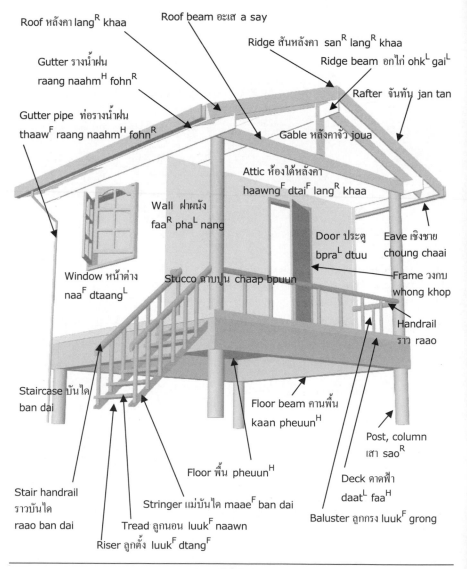

Roof หลังคา lang^R khaa

Roof beam อะเส a say

Ridge สันหลังคา san^R lang^R khaa

Ridge beam อกไก่ ohk^L gai^L

Gutter รางน้ำฝน raang naahm^H fohn^R

Rafter จันทัน jan tan

Gutter pipe ท่อรางน้ำฝน thaaw^F raang naahm^H fohn^R

Gable หลังคาจั่ว joua

Attic ห้องใต้หลังคา haawng^F dtai^F lang^R khaa

Wall ฝาผนัง faa^R pha^L nang

Door ประตู bpra^L dtuu

Eave เชิงชาย choung chaai

Window หน้าต่าง naa^F dtaang^L

Stucco ฉาบปูน chaap bpuun

Frame วงกบ whong khop

Handrail ราว raao

Staircase บันได ban dai

Floor beam คานพื้น kaan pheuun^H

Post, column เสา sao^R

Stair handrail ราวบันได raao ban dai

Floor พื้น pheuun^H

Stringer แม่บันได maae^F ban dai

Deck ดาดฟ้า daat^L faa^H

Tread ลูกนอน luuk^F naawn

Baluster ลูกกรง luuk^F grong

Riser ลูกตั้ง luuk^F dtang^F

English/Thai words and phrases

House	บ้าน baan^F
Footing	ฟุตติ้ง foot^R ing^F
Post, poll, column	เสา sao^R
Basement	ห้องใต้ดิน haawng^F dtai^F din
Beam	คาน kaan
Floor	พื้น pheuun^H
Floor beam	คานพื้น kaan pheuun^H

Floor joist (horizontal member usually sitting on beam and supporting the floor)

ตงพื้น dtong pheuun^H

Ground, floor, sub floor, foundation	พื้น pheuun^H
Wall	ฝาผนัง faa^R pha^L nang
Ceiling	เพดาน phaeh daan
Door	ประตู bpra^L dtuu
Handle (door)	ด้าม daam^F
Hinge	บานพับ baan phap^H
Lock	กุญแจ goon jaae
Key	ลูกกุญแจ luuk^F goon jaae
Window	หน้าต่าง naa^F dtaang^L
Window pane	กระจกหน้าต่าง gra^L johk^L naa^F dtaang^L
Door or window screen	มุ้งลวด moong^H luaat^F
Shutters for a window	บานเกล็ดหน้าต่าง baan glet^L naa^F dtaang^L
Bolt (of a lock)	กลอน glaawn

Frame (door/window)	วงกบ whong khop
Staircase, steps, ladder	บันได ban dai
Handrail	ราว raao
Staircase handrail	ราวบันได raao ban dai
Baluster	ลูกกรง luuk^F grong
Stringer (staircase frame)	แม่บันได maae^F ban dai (mother of the stairs)
Tread	ลูกนอน luuk^F naawn (sleeping child)
Riser	ลูกตั้ง dtang^F luuk^F (standing child)
Roof	หลังคา lang^R khaa
Roof tile	กระเบื้องหลังคา gra^L beuuang^F lang^R khaa
Attic	ห้องใต้หลังคา haawng^F dtai^F lang^R khaa
Rafter (sloping beams)	คานค้ำหลังคา kaan kam^R lang^R khaa
Roof beam	อะเส a say
Ridge	สันหลังคา san^R lang^R khaa
Ridge beam	อกไก่ ohk^L gai^L (chicken breast!)
Purline (cross members supporting roof cover)	แป bear
Eave (overhanging lower edge of roof)	เชิงชาย choung chaai
Gable (triangular shaped area at ends of roof)	หลังคาจั่ว joua
Gable end	หลังคาจั่ว joua
Gutter (rain gutter)	รางน้ำฝน raang naahm^H fohn^R
Gutter pipe, downspout	ท่อรางน้ำฝน thaaw^F raang naahm^H fohn^R

ROOMS

Room	ห้อง haawng^F
Bathroom, toilet	ห้องน้ำ haawng^F naahm^H

Bedroom	ห้องนอน haawng^F nown
Kitchen	ห้องครัว haawng^F khruaa
Living room	ห้องรับแขก haawng^F rap^H khaaek^L
Rec. room, den	ห้องนั่งเล่น haawng^F nang^F lehn^F
Front porch, balcony	มุข mook^H
Closet, small room	ห้องเล็ก haawng^F lek^H
Basement	ห้องใต้ดิน haawng^F dtai^F din
Attic	ห้องใต้หลังคา haawng^F dtai^F lang^R khaa

Chapter 11

Concrete and form work

Almost all structures will start with concrete and steel. Only concrete should come into contact with the ground. The success of concrete work is based mostly on preparation. By the time the concrete goes in, 90% of the work is done.

See http://en.wikipedia.org/wiki/Concrete for great information about concrete.

Construction of forms and reinforcing steel structures are critical to the long term structural integrity of your building

Concrete is a science, but unfortunately, in Thailand, it's usually not done very scientifically. Concrete is a mixture of Portland cement, fine aggregate (sand), course aggregate (rock or gravel) and water mixed thoroughly in the correct proportions.

The strength of concrete depends on 3 factors:

1) The proportions of cement, sand, rock and water in the mixture

2) How well the air pockets are removed from the poured concrete

3) How long it has to cure and the curing conditions

In all of the above factors, I feel that Thai builders generally do a bad job.

Types of cement in Thailand

Cement is typically available in 50kg bags. The two most popular cement types are "ปูนช้าง bpuun chaang", elephant cement and "ปูนปีเสือ bpuun seuua", tiger cement. Bpuun chaang, as the name suggests is stronger and is used for structural concrete for footing, posts, beams, and floors. Bpuun seuua is stickier and smoother and is used for cement mortar for concrete block walls, tile underlying and chaap (rendering). "ปูนเพชร bpuun phaeht", diamond cement is similar to bpuun chaang, perhaps a little stronger.

Also, "ปูนกาว bpuun gaao", glue cement is often used for tiling. The green crocodile brand is used for normal tile and the red crocodile for swimming pools.

Superblock and qcon (autoclave aerated concrete block) has its own special cement.

Cement/water proportion

The ratio of water to cement will control how strong your final concrete is. The more water that is in the concrete mix, the weaker your concrete will be.

This graph shows the relationship between the amount of water in the concrete as a ratio of water to cement, and its effect on the concrete strength (after 28 days).

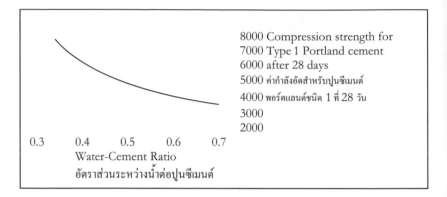

8000 Compression strength for
7000 Type 1 Portland cement
6000 after 28 days
5000 ค่ากำลังอัดสำหรับปูนซีเมนต์
4000 พอร์ตแลนด์ชนิด 1 ที่ 28 วัน
3000
2000

0.3   0.4   0.5   0.6   0.7
Water-Cement Ratio
อัตราส่วนระหว่างน้ำต่อปูนซีเมนต์

The graph above shows that by doubling the amount of water in the concrete mix, you will approximately half its strength!

Concrete should be firm enough that if you form a tower about 1 foot (30cm) high and about 4 inches (10cm) diameter, it should droop no more than about 3 or 4 inches (7-10cm). If it drops instantly into a pile of rock swimming in cement soup, (tom yam hin), you have a big problem!

You can do this test yourself with a 30cm long section of 4" water pipe. Fill it with concrete, slide the pipe off and see what happens.

I find that Thai builders love to make concrete too wet, because it's easier to work with. Keep a close eye on the consistency of the mix and tell them if you are not satisfied. The graph above shows how water reduces the strength of concrete. It also causes cracking and makes the concrete porous.

After numerous failed attempts to get dryer cement by saying "add less water", I finally found a way to get the concrete I want. The following is an important tip for communicating with Thai people in general. **Don't tell Thais what you don't want, tell them what you want!** On my friend's swimming pool, I asked the man working the cement mixer how many buckets of sand and how many buckets of rock they normally put in the mixer with one bag of cement. The answer was 10 rock and 12 sand. I told them to use 8 rock and 10 sand and add only enough water to make it sticky. Following these instructions, I got perfect cement every time. The pool floor and walls when in perfectly and are unbelievably strong.

Also, use plasticizer to maintain workability and while reduce water content (http://en.wikipedia.org/wiki/Plasticizer) .

The water in concrete should be clean and not salty. Concrete books say it should be good enough to drink. I wouldn't drink the water coming out of my pipes, but it is good enough for concrete.

Air pockets in poured concrete

Freshly poured concrete is full of air pockets. Air does not support any weight (surprise, surprise!). It is vitally important that the air is shaken out of the concrete before it hardens. This is usually done by stabbing or poking it repeatedly with a piece of steel rod or a concrete vibrator.

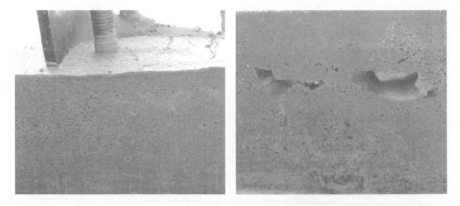

These 2 pictures show the effect of vibrating more or less air out of the same concrete in 2 different places. The left side shows the area under the post bases where the concrete was poked for about 2 minutes. As you can see, the air bubbles are very small. The right side shows where the concrete was not vibrated for long enough. This air pocket is about 2cm long and 1cm high.

You can buy a concrete vibrator for bigger jobs for about 3-10,000 baht. If you do not use a concrete vibrator, I suggest you tell your builder you want 2 extra people on concrete days that do nothing but vibrate the concrete. And check that it is what they actually do.

If concrete is properly vibrated, it will become considerably heavier since the air is forced out and replaced by concrete. This will put more stress on the form work and can break or bend the forms, especially if the builders at not used to making forms or concrete correctly. This happened to me on my swimming pool walls. It took two weeks with a concrete saw to correct it!

The concrete in this picture (below) was not adequately vibrated and the steel was too close to the forms. The concrete did not get under the steel reinforcing bar so it will not have the benefit of steel reinforcement and the steel will rust out over time.

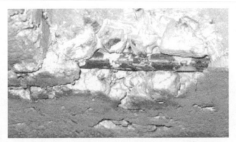

I suspect that some Thai builders think that by making the concrete very wet, the concrete will simply find its own way around steel and into tight corners and the bubbles will just float to the surface by themselves. This picture (left) demonstrates they are wrong on all counts. Wet concrete is easier to work than dry concrete but it still needs vibration to get the air out and wet concrete is inherently less strong than dry concrete anyhow.

Sometimes you may find it is impossible to get your builders to do a good job of vibrating the concrete. I finally asked my wife do it.

Curing concrete

Concrete gains most of its strength in the first 28 days after it is poured. Think of those first 28 days like it's a new baby. You need to take extra care not to over stress it (by loading too much weight on it) and it has to cure properly.

Concrete gains strength by curing NOT BY DRYING!! It must be protected from drying too quickly, which in Thailand, in the dry season is admittedly a big challenge.

If concrete dries too quickly, it will not have a chance to cure and the concrete will be weak.

You should leave wood forms on as long as possible, both to provide support and to stop it drying too quickly. This is especially important on structural components like beams, joists and posts.

Also cover new concrete with something to protect it from the sun and try to keep it moist. The Thais will think you are crazy, kon baa!, watering concrete, especially after you have spend all morning complaining the mix is too wet, but it is very important you look after your new baby for the first 28 days. You cannot fix it later (although the builder will try by patching it up with cement mortar!)

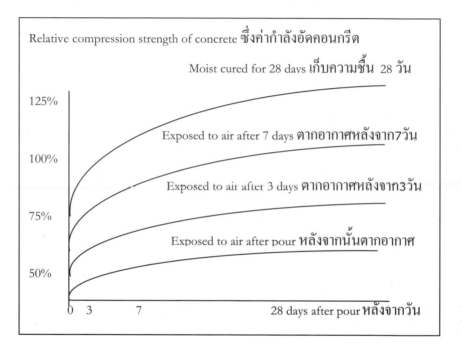

The graph above shows the effect of exposure of concrete to the air after pouring. Concrete that is exposed to the air immediately after pouring will only reach 50% of its ideal strength and will stop curing after 28 days. Concrete that is protected from drying for a full 28 days will gain up to 125% of its ideal strength in 28 days and will keep getting stronger.

If properly made and cured, concrete should be sufficiently strong in 7 days to allow work to continue, but do not put heavy loads on slabs for a full 28 days.

The Hoover dam in America is still curing, 70 years after it was built. See http://www.usbr.gov/lc/hooverdam/History/essays/concrete.html. Here is an excerpt from this essay:

"One of the problems was that in order to produce the strength concrete required, a **very dry mix** had to be used. There was very little time available to move the concrete from the mixing plant to the dam. If too much time was taken, the concrete would take its initial set still in the dump buckets and would have to be chipped out by hand. For this reason, the men who operated the cranes which moved the buckets into place were some of the highest paid workmen on the project, earning $1.25 per hour. As each bucket was dumped, seven puddlers used shovels and rubber-booted feet to distribute the concrete throughout the form and **pneumatic vibrators to ensure there were no voids.**"

Ready-mix

You may have access to ready-mix concrete from the big rotating drum concrete truck. Ready-mix usually costs 10 to 30% more than mix on site, but the quality may be better than on site mix (see comments above about cement/water ratio). However, even with ready mix it is important to check the wetness of the concrete as the concrete company may want to make it too wet to get it out of the truck easier. I suggest you keep a few bags of cement handy. If it is coming out too wet, tell the mix operator to add more cement to the mixer drum to improve the cement to water ratio.

The main disadvantage of ready mix is you need to accurately calculate the volume of concrete required for a job. If you end up with too much, it's wasted; too little, you may have to pour another day which will result in a joint which is never as good as a single pour. This happened to me on my swimming pool. The last truck of the day didn't bring a full load and I was about ½ m^3 short of finishing the floor. Fortunately I had sand, cement and rock handy and the cement truck people loaded the ingredients in by hand and mixed the remaining ½ m^3.

One problem you are likely to face with ready-mix (besides, can you get the truck to your site), is that concrete pumps are not commonly available in Thailand except for large commercial buildings in big cities. In America you will almost always rent a concrete pumping service when you have the concrete truck come to your job. In Thailand, it's people with buckets! The problem is you need a lot of people to move that much concrete before it starts to harden, so you may find your builder isn't on board with the idea of ready-mix. Talk to your builder and if you are sure you want ready-mix, tell him to prepare for it.

If you need many trucks for a complete pour, check how long it will take for the truck to return. If you are far away from the concrete company, it may take several hours for the truck to return and the previously poured concrete will have started hardening already, possibly producing a weak joint.

When using ready-mix, the comments above still apply. It must have the air vibrated out and be protected from drying and excess loading.

On-site mix

On site mix seems to be the norm for houses in Thailand. It is certainly more convenient because you can mix as much as you need, when you need it and potentially have more control over the speed and quality of the pour.

I highly recommend your builder uses a powered concrete mixer! I have seen many quite large houses been built where the builders are mixing by hand. On top of everything else you have to deal with, like concrete too wet, full or air and drying too fast; bad mixing is just too much! If your builder doesn't have a mixer, I suggest you rent one (unless it's a very small job).

Pour in a day

I highly recommend pouring floor joists in one session, usually one day. If concrete is poured in two or more sessions, and by that I mean letting part of it to dry before the whole structure is poured, you will have a weak point at the joint.

You should build the complete concrete form work for the floor joists so the pour can happen in one session. Your builder may try convince you that it is too expensive to build all the form work, and that it is fine to do half now, move the forms, and do half later. In my house, the extra wood required to finish the forms completely was about 10% more than I had already spent, about 8,000 baht. If I had allowed the builder to pour half then move the forms that would have exposed the first half to fast drying conditions, which as discussed, is a very bad idea.

You should make sure you have enough cement, sand, rock and water to finish the pour.

Electrical service is often unreliable in Thailand so if you are using an electric concrete mixer, it may be a good idea to rent a backup generator if you are worried about the power going out.

Take particular care that unsupported structures like overhanging decks joists are poured at the same time as the surrounding joists that will support the weight and pay extra attention to vibrating the concrete around those joints.

Concrete forms

Above ground concrete will be poured into forms ("shutters" in England), most likely wood or concrete (concrete pipe for example).

Forms made from wood

I was shocked to find I had to spend over 110,000 baht on wood for the concrete forms for my house.

Ideally your builder will have a large supply of wood to build the forms from a previous job. You should check before you hire a builder, it can make a big difference to the cost!

Some builders like to use coconut because it is cheap. However, it is not dimensionally accurate (assuming its rough cut with a chain saw) so the accuracy of your concrete structures will likely be a bit off with coconut.

If you do buy nice wood, ask your builder to take reasonable care of it so it can be used again. You will likely use it again for scaffolding when building the roof, temporary stairs and a host of other odd jobs. After use, you can either sell it to another building project in town or clean it up and use it again for wood components in your house, or a very expensive garden shed! Some people recommend soaking form wood with preservative, diesel or old engine oil before use, so it can be used again and again for forms.

Shoring up wood forms

Wood forms are required to hold a lot of weight when the wet concrete goes in. The last thing you want on concrete pour day is for the forms to spread apart, sink or break.

This actually happened to me in America when I was paying someone to help me make a garage floor. He did not brace the concrete forms well enough and I did not know any better and the ground was very wet after a heavy rain. The shoring posts sank into the ground and the side of the floor slab bowed out about 5 inches at the middle. We continued with the pour after adding a bit more bracing, but the guy I hired to help spent the next 2 weeks with a concrete saw fixing his mistake, and I paid for the extra concrete!

After the forms are built and just before the pour is scheduled to start, push the forms sideways and down with your foot as hard as you can, all around. If the forms move under the weight of your foot, they will move under the weight of the concrete. Have them fixed. If the ground is wet, take extra precautions that the weight is spread over a large area.

Tell your builder not to start pouring concrete until you or your project manager have checked the form work and given him the go ahead. There is no building inspector in Thailand, so builders are used to doing everything, however and whenever they like. You must have time to check the forms; once the concrete pour starts, it is too late.

My builders use a lot of wood to brace the side walls of the beam forms.

A lot of this bracing wood could have been avoided by using form ties. Form ties are steel rods with wing nuts on either end that are used to connect the side walls together.

Leave shoring and wood forms in place as long as possible, 28 days is ideal. This will protect the new concrete from overloading before it reaches working strength and protect it from drying too fast in the baking Thai sun. The picture above is my house about 1 month after the floor joists were poured.

By contrast, the picture on the right shows a quite large building (about 15m x 20m), on a steep hillside. The builder is using shoring about every 2 meters, and using small support logs to save money.

The floor joists are much larger and heavier than my smaller house.

The picture on the left shows a finished concrete post on the same job. I don't know what happened here, but it doesn't look good!

This column is supporting a large overhanging deck (about 3m x 8m), same as the one shown below. This it is not a good place to have a weak structural post (there's never a good place!).

I also don't like the structural design of this overhanging deck, which is also supporting the roof. For a few thousand extra baht they could have added another beam in the middle, running front to back. This deck is overhanging a steep hill. It looks like it will be a restaurant. You can be sure my family and I will not be eating there!

This building used plywood floor forms. You can see the underside of the floor looks nice compared to pre-cast concrete floor slab method.

Forms made from concrete

A simple, quick, accurate and inexpensive way to make posts is to use concrete water pipes for forms. Concrete water pipe comes in many different, convenient sizes, is easy to work with (join, cut, etc) and protects the concrete inside from drying too fast. In America, resin impregnated cardboard tube (sonotube) is usually used for this size of job. Sonotube or equivalent does not seem to be available in Thailand.

If concrete water pipes are used, the builders will hammer steel rods into the sides of the pipe for attachment to the wall. At my house, one of the concrete posts exploded while hammering the rod into the post and most of the concrete fell out.

If this happens to you, I suggest you have the whole thing removed, cleaned and start over with a new pipe. Do not patch up concrete in major structural components.

Note the importance of dressing appropriately when it's 38 ^{0}C in the shade! Working like this would kill the average farang.

Above ground concrete floors will be poured on top of pre-cast concrete slabs or plywood forms. Pre-cast concrete slabs are usually 30 or 35cm wide, 5cm thick and various lengths in increments of 0.5 meters. They are far faster to use and cheaper to set up than building floor forms out of plywood.

They are also very heavy so it's a good idea to have the delivery truck, which usually has a crane on it, place the slabs directly on the floor joists. Be careful not to over load the floor joist, especially on new concrete. Leave the shoring in place until after the floor is finished and have the workers move the slabs around as the crane drops more on.

Check that there are no large holes in forms or between slabs that will let concrete leak out. If concrete leaks out it will leave an air pocket and will not be strong. Small holes will probably be filled with wet paper concrete bags. Big gaps should be fixed with adequately braced wood or concrete.

Pre-cast concrete slabs do not look very attractive when the floor is visible from the under side.   You may want your builder to smother over it with cement mortar.

For more valuable information on concrete construction please read the chapter on swimming pools.

English/Thai words and phrases

Concrete	คอนกรีต khaawn greet^L
Reinforced concrete	คอนกรีตเสริมเหล็ก khaawn greet^L seerm^R lek^L
Cement	ปูนซีเมนต์ bpuun see maehn
Water	น้ำ naahm^H
Sand	ทราย saay
Put (to put)	ใส่ sai^L
Put (to put)	ทา thaa
Gravel, stone	กรวด gruaat^L
Stone, rock	หิน hin^R
Steel	เหล็กกล้า lek^L glaa^F
Reinforce (make stronger)	เสริมกำลัง seerm^R gahm lang
Form (shuttering)	แบบ baaep^L
Shoring	จุน joon
Cement mixer	เครื่องผสมปูนซีเมนต์ khreuuang^F pha^L sohm^R bpuun see maehn
Cement mixer (common)	โม่ mor^F
Vibrate, shake	สั่นสะเทือน san^L sa^L theuuan

Weld	เชื่อม cheuuam^F
Water-Cement Ratio	อัตราส่วนระหว่างน้ำต่อปูนซีเมนต์ at-raa suan^L ra^H waang^L naahm^H dtor^L bpuun see maehn
Compression strength	ค่ากำลังอัด kha^L gahm lang at^L
To be exposed (verb)	ตาก dtaak^L
To be exposed to sun	ตากแดด dtaak^L daaet^L
To be exposed to air	ตากอากาศ dtaak^L aa^M gaat^L
To check something	ตรวจดู dtruaat^L duu

Please check the forms again. I think they will break when the concrete goes in

กรุณาตรวจดูแบบอีกผมกลัวจะแตก ga^L roo$^{H'}$

naa^M dtruaat^L duu baaep^L eek^L ,phohm^R gluaa^M ja^L dtaaek^L

There is a hole in the form. Please fill it   แบบมีรู อุดรูด้วย baaep^L mee ruu oot^L ruu duay^F

The concrete is too wet, put less water in it คอนกรีตเปียกมากเกินไป ใส่น้ำน้อย

กว่านี้   khaawn greet^L bpiiak^L maak^F geern bpai sai^L naahm^H naawy^H gwaa^L nee^H

You must shake the air out ต้องสั่นสะเทือนอากาศออก dtaawng^F san^L sa^L theuuan aa gaat^L aawk^L

Please cover up the concrete, it must not dry too fast   คลุมคอนกรีต ไม่ให้

แห้งเร็วเกินไป khloom khaawn greet^L , mai^F hai^F haaeng^F reo geern bpai

Chapter  12 Steel

Concrete reinforcing steel

Reinforcing steel, or rebar as it is called in America, is required for any concrete structure. Your architect will specify the size, amount and design of reinforcing steel that will be placed inside footing and forms.

Thailand uses the ASTM standard sizes for reinforcing steel:

#2 – 6mm
#3 – 10mm - saam[R]
#4 – 13mm - see[L]
#5 – 16mm - haa[F]
#6 – 19mm - hohk[L]
#7 – 22mm - jet[L]
#8 – 25mm
#9 – 29mm
#10 – 32mm

It is usually supplied in 10 meter long rods. Number 4, 5 and 6 steel is usually used for structural components in footings, joists, posts, etc in houses. Welded wire mesh or #2 steel will likely be used for reinforcing the floor slabs. #2 is also used for 'stirrups', box sections running perpendicular to the main steel rods in beams and posts.

Steel rods are available with ribs (lek[L] kor[F] oi[F]) or smooth (lek[L] glom). Ribbed will be labeled "DB" on architectural drawings and smooth labeled "RB". For example, 5-DB 16, means 5 pieces of 16mm ribbed steel. Stir RB 6 @ 0.10 means place a stirrup (perpendicular bracing) using smooth 6mm steel at 10cm spacing. All steel connections must be tied with steel wire. 2 pieces are recommended.

Ribbed steel is typically a little more expensive and thinner on average than smooth steel of the same size.

Check that the ends of steel rods bent over into a nice big hook so it grips the concrete.

Placement of reinforcing steel in footings and forms

Probably the most important thing I'm going to tell you about building your house in this book is this:

Reinforcing steel must be raised off the floor and separated from the side walls of footing and forms for the concrete to be structurally sound! If the steel can come into contact with moisture, IT WILL RUST, and eventually be eaten away. Then your house will be sitting on Swiss cheese!

Also, the steel rods need to be well inside the concrete to provide it with structural strength and fire resistance. On underground concrete use 10-15cm clearance from the ground; on above ground concrete 5–10cm is acceptable. If you live in a

marine climate, where rust is a big problem, you can leave a little more. In the photo on above, the steel rods are touching the wood forms. The builders were perfectly happy with this. When I told them to fix it, they said they would fix it later! How do you fix this later? Replacing the concrete is the only way I can think of! I told them to cut it out, which took ten minutes of complaining and one minute of work (right).

Make sure you understand your architect's specifications about the placement of steel inside footings and forms and make sure the builder follows the design and leaves enough space between the steel and the walls. If your architect does not specify, ask why!

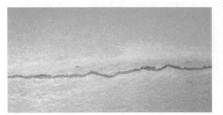

The builders will also try to convince you that steel touching the walls of the forms in no problem because they can cement stucco (render, chaap) over it later. This will certainly cover up the problem, but in no way will it fix it. The steel must be inside the concrete to provide structural support; embedded in the edge is not enough. Also, the cement will not stop water penetrating into the steel. The picture (above) shows a crack where the cement stucco has separated from the concrete beam, only one week after it was applied.

You must check steel clearances prior to pouring concrete. If you only check one thing on your house, CHECK THIS.

If is very important that the steel is raised above the floor in such a way that it cannot fall while the concrete is been pour or vibrated. In America you can buy concrete blocks with wire ties poking out of the top. The

wire tie is used to secure the concrete block to the steel. In Thailand, I have not seen these blocks in shops so you should make them on site or use broken concrete block. **Do not use wood**! Wood will be eaten away in a few years leaving the steel exposed to water. My builders used some wood blocks; fortunately I caught it before the concrete went in.

Steel beams, joists and rafters

Beams, joists and roof rafters are often built for steel girders. The major advantage of steel over wood is, it's always straight and is not susceptible to bugs. It is however susceptible to rust so prime and paint well.

Steel girders come in a variety of shapes and thicknesses. 'U' and box sections usually have a wall thickness of 6-8mm are usually used for beams. 'C' sections are lighter, (2-4mm wall thickness) and therefore cheaper than 'U' and are usually used for joists and rafters.

The other big advantage of steel over wood is most Thai builders know how to weld but few seem to know how to work with wood correctly. However, steel structures are very ugly and will likely require covering with something.

Steel and wood structural components are approximately the same price (at least where I live). A 4" 6.5mm wall thickness U beam is about 216baht/m, an equivalent strength 2x8 wood beam is 218baht/m but the wood takes more prep and finishing so perhaps the wood is a little more expensive.

Other steel components

Joining wood to concrete

The traditional way to join a wood post to concrete in Thailand is what I call the "half and half" method and Thai's call the "lock". Half of the wood post is cut away at the base and half of the concrete is cut away at the top; the two are overlapped and a bolt or two is used to bind it together.

In America, and I expect in Europe, a building inspector would probably burn your building permit and condemn your house if he saw this method in use.

By cutting the wood and concrete, you are halving the strength of the join. If you are using 6"x6" posts, you will really be using 6"x3" posts because, like a chain, the structure is only as strong as its weakest link. Technically speaking, the compression strength will not be adversely affected by the half-and-half method (unless the joint breaks apart as shown in the picture on the right). But the lateral (sideways) strength will be reduced. This is important because typhoon and earthquakes do happen in Thailand. A good strong breeze could blow this bungalow off its foundation.

The preferred way to connect wood to concrete (and wood to wood if joining in line) is with a steel plate of some kind. In America, Home Depot or any big building shop will have a variety of steel plates, (usually Simpson Strong Ties, http://www.strongtie.com). Manufactured steel ties seem to be hard to find in Thailand. I had to design my own and have my local steel shop make them.

One of the great things about Thailand is that there seems to be specialty shops in every city and town that charge a handful of baht to custom make things for you. If you order steel items that you end up not using, keep the steel for future jobs. The steel cost is probably 90% of the cost of the component so it you need something else made, you can save a lot of money by re-using the steel.

Post bases

Post bases are U shaped steel plates that are either embedded in or bolted to the concrete. The wood post sits inside the U and is bolted through, usually with two big steel bolts.

Posts bases can be embedded inside the concrete if the concrete structure is big enough that the post base itself will not cut into the concrete too much as weaken the concrete.

The problem with embedding the post base in the concrete is that it must be accurately positioned, checked for square and vertical BEFORE the concrete goes in. And it must not move while the concrete is being poured. Once the concrete is in, it's not moving anywhere!

I prefer to place steel bolds inside the concrete, poking out about 2cm above the finished concrete level.

The steel structure in this picture (left) is for reinforcing an 8" concrete post (below). Use different length bolts so the bolt heads do not all end at the same level and create a weak seem in the concrete.

Weld the bolts to the reinforcing steel to keep them in place as the concrete is poured and provide addition bonding strength with the concrete.

In America, you would buy a J bolt for this job which, as the name implies, is shaped like a letter J. The bottom of the J hooks inside the concrete. Carriage bolts (above) seem to work well when welded to the reinforcing steel.

After the concrete is poured and hardened, the U shaped steel post base can then be drilled and attached to the concrete with washers and nuts.

Since the bolt positions will likely not be exactly where you expected them to be, it is a good idea to wait until the concrete is finished before cutting the holes in the post base.

To cut the holes in the correct place, sit the post base on top of the bolts and mark the bolt positions with a pencil. Cut the holes a bit bigger than the bolts so you have space to adjust the alignment before tightening down the nuts.

Place a small amount of mortar under the post base before tightening down the bolts to make a

nice solid, level seat for the steel.

Clean and paint the inside and outside of the steel with a rust preventing primer. Just before the post is installed, apply silicon or latex sealer to avoid any chance of water getting inside the join.

Because the nuts and washers are protruding above the floor of the post base, the posts will need slots cut in to accommodate them. Since each post is likely a bit different, make a cardboard pattern for each post base and use it as a guide to drill/route the holes in the post bases.

Apply wood preservative to the post base and fill the holes with silicon sealer prior to final installation.

Because some of the methods described in this book may be unfamiliar to Thai architects and builders, it is essential you communicate the information clearly and accurately. I draw complex and unfamiliar designs on my computer and demonstrate it to my builder and the foreman, by rotating the computer model around in 3D.

I also demonstrate the sequence things will go together by turning on "layers" in Rhino3D in construction sequence. (Rhino3D is described in Chapter 7, Architects, design and permits).

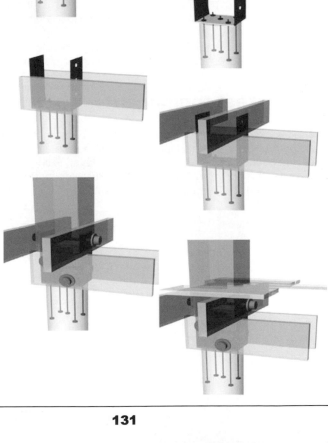

Joining wood to wood

Thai builders also like the half-and-half technique for joining structural (posts, joists, trusses, etc) wood to wood. This has the same disadvantage as half-and-half concrete/wood joist, except it is potentially even worse for horizontal members.

If using 2"x8" floor joist and the floor joist it cut to 1"x8" at the post join, then you really have no more than 1"x8" floor joists, WHICH IS NOT ENOUGH.

A better way is to use lap joints (overlapping joins) or butt joints (in-line end to end joints) with a steel plate connecting the two joists at the post and 4 bolts (2 for each joist) through the post.

Sizing build it yourself steel ties

I suggest you go to the Simpson Strong Tie web site, http://www.strongtie.com, where you will find detailed design specifications for their products. Use these as a guide for designing your own ties, and overbuild it a bit to be safe.

You can also print out the pictures from the strongtie web site and show it to your builder and steel shop to prove you are not crazy! farang baa.

Care of steel components

Never allow exposed steel to come into prolonged contact with water. It will rust and become useless. Steel posts bases must be the either raised above the floor level or embedded in concrete above floor level. Paint, spray or dip the inside and outside of steel components with a rust preventing primer or zinc paint (better if you can find it) prior to final assembly.

English/Thai words and phrases

English	Thai
Steel	เหล็กกล้า lek^L glaa^F
Steel wire	ลวดผูกเหล็ก luat^F pook^L lek^L
Ribbed steel	เหล็กข้ออ้อย lek^L kor^F oi^F
Smooth (round) steel	เหล็กกลม lek^L glom
Stainless steel	สเตนเลส sa^L dtaehn laeht^F
Reinforce (make stronger)	เสริมกำลัง seerm^R gahm lang
Steel plate	บล็อคเหล็ก block lek^L
Post base	กกเสา gohk^L sao^R
Weld	เชื่อม cheuuam^F
Rust	สนิม sa^L nim^R
The steel is too close to the soil	เหล็กกล้าใกล้ดินมากเกินไป lek^L glaa^F glai^F din^M maak^F geern^M bpai^M
Please lift the steel up so it does not touch the soil	กรุณายกเหล็กขึ้น ไม่ให้แตะดิน ga^L roo^H naa^M yohk^H lek^L kheun^F ,mai^F hai^F dtae^L din
I'm afraid it will rust	กลัวจะเป็นสนิม gluaa bpen ja^L bpen sa^L nim^R
Please paint the steel with primer	กรุณาทาสีรองพื้น ga^L roo^H naa^M thaa^M see^R raawng^M pheuun^H

Chapter 13 Wood

Wood in Thailand

Wood in Thailand is often much harder than wood used for construction in America and Europe. Harder can mean stronger, but not always so beware if you think you can use less wood for structural components than would be used in the West.

In America, when we talk about 2x4 we actually mean about 1¾" x 3½" and similarly of 2x6, is 1¾" x 5½", etc. This is because the 2"x4" is the size of the wood before it was dried and planned. In Thailand, 2x4 is pretty close to 2" by 4". If the wood is planed, they will usually call it 1½" by 3½".

Strangely, this seems not to be the case for plywood. I ordered 10mm thick plywood and the bill said 10mm, but the wood was actually about 7.5mm think. I asked my supplier and she said that is normal for Thailand. In any case, if it is a special order, you should ask your suppler how thick the wood will actually be. Plywood comes in US standard 4x8 sheets which is rather inconvenient for sub-floors because wood strip flooring often comes in meters, so the joins do not match up!

As a big wood fan, I get very excited about choosing wood for my house (hey, it could be worse, at least I don't go to Star trek conventions!). In America, in Home Depot, its Pine or Fir all the way for general construction. Oak, Redwood and other "precious" woods are so expensive they can only be used for decorative components

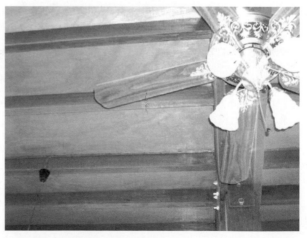

like stairs, frames, decks, etc.

In Thailand we have a wonderful selection of beautiful woods. Wood is not cheap in Thailand but tropical hardwoods, which would cost a fortune in the West, are about the same cost as basic construction woods in America and Europe. I left my ceilings (right) unfinished (except for sanding and varnishing the joists and plywood sub-floor) because it looks so nice, is free (having already paid for the floor above) and I don't like cavities where creatures can take up residence. Note that because the electric cables for the lights are visible I painted them brown to match the wood.

Thai builders often leave wood un-sanded and un-varnished. I prefer to have all the wood that will be visible after the house is finished, sanded and varnished. Varnish (Polyurethane) will protect the wood and it looks more beautiful too. You should tell your builder if you plan to have the wood finished so he can plan ahead and figure out how to charge for the labor. Use exterior grade Polyurethane, even for interior wood because it provides better protection.

If ordering wood, it may be best to order lengths the maximum that will fit on a delivery truck (usually 7 to 8 meters). You may need different lengths for your job, some long, some short. By ordering all long lengths, you can choose the best longer pieces and cut the not so good ones for your smaller needs. I needed 4, 6m 8x8 and 12, 3m 8x8 posts. I ordered all 6m wood and chose the best four pieces (straightest, no damage or cracking, nice color match) and cut the rest for the 3m. This is particularly import and for long beams and joists. Order all the wood at the maximum span and use the straighter pieces in the important places. Send the curved ones back to the shop if you can or cut and user where shorter ones will suffice.

"Green" wood from the forest

If you are designing for the natural look, your builder may use logs for structural posts, joists, trusses, etc. You should check that wood it obtained legally. It should have documentation to prove it. This documentation is necessary in case the police check the delivery truck. Illegal wood can be confiscated and you could be in big trouble for having illegal wood on your site.

Fresh cut (green or wet) wood has from 30 to 300% moisture content. As it dries it will shrink. If the drying process is not controlled it will warp and crack. Do not allow green wood to sit in the sun, it will dry too quickly and will bend and twist.

If you are not sure about the origin of your wood, or if it was dried properly, keep it protected from the sun as long as possible, certainly until it feels totally dry to the touch. To be sure, hammer a big nail into the wood and see if any sap comes out.

If you suspect doors, windows or frames are not totally dry, stack them inside with an air gap between them and keep a fan blowing over them for several weeks to help them dry evenly.

Preparing and cleaning rough wood

Your wood shop will probably stock rough cut lumber. You may choose to "clean" (plane) the wood if it is to be used in a prominent, visible location. Most wood shops will clean it before delivery if you ask. Some wood may need to be cleaned on site, especially if it is likely to be scraped or knocked about during delivery.

Here a builder is planning an 8x8 wood post with an electric planner. For bigger jobs like this, your builder should use a 5 ⅜" blade planner to minimize ridges in the final wood and to get the job finished faster.

If rounding over corners, you will get a nicer looking, more consistent round over with a router. The builders should use many small passes over the wood to minimize the chances of damage to the bit and the wood.

Care and preservation of wood

While it was happily minding its own business, growing in a tropical rain forest, your wood was living on sun and rain. Now sun and rain are its mortal enemies!

Protect wood, especially new wood, from sun and rain. This is true for storage, during construction and after the house is finished. Check with your architect that wood doors, windows, frames, posts and everything

else wood is protected from the sun and rain as much as reasonably possible. The useful life of your wood will mostly depend on how much exposure to the elements it gets.

While storing and during construction, raise wood above the ground and cover with blue plastic sheeting (actually, the color is not important). Plastic sheeting costs about 1000 baht for a 100 meter roll.

While working on the wood, try to provide a shaded area to keep the wood and the workers cool. If your house is raised, have the workers store and prepare wood under the house.

Pay particular attention to decorative or detailed wood and protect it from sun at all times prior to applying polyurethane. I have some turned wood posts that were installed in a place with exposure to sun. The post quickly deteriorated, cracked and discolored in the sun. I wasted two days filling and sanding and the post will never look as good as new. I should have applied stain and polyurethane before installing them in a sunny exposure. I would likely have had to patch up the polyurethane after construction was finished but the vast majority of the wood would have remained in pristine condition.

Now I have learned my lesson. On my friends house I have the builders put **ALL** the arriving wood under the house where they sand it, apply preservative and one or two coats of polyurethane **BEFORE** I allow them to install it on the house. The builder will complain and tell you they can do it later. Insist that it is done before hand or expect the wood to be cracked, discolored and ugly forever.

My builders were constantly hammering nails into the wood posts and beams to make temporary structures such as scaffolding for working on the roof. This left many ugly nail holes which needed filling later. Had I though of it sooner, I should have had them find other ways to make temporary structures. If nailing into the posts is necessary, nail in a place that will not show such as under a hand rail mounting point.

Termites and other wood destroying insects can and will eat any wood components in your house. Never put wood into contact with the ground or water unless it is pressure treated with preservative and even then, I would not put wood in the ground for structural components of a house.

Ideally your wood supply shop can supply pressure treated wood. If not, buy a good wood preservative and have it applied to the wood before it is installed so it gets into the places that will be impossible to reach after installation.

Some woods such as teak are naturally bug resistant, most woods are not.

Wood for concrete forms

Wood for concrete forms was discussed in detail in the chapter on concrete. 2x3 is usually used for support structures and 1"x6", 1"x8", 1"x10" or plywood for form walls.

Coconut and bamboo are often used for forms because it is cheap, maybe free if you have a lot of it on your land.

Wood for the forms can be a significant part of the cost of the house. On my 110m² floor I used 2680 meters of 2x3 and 712 meters of 1x8, a total cost of about 110,000 baht. The wood can usually be reused for other building jobs or in the house. (The guy in black is me checking the post base bolts).

The consequence of not using enough wood can be seen in the photos on Shoring up wood forms page 117.

If you plan to use the wood forms again, paint or roll diesel or old engine oil (usually free) on the wood before pouring concrete. This will make the forms easier to remove with less concrete stuck to the wood and protect from bugs.

Wood floors

The traditional Thai wood floor uses planks, typically 1x6, 1x8 or wider, nailed directly to the joists. Usually, either by design or by shrinkage, there is a gap between the boards. There's even a word in Thai for the gap between floor boards; laawng. The gap makes sweeping the floor quite easy, the dirt falls straight through, so its best if there is not another floor below!

In Ko Phangan, several of the cheaper bungalows use coconut wood for the floor, which actually looks quite nice. But coconut must be sanded and varnished. If splinters get into your skin it can get irritated and infected for weeks. Technically speaking, coconut isn't considered a wood at all, it's a grass. If using coconut, you should only use the outer wood for old trees that have stopped producing. In the north, Teak is often used for the floor, walls and everything else, making many old village houses worth more in wood than they are worth as a house.

The less traditional way to make wood floors is tongue-and-groove strip wood flooring or manufactured parkea as in America and Europe. T&G as it is usually called has interlocking tongues and grooves cut into the sides and optionally the ends. You should buy the type with the T&G on the ends, not only the sides. This will look nicer at the joins and will not separate as much over time.

Solid wood will have some slight variation in width and thickness between pieces of the same lot. You should buy all your wood flooring from one lot to minimize variations. The wood should be nailed down to the sub-floor using a pneumatic finish nail gun, NOT WITH A HAMMER. A nail gun will give a neater finish and be less likely to separate. You can also glue it to the sub-floor.

Nail into the floor joists only and glue everywhere if you plan to leave the ceiling below open. Nails poking through the ply look very ugly.

Solid wood will arrive planed but unfinished. It will require sanding to level it and prepare it for varnishing (use exterior grade polyurethane, not varnish). You may need to hire a specialist floor maker if your builder is unfamiliar with this type of wood floor.

T&G strip wood flooring should sit on top of a sub-floor, usually made from plywood. In America you would typically use from ¾" to 1 ¼" T&G plywood. In Thailand, the norm seems to be 10mm to 15mm which will make your floors a little bouncy but structurally fine.

Laminated wood (parkea) floors are also very popular in Thailand. Typically laminated wood flooring is about 6mm thick, 5-10cm wide and varying lengths. Because it is manufactured, it should have very consistent width and thickness. It will usually arrive already finished (varnished), so it only needs to be installed.

Laminated floors are cheaper and faster to install than solid wood and are relatively easy to replace or floor over. Solid wood can be sanded many times and can last for 100 years or more if looked after properly. My house in America has 110 year old oak floors that look like they are good for another 100 years.

Solid or laminated T&G flooring is not recommended for outdoor use or decks which can get wet. For wet areas, use 2x6 planks and leave a space of about 1cm between planks for water and debris to drain though. Use a wood which is naturally resistant to water problems and finish with wood sealer or preservative and exterior grade polyurethane to be sure. Use stainless steel screws to attach the planks to the joists. Nails will pop out over time. Glue will probably not help.

Sorting the wood

Inevitably, your wood deliveries will contain some less than perfect pieces, hopefully not too many.

Sort out the worst pieces, ones with twists, bends, knots, cracks, etc. and mark them somehow, maybe a big red 'X'. There will be many places where smaller lengths are needed, such as blocking between floor joists and roof rafters. Tell your builders to use the bad wood for these smaller jobs where bends and twists will not be significant and knots can be cut out and thrown away.

It really pays to sort the wood first. The builders will typically slap up the first piece of wood that comes to hand. For beams, joists and rafters, lay all the wood side by side and check for curvature. There will always be curvature in real wood to some extent. I find it's easier to cut wood, especially beams, straight before installing. For rafters, a little curvature may be acceptable if it is consistent, for all rafters. Mark the high or low side with masking tape so that the builders place them consistently. Failure to do this will result in a lot of plaining later to level everything.

Thai builders seem not to have the same sense for the aesthetics of the finish details as we would like in a high quality job. A little subtle help is sometimes needed.

English/Thai words and phrases

Wood   ไม้ maai^H

Hardwood   ไม้กระยาเลย maai^H gra^L yaa leeuy

Plywood   ไม้อัด maai^H at^L

Teak wood   ไม้สัก maai^H sak^L

Hardwood of the *Serianthes grandiflora* tree   ไม้ซาก maai^H saak^F

Bamboo wood   ไม้ไผ่ maai^H phai^L

Gra-thing (a hardwood tree similar to mahogany) ไม้ไม้สน maai^H gra^L thing^M

Fir or pine wood   ไม้สน maai^H sohn^R

Carpenter   ช่างไม้ chang^F maai^H

Chiang Mai (the city)   เชียงใหม่ chiang mai^L

To work with wood   ทำงานช่างไม้ thahm ngaan chang^F maai^H

A cut tree, log, timber, lumber   ซุง soong

Wood grain   ลายไม้ laay^M maai^H

Preservative

Termite   ปลวก bpluaak^L

Straight   ตรง dtrohng

Bent   โก่ง gohng^L

Twisted   ขด khoht^L

New wood doesn't burn, does it? (lit. wood new not burn, right?)
     ไม้ใหม่ ไม่ไหม้ ใช่ไหม maai^H mai^L mai^F mai^F chai^F mai^R

Classifier for a none flat wood   ตัวdtuaa

Classifier for a tree or vertical post   ต้น dtohn^F

Classifier for a flat wood (plywood, 1x4 flooring, 1x8, etc) แผ่น phaaen^L

Classifier for a logs ท่อน thaawn^F

I want 5, 3 meter, 2x4's ผมต้องการ 2x4 นิ้ว 3ม. 5ตัว phom dtaawng^F gaan^M seuu^H song khuun see niu^H, saam met, haa dtuaa

How much is a sheet of 15mm plywood? ไม้อัด15 มม.แผ่นละเท่าไหร่ maai^H at^L sip^L haa^F min phaaen^L la^H thao^F rai^L

Chapter 14
Fasteners and hardware

Nails are the mainstay of wood construction in Thailand. Drywall screws are commonly used in America for many construction uses but seem not to be popular here. Maybe because the wood is so hard, it is difficult to get screws in and screwdriver bits are expensive.

For concrete forms and other temporary structures, the nails should not be completely hammered in, to make dismantling easier.

Carriage bolts are usually available in most building supply shops and should be used for connecting larger structural wood components. I have seen many instances where the nut was only hand tight, or actually falling off the bolt. On important structural joints, have the nut welded to the bolt for extra security.

White latex glue is often used for a host of building jobs, but it is not very strong and not water proof. For fine woodwork, I prefer "Bosney" glue, a plastic resin glue that is very strong, can be used as a filler, sanded and matches darker wood colors perfectly.

The generally accepted view is that the bast hardware for doors, windows, etc. is from the German company "Hafele". Hafele hardware is available at many larger building supply shops. Hafele has a phone book sized catalog available in English and Thai with every piece of door and window hardware know to mankind. http://www.hafele.com/th/en/

English/Thai words and phrases

Classifier for nails, screws, bolts, etc.

Nail	ตะปู dta^L bpuu
Concrete nail	ตะปู dta^L bpuu
To nail (verb)	ตอกตะปู dtaawk^L dta^L bpuu
Screw	ตะปูเกลียว dta^L bpuu gliaao
Screw	ซครู sa^H gruu
Philips, cross head crew	ตะปูเกลียวหัวแฉก dta^L bpuu gliaao huaa^R chaek^L
Flat head screw	ตะปูเกลียวหัวแบน dta^L bpuu gliaao huaa^R baaen
Bolt	ลูกกลอนดาน luuk^F glaawn daan
Nut	เกลียว gliaao
Nut and bolt	ลูกกลอนดานและเกลียว luuk^F glaawn daan lae^H gliaao
Washer	วงแหวน wohng waaen^R
Glue	กาว gaao
Staples	แม็ก maek^H
Wall anchor	พุก phook^H
Hook	ตาขอ dtaa khaaw^R
Angle bracket	เหล็กฉาก lek^L chaak^L

Chapter 15

How and where to buy materials

Shopping around, dual pricing and where to buy

The Thailand Land and Building forum has a directory of recommended building services and building suppliers. If you have a builder, building supplier, lawyer etc. that gave you great service, please share your recommendations with others at http://buildingthailand.com/forums.

Dual pricing (farang price vs. Thai price) exists to some extent in Thailand, but the real dual pricing happens between people who know what something is worth and people who don't, Thai or farang. Your best protect against dual (or high) prices is to shop around and bargain.

Having your builder order some materials will help but you should also have your Thai friend check the price just to make sure there is no added mark-up.

The cost and quality of some materials such as concrete and steel are probably about the same at all the suppliers in your area. It may be worth shopping further a field to get a better price but check the added delivery cost to see if it makes it worth the trouble. I once found myself paying 3000 baht for a truck from Surat Thani to deliver 1000 baht of rock!

Wood will vary a lot in quality and choice in different parts of the country. Buying locally may be better, even if the price is higher, because you can see what you are buying before you have it delivered or send it back if you are not happy with what you get.

For special order wood, shop around; research the type of wood you are planning to buy as much as you can. Look at it in use in other buildings. Ask how old the trees are and how long has it had to dry. You do not want wet wood directly from the forest; it will bend and crack in the sun.

If buying logs, ask where they are coming from. They may be illegally cut. If illegally cut logs are found on your site, they will be confiscated and you could be in a lot or trouble. Also they are most likely very green (wet) and could be a problem if not dried properly.

Protect wood from sun and rain while it is stored on your site and even after it has been installed if possible, at least until you feel it has dried sufficiently.

There is a street in Bangkok called Soi Prachanarumit in Bang Po, close to Bang Su station. There are literally hundreds of wood shops, selling everything from structural wood, to wood flooring, hand rails and decorative trim, furniture, doors, windows and hardware, tools, you name it. I bought my wood floors, door handles and hinges there, got beautiful wood and saved a fortune.

Soi Prachanarumit occasionally has a street fair where you can get even better deals on door handles, hinges, etc. Check http://thaivisa.com for announcements.

Manufactured floor tile can be found in any reasonable size town. Marble and granite may be harder to find. Marble and granite is mined in Saraburi, about 1 hour north of Bangkok. You will find an excellent selection and very good prices in several shops on Highway 1.

In the north of Thailand, in the villages around Chiang Mai, and perhaps other areas, you will find many small houses for sale, made of teak. Since teak wood lasts pretty much forever, this is a good source for some beautiful old wood at reasonable prices. You will likely need a Thai friend to do the negotiation for you; the villagers will not know what to make of a farang trying to but their house.

Living up country

If, like me, you live a long way from Bangkok or a major city, you will no doubt find yourself making far too many visits to the big city for things you cannot buy, or are too expensive in your local store. It is very important to get phone numbers and if possible brochures from shops that are useful. I got a few power tool brochures from a tool shop in Surat Thani and when I need a tool or tool  supplies, I order over the phone and have it sent to Ko Phangan on the night boat, saving a whopping 30-50% over local prices!

On one occasion, I bought some simple metal angle brackets for attaching the handrails to the posts. I bought them from a shop in Bangkok that specializes in hardware stuff but unfortunately forgot to get a phone number or address.

I found the brackets very useful for several other jobs, including the stairs, kitchen cabinets etc. but was unable to find anything like them locally. So I had to spend two nights on the train and over 1000 baht to go back to Bangkok to buy 200 of the ******* things!

If you are building a long way from any building supply shop at all, you or your project manager will have to employ extraordinary powers of planning and management to keep the flow of materials and tools running smoothly. I live 20 minutes from town which has 3 reasonably well stocked hardware shops. I needed to buy something every day and some days I went 2 or 3 times. Items like drill bits, screws, nuts and bolts, and especially plumbing fittings are hard to plan for and can bring a project grinding to a halt until you have them in hand. If you are not easily able to visit a building shop easily, plan on overstocking for your job. If possible, find a shop that will take back what you do not use then buy lots of all the small stuff you will likely run out of, like sand paper, drill bits, screw driver bits, plastic pipe fittings and glue, etc. etc. etc.

Internet resources

Internet shopping has not developed significantly in Thailand the way it has in America. You can buy items from overseas but the cost of shipping and import duty would probably make them too expensive.

http://www.buildingthailand.com has an extensive database of legal, accounting and building professionals and building supply stores organized by geographical area. buildingthailand.com also has a classified notice board for used items and a forum where other land owners and home boulders discuss their problems and solutions. Anyone can join the forum and post their question to the user group. I or someone else will usually answer within a day or so with a well informed answer.

Thaivisa.com, the number one portal for farangs living in Thailand, has an excellent forum: http://www.thaivisa.com/forum/index.php?showforum=59 for real estate and building issues.

On http://www.bahtsold.com you will find classified advertisements for real estate, business services and articles for sale.

http://www.coolthaihouse.com/blog has many stories from farang home owners' experiences in Thailand.

Fake branded items

Many brand name items, particularly Makita, are fake Thai or Chinese items. The fake items are often 1/3 the price of the real thing but often are less than 1/3 as long lasting. Cheap saw blades in particular can cost more in the long run because they put more strain on the saw.

Nepotism

Everyone seems to be related to everyone else in Thailand. There's a good chance your builder is related to the owner of one of the local building supply shops. That may be a good thing; maybe you will get a good discount or better materials, but like everything else, shop around and check prices from other suppliers for yourself, especially on more expensive items.

Deposits for special order items

I have created my own law about paying deposits for special order items like custom doors, wood, tile, etc. "Philip's law of inverse deposit/satisfaction ratio" states that the more deposit you are required to pay; the less likely you will be satisfied with the product or service.

Case in point; I ordered 20, 8x8 wood posts from my local wood shop, over 80,000 baht of wood. The wood had to be special ordered and shipped from Malaysia. The wood shop owner didn't ask me for a deposit and gave me a delivery date which she actually beat by 2 weeks. I was really happy with the wood when it arrived, beautiful color and grain, straight, no knots.

She obviously knew she could sell the wood to someone else easily if I changed my mind and left her holding the wood.

I ordered some custom teak doors from another supplier, he initially asked me for 20% deposit which I thought was reasonable, but half way into the job he asked me for another 40% which I refused to pay. When the doors arrived, I was less than satisfied with the quality.

Building materials have legs!

I find the Thai people very honest in general. I have heard many stories and have personally experienced many incredible acts of kindness, honesty, selflessness and generosity from Thai people, often from complete strangers.

However, a friend once told me that the Thai sense of honesty, for some reason, does not extend to building materials. Like software and DVD's in Pantip Plaza,

they are considered public domain!

You will need to build a secure storage shed for your valuable building materials or find some way to protect them from theft, as well as sun and rain.

Many times, your workers will live on the building site. They will build a temporary house for themselves first. This is a good way to protect your stuff since they can watch over it. However, the builders may help themselves to a few items, so keep a close watch on your stuff.

Have a building schedule worked out ahead of time so you can plan for deliveries of materials and not have them sitting around too long. However, be careful not to be too "just in time". Sometimes, materials can be out of stock or there are problems with delivery and the building may stop.

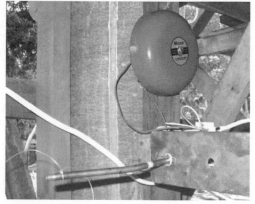

I made a home brew security system of my site. At night, I run fishing line around the site on coconut trees, at waist height (above dog height). The fishing line is connected to an electric switch, which if triggered by someone walking into the fishing line, will sound a bell and turn on a spot light. The whole kit cost about 1000 baht and the parts were available in my local hardware shop.

Delivery

Depending on where you live, delivery cost of materials may be 5% or more of the cost of your house. Check that delivery trucks can get to your building site. You may have to build a temporary road, or patch the worst spots of the current road, for the larger trucks.

It is a big advantage if you can get larger trucks to your site. If heavy items must be transferred to a 4 wheel drive pickup, that will add time and expense to the project.

Research all the available delivery options in your area. I was happily surprised to find there is a night boat from Surat Thani to Ko Phangan which carries loose freight (but not vehicles). I was able to buy bathroom fixtures and doors in Surat for a far better price than available in Ko Phangan and the delivery only cost 600 baht.

If your part of the country produces goods that are shipped to other parts of Thailand, talk to the companies that do the delivery. They may have empty trucks coming back to your town that could pick up supplies for a discount price.

When materials arrive, you or your project manager should check that everything on the bill is present and in good condition. You may need a Thai person to read the bill. You may pay most, or all of the bill when the delivery arrives, so plan to have plenty of cash on hand, especially for weekend deliveries when the bank is closed. Delivery drivers never carry cash, so don't expect them to change 1000 baht notes; keep some small money in your pocket or be prepared to give a big tip.

It is also a good idea to check that you actually ordered some deliveries. With all the wood, concrete and steel showing up at your site every day, it's easy for some suppliers to get a little "over zealous" and send things you never ordered or wanted!

English/Thai words and phrases

Deposit	ค่ามัดจำ khaa^F mat^H jahm
Discount	ลด loht^H
Fake	ของปลอม khaawng^R bplaawm
Guarantee	รับรอง rap^H raawng
Deliver	ส่ง song^L
Deliver	การขนส่ง gaan khon^R song^L
Truck driver	คนขับรถบรรทุก khohn khap^L roht^H ban^L thook^H
How much does this cost?	นี่เท่าไร nee^F thao^F rai
Can I get a discount?	ลดได้ไหม loht^H dai^F mai^R
Can I get a discount if I buy 10?	ซื้อสิบอันลดได้ไหม seuu^H sip^L an, loht^H dai^F mai^R (note, the classifier "an" will change depending on the item)
How much is the deposit?	ค่ามัดจำเท่าไร khaa^F mat^H jahm thao^F rai
Will you take 10% deposit?	ค่ามัดจำสิบเปอร์เซ็นต์ได้ไหม khaa^F mat^H jahm sip^L bpuuhr sen dai^F mai^R
Is this really Makita?	ของแท้ไหม khaawng^R thaae^H mai^R
How long in the guarantee	รับรองนานเท่าไหร่ rap^H raawng naan thao^F rai^L
Can you deliver to ...	ส่งไป...ได้ไหม song^L bpai ... dai^F mai^R
How much does it cost to deliver to ...	ส่งไป...เท่าไร song^L bpai ⋯ thao^F rai
When can you deliver to ...	ส่งเมื่อไร song^L meuua^F rai
Do you need anything else?	รับอะไรเพิ่มไหม rap^H a^L rai pheerm^F mai^R

Chapter 16 Tools

Philip's first rule of tools: "every baht you spend on tools will be repaid ten times over with faster work and a better quality result". Maybe ten times is an exaggeration, but in every case where I have thought about buying a tool and decided not to, to save money, I have either suffered with inferior quality work or bought the tool and redone it later.

Thai builders are experts at making do without the right tool or no tool at all, but the quality of the end result will likely show it. If you want high quality construction and finish work and your builder doesn't have the right tool, buy it.

Makita and Bosch (made in Malaysia) are the popular name brands for power tools in Thailand. Makita is usually about 5% more expensive than Bosch but in my experience is better made and lasts far longer than Bosch. There are a host of generic Chinese tools available which often have strong motors but lack the refinement and accuracy of the name brand tools.

If coming from the UK you could bring power tools with you, but since the US is 110V you would have to use a very big voltage converter for US tools. However, 18.8V cordless drills, commonly available in America are not available in Thailand or Malaysia for some reason.

The hard wood in Thailand is very hard on power tools. Buy new drill bits and blades often to avoid overstressing the tool. Your builders will somehow make the dullest drill bit or saw blade go through the hardest wood but will burn out the motor in the process. One of my drills got so hot; it was too hot to touch, 20 minutes after the power was turned off, and it was totally destroyed. Usually you can have power tools repaired for simple things like worn out brushes.

Building my house, my builders totally destroyed one power drill, one power saw, and all my other tools took a heavy beating. The builders went through 5 saw blades (800 baht each), 80 drill bits, about 10000 baht in sandpaper (although I would have happily spend more if the builders would use it!) and about 150 screw driver bits, for a grand total of about 18,000 baht in tools and tool supplies.

Sometimes, a worn out screw driver bit can be reground and used again for a short time.

There are many simple and effective tools in Thailand. For example, the usual way to check for level, especially over larger distances like 2m or more, is with a clear tube, about 1cm diameter, filled with water. Two people will hold the tube, one at each end and mark the water levels as horizontal reference points; simple and effective! The standard concrete chisel is a concrete nail and a piece of rubber water pipe, which works remarkably well.

English/Thai words and phrases

Tools	เครื่อง khreuuang^F
Hand tool	เครื่องมือ khreuuang^F meuu
Power tool	เครื่องไฟฟ้า khreuuang^F fai faa^H
Tool belt	สายคาดเครื่องมือ saay^R khaat^F khreuuang^F meuu
Hammer	ค้อน khaawn^H
Sledge hammer	ค้อนขนาดใหญ่ khaawn^H kha^L naat^L yai^L
Jack hammer, pneumatic drill	เครื่องเจาะหิน khreuuang^F jaw^L hin^R
Nail gun (air gun)	ปืนลม bpeuun lohm
Staple gun	ที่ยิงเย็บกระดาษ thee^F ying^M yep^H gra^L daat^L
Compressor	อัด (ไล่ลม) at^L lie^F lom^H
To hammer (verb)	ทุบ thoop^H
To nail (verb)	ตอกตะปู dtaawk^L dta^L bpuu
Screwdriver	ไขควง khai^R khuaang
Philips/crosshead screwdriver	ไขควงแฉก khai^R khuaang cheerk
Flat-head screwdriver	ไขควงแบน khai^R khuaang baaen
Power screwdriver	ไขควงวัดไฟ khai^R khuaang wat fai
Screwdriver bit	ไขควงลม khai^R khuaang lohm
Pliers'	คีมปากคีบ kheem bpaak^L kheep^F

Needle nose pliers'	คีมปากจิ้งจก kheem bpaak^L jing^F johk^L
Wrench/spanner	ประแจ bpra^L jaae
Adjustable wrench/spanner	กุญแจเลื่อน goon jaae^M leuuan^F
Saw	เลื่อย luuay^F
Hand saw	เลื่อยมือ luuay^F meuu
Power saw	เลื่อยไฟฟ้า luuay^F fai faa^H
Circular saw	วงเลื่อย wohng luuay^F
Miter saw	เลื่อยตัดฉาก luuay^F dtat^L chaak^L
Table saw	เลื่อยตั้งโต๊ะ luuay^F dtang^F dto^H
Jig saw	จิ๊กซอ jig saw
Drill	สว่าน sa^L waan^L
Electric drill	สว่านไฟฟ้า sa^L waan^L fai faa^H
Hand drill	สว่านมือ saL waan^L meuu
Drill bit	ดอกสว่าน daawk^L sa^L waan^L
Drill stand	ขาตั้งยึดสว่าน khaa^R dtang^F yeut^H sa^L waan^L
To drill a hole (verb)	เจาะรู jaw^L ruu
Chuck	หัวสว่าน huaa^R sa^L waan^L (lit: head of drill)
Chuck key	ลูกกุญแจไขสว่าน luuk^F khai^R goon jaae sa^L waan^L
To saw/ to cut (verb)	เลื่อย luuay^F
To join, connect	ต่อกัน dtaaw^L gan
Axe	ขวาน khwaan^R
To cut with an axe	ฟัน fan
Spade/shovel	พลั่ว phluaa^F

Welder (tool)	เชื่อม cheuuam^F
To weld (verb)	เชื่อม cheuuam^F
Soldering iron	เครื่องบัดกรี khreuuang^F bat^L gree
Blower	เครื่องเป่าลม khreuuang^F bpao^L lohm
Sander	เครื่องขัด khreuuang^F kut
Orbital sander	เครื่องขัดโคจร khreuuang^F kut kh<u>o</u>h jaawn
Belt sander	เครื่องขัดสายพาน khreuuang^F kut saay^R phaan
Sand paper	กระดาษทราย gra^L daat^L saay
Sand paper belt	กระดาษทรายสายพาน gra^L daat^L saay saay^R phaan
Sand paper disk (simple flat type)	ใบขัดหัวหมู bai khat^L huaa^R muu^R (lit: sheet sand pig's head! I don't get it either)
Sand paper disk (with many small overlapping sheets)	กระดาษทรายเรียงซ้อน gra^L daat^L saay riiang saawn^H
To sand (verb)	ขัด khat^L
Grinder	เครื่องเจีย khreuuang^F jiia
Router	ราวเตอร์ rou teer
Concrete mixer	คอนกรีตผสมสำเร็จ khaawn greet^L pha^L sohm^R sam^L ret^F
Concrete vibrator	สั่นสะเทือนคอนกรีต san^L sa^L theuuan khaawn greet^L
Crane (for heavy lifting)	ปั้นจั่น bpan^F jan^L
To lift	ยก yohk^H
Bending bar (to bend steel)	ประแจดัดเหล็ก pa jeer dtat lek^L
Bolt cutter	เครื่องตัดเหล็ก khreuuang^F dtat^L lek^L
Tape measure	ตลับเมตร dta lap maeht^F

To measure (verb)	วัด wat^H
Meter	เมตร maeht^F
Centimeter	เซ็นติเมตร sen dti^L maeht^F (usually sen)
Millimeter	มิลลิเมตร min li^H maeht^F (usually min)
Foot	ตีน dteen
Inch	นิ้ว niu^H
½ inch	ครึ่งนิ้ว khreung^F niu^H
5 ¼ inch	ห้า เศษหนึ่งส่วนสี่ครึ่งนิ้ว haa^F saeht^L neung^L suaan^L see^L niu^H
To measure (verb)	วัด wat^H
Square (tool)	เหล็กฉาก lek^L chaak^L
Level, spirit level	ไม้ปรับระดับ maai^H bprap^L ra^H dap^L
Plumb bob	ดิ่ง ding^L
Plumb line, line with a plumb bob	สายดิ่ง saay^R ding^L
String	คุณ khoon
Clamp	คีมหนีบ kheem neep^L
Plane (tool)	กบ gohp^L
To plane (verb)	ไสกบ sai^R gohp^L
Chisel (tool)	สกัด sa^L gat^L
A curved chisel for carving wood	สยุ่น sa^L yoon^L
To chisel, to engrave, sculpt (verb)	สลัก sa^L lak^L
File (tool)	ตะไบ dta^L bai
To file (verb)	ตะไบ dta^L bai
Rasp, large coarse-toothed file	บุ้ง boong^F

Paint brush	แปรงทา bpraaeng thaa
Paint roller	ลูกกลิ้งทาสี luuk^F gling^F thaa see^R
Spray paint (can)	สีพ่น see^R phohn^F
To paint (verb)	ทาสี thaa see^R
Clockwise direction	หมุน moon^R
Counter-clockwise direction	หมุนเวียน moon^R wiian
Like this, but …	แบบนี้แต่ baaep^L nee^H dtaae^L...
Like this, but bigger	แบบนี้แต่ใหญ่กว่า baaep^L nee^H dtaae^L yai^L gwaa^L
Like this, but smaller	แบบนี้แต่เล็กกว่า baaep^L nee^H dtaae^L lek^H gwaa^L
Like this, but longer	แบบนี้แต่ยาวกว่า baaep^L nee^H dtaae^L yaao gwaa^L
Like this, but shorter (in length)	แบบนี้แต่สั้นกว่า baaep^L nee^{ll} dtaae^L san^F gwaa^L
Like this, but shorter (in height)	แบบนี้แต่เตี้ยกว่า baaep^L nee^H dtaae^L dtiia^F gwaa^L
Like this, but taller	แบบนี้แต่สูงกว่า baaep^L nee^H dtaae^L suung^R gwaa^L
Where can I buy a	ซื้อ ... ที่ไหน seuu^H ... thee^F nai^R
Where can I hire (rent) a	เช่า ... ที่ไหน chao^F ... thee^F nai^R
Can I order it?	สั่งได้ไหม sang^L dai^F mai^R
How long will it take to arrive?	นานเท่าไหร่จะมาถึง naan thao^F rai^L ja^L maa theung^R
This is broken, can you fix it?	มันชำรุด ซ่อมได้ไหม man chahm root^H, saawm^F dai^F mai^R

Chapter  17 Building the house

Residential construction in Thailand

Residential construction in Thailand is almost entirely based on the post and beam concept. By this I mean that the main structure of the house is composed of vertical posts or columns, made from either concrete or wood, and horizontal beams (concrete or wood) supporting the floors and the roof. This differs significantly from common residential building in the US and UK where the walls (wood or steel studs or brick) provide support for the floors.

The idea of posts is so heavily embedded in Thai people's minds that the size of a house is often described by the number of posts. Beam span is typically 2.5 to 5 meters so a 12 post house is probably about 8m x 12m. The first thing a builder will often ask when asked to build a house is, "how many posts?"

Typically (but not always), posts will rise, uninterrupted, from footings to roof beams. Exterior and interior walls should be placed to provide lateral support for the posts and to hide the posts as much as possible so they do not take away space from the inside of rooms.

Setting up the guide lines

The first job when starting to build a house is to set up string lines and reference points. Stakes that hold string lines should be strong and securely hammered into the ground so they will not move, even if someone walks into them. If the string lines move after setup, the problems caused later will be huge!

String lines will guide the builders when they place footings, walls and columns. It is critical that the strings lines are set up correctly. Corners must be square and walls parallel. All reference lines should be at the correct height. Mark a height reference on an immovable post or a slow growing tree and use that as the master height reference when building foundations and floors.

To check the squareness of corners, you cannot rely on a small carpentry square; you will need to know a little math. Pythagoras tells us that the sum of the squares of 2 sides of a right angle triangle is equal to the square of the hypotenuse.

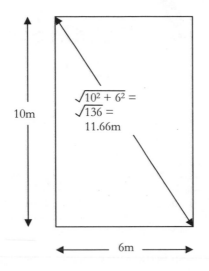

$$\sqrt{10^2 + 6^2} =$$
$$\sqrt{136} =$$
$$11.66m$$

10m

6m

Measure the distance along the string lines from corner to corner. Verify it is consistent with the plans. Using a calculator, find the square of the each side's length. Add the squares of the 2 lengths together then take the square root to get the hypotenuse (corner to corner distance). This number should be 5-40% bigger than the larger of the 2 side lengths. In the example above, a 10m x 6m rectangle has a 11.66m hypotenuse. Measure the distance between corners of your string lines. **If it is not EXACTLY the distance you just calculated, the area is not square and everything else that follows will be WRONG!!!** Your builders will need to move the stakes and reset the string lines until everything is the correct size and square.

Footings and basements

Footings should be built on stable, compacted, undisturbed, soil, rock, sand or clay, to minimize settling (sinking of the footings). The base of the footing should be compacted with a footing compactor or a steel plate and a big hammer. Note that a footing compactor machine applies more concentrated pressure than the small vibrating foot compactor used for roads.

The loading on all footings should be about equal as measured by load per surface area. Your architect should take loading and settlement into account while designing the footings, but you may find the ground under the footings is not consistent in all places. This may be especially true if there are large rocks in the ground, your site is on a slope or the footings are in the path of natural drainage. If your foundation is partly supported by large rocks, the area supported by the rock will likely never move, but the rest of the foundation may settle. This could cause cracking in the foundation, so it may be better to design around the rocks or remove them.

Footings can be dug by hand or with a backhoe (mechoe). Digging by hand usually produces a cleaner, squarer, more accurately sized hole. If using a back hoe, the hole may end up bigger than the plans. If this is the case, use more concrete, do not backfill around the sides with soft soil.

After the footing holes are dug, you should check the hardness of the footing floor. Find a 2x4 wood post which will be used to test the hardness of the floor. Hammer a wooden stake in the ground somewhere to use as a height reference. Using a "water tube" level, mark a line on the post from a point on the reference stake. Hammer the post into the ground at several test points around the footing floor. At each test point, use the same number of hammer blows (say 5), and try to use the same hit pressure. Measure the amount of sinking of the test post at each test point. Ideally, the amount of sinking will not vary by more than 10% from the other test points. If there is too much sinking at any point, do more compacting. If there is too little sinking in one footing, you may need to get expert help.

You should do a soil engineering analysis of your site if you are on a slope or have uneven compaction rates.

If you encounter unexpected problems while digging the footings, talk to your architect. Settling will cause cracks in the floor and potentially serious structural problems, usually years after the architect and builder have been paid and forgotten all about you.

Some building experts recommend rock and sand be placed under footings (i.e. before the concrete goes in) but this is not common in American buildings. Check with your architect.

Basements are not commonly used in Thailand but I think they are a good idea as a way to avoid the heat! I do not plan to go into the details of basement construction because my house in Thailand does not have one, and I do not feel qualified to talk about basement construction here. I did have a basement in my house in California and had problems with the walls cracking under the pressure of the soil pressing against the walls, as soil expanded and contracted in wet and dry seasons. I also had basement flooding problems in the rainy season, so I had to dig a sump (big hole in the basement floor) and use a sump pump (water pump with a float switch), to pump out the water. If you need a sump pump, you should also think about a backup power source for it. Chances are you will loose power at the most inconvenient time.

If building a basement, please check with a good building reference book such as "Building Construction Illustrated" mentioned in the introduction. The most important design consideration for a basement is drainage around and under the walls and floor.

Floor structures and finishes

Concrete posts

Concrete beams and optionally wood beams will be supported by concrete posts. Concrete posts can be either square (made with wood or steel forms) or round (made with concrete pipe or cardboard (sonotube)). Typically, concrete posts will be 10" diameter or square if sporting a floor and a roof or 8" if supporting only a roof. Posts will be reinforced with 4 to 8 pieces of 12-16mm steel, braced with 6mm steel stirrups on 10-15cm spacing.

Clean the floor or the beam below the posts before the formwork goes in and wash thoroughly before the concrete goes in to assure a good bond between the posts and base concrete.

When pouring concrete into posts it is VERY important that the air is vibrated out as the concrete is poured, not only at the end of the pour. If using a concrete vibrator, use it to vibrate the reinforcing rods which extend all the way to the bottom.

Concrete beams

Concrete floors and optionally wood floors and roof structures will be supported by concrete beams.

Concrete floors

Concrete floors will typically be about 10 to 15cm thick. They will be reinforced with steel mesh. The mesh must be raised above the forms, ideally slightly below half the thickness of the concrete, about 5 to 8cm. The steel mesh can be raised above the forms by pulling up on the steel by hand (painful) or with a steel bar hooked at the end. The pull up method is perhaps better than raising it before the concrete goes on, because it is less likely there will be a void below the steel rods.

The concrete will be supported by either wood forms (expensive) or pre-cast concrete slabs.

If using pre-cast concrete floor slabs, have them delivered directly on top of your floor frame.

Remember not to overload the floor frames. The slabs are heavy.

Check your builder will have plenty of workers when the floor slabs arrive to move them around.

If you forgot to put steel rods or bolts in the posts, joists or footing for things like hand rail posts and stair bases, this is your second chance to do it. Do not try to put major structural steel connectors in the floor at this point. It is too late; they must go in the thick concrete of the footings, joists or posts.

Concrete floors are typically finished with tile or wood. Carpet is not common in Thailand and I would not recommend it. Who knows what would be living in that thing!

Tile will be placed on a 3-5cm bed of cement, so the finished floor level will be 4 to 7cm above the concrete sub floor level. This is usually done after the majority of the structural construction is finished so the tile does not get damaged by the builders.

Marble is very weak and will crack if you sneeze on it, so as with any tile, it is important to have a solid, flat, base.

Some experts recommend a membrane (plastic sheet) be placed between the concrete sub floor and the tile mortar bed. The tile bed will then be mechanically isolated from the sub floor, so in the event of slight movement or cracking of the sub floor; the tile will not be damaged. The mortar bed should be reinforced with steel mesh if a membrane is used. I did not use a membrane but my sub floor is about 10cm thick so I don't think it's moving anywhere.

If using wood on top of concrete, the wood flooring will be attached to "sleepers"; strips of pressure treated wood sitting on top of the concrete sub floor. I would not like to think about the interesting things you would have living in the space between the concrete floor and the wood floor, but it's up to you, "daam jai khun".

Wood floors

Wood floors will be built on a horizontal frame consisting of beams (kaan) and joists (dtong). There are more joists than beams. The beams and joists will be connected to the vertical posts or columns (sao). The holy grail of Thai building is the "lock" as my builder calls it. A lock is a horizontal notch or channel cut into the post that the beam or joist rests in.

The "lock" is not a common building technique in America because it weakens the posts. However, you will have a very hard time convincing your builder not to use the lock method so I suggest you use posts 2" wider that the architect recommends so after the lock is cut in the posts, you still have enough core wood to ' be structurally sound.

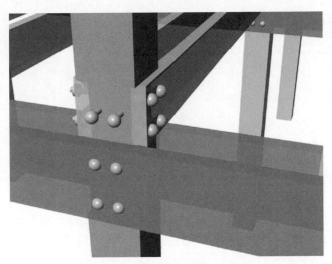

In wood frame construction, the compression (downward) strength of wood is probably more than adequate for the normal loads of the floors and roof. The more likely cause of structural failure is from lateral (sideways) forces that would occur in a strong wind or an earthquake.

For this reason, it is important to create a structure that is very resistant to sideways bending pressure. Cutting a notch out of a post and filling it with a beam or joists will not substantially reduce the compression strength but will reduce the lateral strength.

In my house, I did get some compromise on the lock principle. I used 2x8 beams and 2x6 joists but told the builders to only make a 1" notch for the lock. That way, the beams and joists can sit snugly inside the post, the Thai way, but the post is not weakened as much as a 2" notch would be. Also, I used 4 bolts for each post/beam and post/joist connection.

In this picture, notice how the notch is about half the depth of the joist. NOTE, the rim joist (see below) is not shown for clarity, but you can see the rim joists 2 bolts.

This is a view of a typical floor structure. Beams and joists are cut away in the front right corner to show detail of the post.

Floor joist ตงพื้น dtong pheuun[H]

Rim joist ไม้ปิดหัวตง maai[H] pit huaa[R] dtong

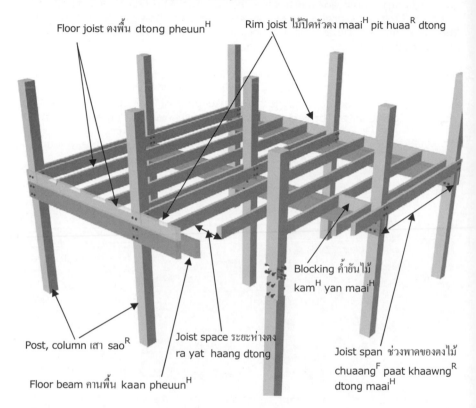

Blocking ค้ำยันไม้ kam[H] yan maai[H]

Post, column เสา sao[R]

Joist space ระยะห่างตง ra yat haang dtong

Floor beam คานพื้น kaan pheuun[H]

Joist span ช่วงพาดของตงไม้ chuaang[F] paat khaawng[R] dtong maai[H]

At posts, I recommend using 2 beams and 2 joists, one either side of the post, so the loading on both sides is approximately even. This will help reduce uneven lateral loading. Think about carrying a very heavy object in one hand and balancing on one foot, very hard! If the heavy object was split in 2 and held, one half in each hand, balancing on one foot would be much easier. It's the same for your posts.

Joist space, the distance between joists, will usually be 16" or 24" on center if using a plywood floor (plywood in Thailand is 4'x8'), or 25cm or 50cm if using planks directly on the joists. The joists that are not connected to the posts will need lateral support to stop them falling over like a wall of dominos. A rim joist connecting the ends of the joists together will provide lateral support and make the structure look neat and tidy.

In addition to the rim joists, it is a good idea to use blocking, wood blocks perpendicular to the joists, at regular intervals; for example above an interior wall. This will help prevent the "domino effect" and act as a fire and sound barrier between rooms.

Joist span (chuaang^F paat khaawng^R dtong maai^H), the unsupported distance between beams, using 16" on center wood joists should be:

- 2x6 up to 3m

- 2x8 up to 3.6m

- 2x10 up to 4.2m

- 2x12 up to 5.4m

If joist spacing is greater than 16", reduce the span or increase the size of wood. These numbers are based on American wood. Remember that an American 2x6 is actually about 1½" x 5½" (disproving the stereotype that everything is bigger in America!). So your Thai, hardwood 2x6 will probably be good for about 20% more span than these numbers. I used 2x6 joists with a 3.3m span; I probably have the strongest floor in Ko Phangan.

Beam span can be estimated as: height = span/15; width = 40% of the height. So for my 3.3m span, that's 22cm or about 9" and 4" width. I use 2, 2x8s (one either side of the post), so that's 8" high and 4" wide but my wood is as hard as solid steel so I think I'm OK.

These engineering numbers are FYI only, your architect or structural engineer should provide you with wood sizes along with all the other details. However, my architect's numbers were approximately half these sizes and I decided I would rather pay a bit more money and do it to American building code standard.

If your beams or joists are longer than 7 meters, it is likely you will have to use more than one piece of wood joined together. Beam joins should ONLY be made at posts and joist joins on top of beams. The two simplest and strongest ways to connect beams and joists are: i) lap join and ii) in-line join with a strap.

Lap join means overlapping the two pieces of wood by at least 10cm (more for beams) and nailing together. In-line joins means the ends are butted up together and a steel plate or wood block is used to reinforce the join. **I strongly urge you not to use the Thai half-and-half method of joining horizontal**

members, if you do, double up everything to compensate (big waste of money).

Have a good supply of bolts, nuts and washers on site in different lengths. Thai builders are experts at improvising when they don't have the right tool or part. But unfortunately that means they tend to make do with something that does not fit instead of simply getting the right part.

Keep all your bolts in boxes, with the size marked on the box so you know when a size is running low and the builders know where to find them.

Bolts must be long enough that there is about 1-2cm of bolt protruding through the nut. Too little and the nut will not have enough grip and could come undone and fall off, too much and you will need to add too many washers which is unnecessary and looks ugly.

Bolts are usually ⅜" or ½" diameter and are available in increments of 1". Unless you are making a very small structure, I would always use ½"; the cost difference is minimal and the bolt is much stronger.

 Check that your builder is using the right size bolt for the job. I found several examples where the builders had used bolts either too short,  and dug a hole in the wood (left), or too long, and used a stack of washers (right). It is one of the mysteries of Thai builders that they will spend half an hour creating a botch job when they could have done it right in 5 minutes.

If you find a dug out hole like the picture above, replace the bolt with the right size and use a steel plate to reinforce the wood or replace it.

Floor finishes

Floors can be finished in several materials included concrete, tile and wood.

Joists should be completely level before the sub-floor and finish floor is applied. Level will be checked with a string line and joists that are a little high will be planed down. Low joists will need shims. If your floors are not level you will have many problems later on with the finished floor and furniture.

Wood floor finishes

Wood floor finishes can be solid wood planks, solid wood flooring strips, parquet (short wood strips or squares), or laminated strips.

T&G and parquet floor should not be exposed to rain regularly. Getting wet occasionally is not a problem if the polyurethane is in good condition, but it should be dried quickly. For wood in exposed locations, use solid wood planks and leave a gap between the planks for water to drain away.

Solid wood flooring strips, parquet, and laminate will usually be tongue-and-groove, T&G. If using T&G you should buy the type with the T&G on the ends, not only the sides. This will look nicer at the joins and will not separate as much over time.

Strip flooring should be installed on top of a plywood sub floor at least 15mm (really 12mm) thick.

If the sub floor is not level, you should level it with a floor leveling compound, if you can find it. Floor leveling compound is basically a thin plaster paste that is wet enough to find its own level before setting.

Strip flooring and parquet will swell or shrink a bit depending on temperature and humidity, so it must be allowed to acclimatize to the house for several days or weeks prior to installation. It should have time to settle down before installation or it may buckle or leave gaps.

If using solid wood T&G strips, use a nail gun or a special floor hammer to nail it to the sub-floor. Gluing is also recommended.

I used 45mm nails on my floor and nailed through the plywood and into the joist and glue. The gun cost 4300 baht and 250 baht for 1000 nails. My builder said that sometimes wood floors lift up, but I believe this is because often, builders do not use long enough nails or glue.

Finishing a solid wood floor requires a lot of sanding to level and produce a nice smooth surface for the polyurethane. A stand up type floor sander will be much faster than a belt sander but be careful. If your builders are not experienced using a floor sander, it is very easy to make a mistake and leave a big groove in the floor which may be hard to remove.

Solid wood flooring will cost about 600-1500b/m2 plus 500b/m2 or more for installation and finishing. Parquet will cost about 600-1000b/m2 plus 200b/m2 for installation.

Tile floors

Tile can be natural marble or granite, or ceramic. Most large building supply shops will sell manufactured tile in various colors, designs and sizes. Marble or granite is usually available in larger cities. The best deals on marble or granite are available in the town of Saraburi, about 100km north of Bangkok, where it is mined.

Ceramic tile can be laid on a bed of mortar (cement) or glued down. If gluing, it is very important that the sub-floor is very flat or the tile will crack.

Marble and granite will be laid on a bed of cement mortar. Ceramic tile can cost from about 150-800 baht/m^2, marble from about 300-1500 baht/m^2, and granite from 500-2000 baht/m^2. Installation cost can be from 200 to 700 baht/m^2 depending on the material and complexity of the design.

I put marble floors in my house, using several different colors and a fairly complicated design with curved borders and star design. Cutting and making nice joins in marble is very difficult, especially for curves. If you have a complicated design, find a marble fitter that has experience with complex designs.

It took my marble fitters 10 weeks for 3 to 5 people to do 130 square meters of floor and wall. I bought 150m^2 of marble which covered about 130m^2 of floor and wall area so I actually had relatively little waste, about 15%.

To make a pattern in marble, the workers will first lay the floor in a simple pattern, using the basic tile colors of the design. Then they will cut out the pattern and dig out the cement under the removed tile so that the new tile can be placed and leveled.

The photo below shows the finished marble design. The marble floors, including labor, was about 150,000 baht or about $US4,200. The same job in America and probably Europe would be at lease 10 times that. The marble floors and walls in my house look truly spectacular and well worth the expense.

English/Thai words and phrases

Floor, sub-floor, foundation	พื้น pheuun^H
First floor	ชั้นหนึ่ง chan^H neung^L
Second floor	ชั้นสอง chan^H saawng^R
Post, poll, column	เสา sao^R
Beam	คาน kaan
Floor	พื้น pheuun^H
Floor beam	คานพื้น kaan pheuun^H
Floor joist	ตงพื้น dtong pheuun^H
Rim joist (perpendicular joist end plate)	ไม้ปิดหัวตง maai^{H}pit huaa^R dtong
Blocking	ค้ำยันไม้ kam^H ngan maai^H
Tile	กระเบื้อง graL beuuang
Joist span (distance between beams)	ช่วงพาดของตงไม้ chuaang^F paat khaawng^R dtong maai^H
Joist space (distance between joists)	ระยะห่างตง ra^H ya^H haang^L dtong
Floor tile	กระเบื้องปูพื้น gra^L beuuang^F bpuu pheuun^H
Marble	หินอ่อน hin^R aawn^L
Granite	
To spread cement or plaster	โบก bohk^L
Finishing coat of plaster, spackle	ปูนฉาบ bpuun chaap^L
At the same level	ระดับ ra^H dap^L
To grade, level, flatten	เกลี่ย gliia^L
Space between floor boards	ล่อง laawng^F

The floor joists are not level, please level them ตงพื้นไม่ได้ระดับ ปรับระดับ

ด้วย dtong pheuun^H mai^F dai^F ra^H dap^L, bprap^L

ra^H dap^L duay^F

Walls, windows and doors

Concrete block and brick walls

Typical concrete wall construction is with concrete blocks or bricks, cemented together, and covered with a 2-3cm thick coat of cement to finish. Concrete blocks and bricks available in Thailand are usually very weak. The Cement joints should be reinforced with steel connected to a post or window/door frame.

Small building construction in Thailand is largely based on the use of structural columns (posts) supporting the main loads of floors and roofs. Thai cement block and brick walls tend not to be strong enough for load bearing purposes. This is quite different to the building style in America and Europe where the walls are the major load bearing component of the structure.

There are exceptions of course; if designing without posts, check your architect and builder have experience with post-less construction. Either a stronger, higher quality brick or block or poured concrete should be used.

If you are concerned about the aesthetics of structural post based construction, talk to your architect about embedding the posts within the walls. This can be achieved by making a very thick wall or using double wall construction.

When using posts, from a structural integrity point of view, you should check the construction of the posts and their joints to the horizontal members such as floor joists and roof trusses more than the structural integrity of the walls.

For improved insulation, you could build with double walls. The two walls are built with an air gap of about 10cm between the inner and outer walls. There should be a way to ventilate the hot air that will build up in the air gap, but check that vermin cannot get into the air space through the vents and set up shop.

Some people recommend the inner and outer walls should be tied together to add structural strength. However, if the walls are not load bearing, it is probably not necessary and tying the inner and outer walls together with steel bar will conduct heat.

Headers (lintels)

Headers (lintels) should be made of reinforced concrete (right). Do not put concrete block or brick directly on top of the door and window frames, it will cause the frame to sag or even break and cause cracks in the finished concrete lathe.

The reinforced concrete headers can also be use to

secure wall joins at corners (below).

Since concrete block and brick walls have very little structural integrity of their own, it is a good idea to use seams of reinforced concrete to add structural stability.

The header concrete must be poured into forms built around the top of window and door frames. Do not simply plaster mortar around the steel.

Cement wall finishes

Concrete block and brick walls are often finished with cement stucco (rendering in English). My builders did a good job of making the walls smooth and flat. However, they made several mistakes in the water pipes inside the walls; requiring the walls to be cut open and the repaired. Patching cement stucco never looks as good as the original and in my house, the repairs are very obvious.

The cement used for the wall covering (chaap) should be mixed with a very fine sand to achieve a smooth finish. However, the finish will not be as smooth as plaster or wallboard (sheetrock, drywall, etc).

If you used concrete pipe for the posts and you want the corners of your house square, the builders must cut away a strip of the pipe to expose the inner core of concrete. The stucco cement will be thicker, stronger and attach to the rough inner core better then the smooth outer pipe.

I kept my ceilings open, exposing the floor joists and the underside of the plywood sub floor. The wood is sanded, stained and varnished and in my opinion looks far nicer than a flat drywall ceiling or ceiling tiles.

I didn't notice that my builders got a lot of cement on the plywood (left). Cement leaves a permanent grey stain on plywood and is almost impossible to remove later without damage to the wood, so now I have very unattractive edges on some of the plywood (right).

A simple way to avoid this is to put masking tape and plastic on the wood before the cement is applied. Go back at least 30cm from the wall with the masking to be safe since the water splashes also leave a stain.

Stud walls

Sheetrock (drywall, wallboard, plasterboard, gypsum board) nailed or screwed to studs is also used for walls in Thailand. Since sheetrock is American and UK standard, 4' wide sheets, the studs should be 16" on center. Ideally, the sheetrock should be as long as your walls are high to avoid horizontal seams. However, you may have difficulty finding sheetrock longer than 8'.

Make sure your builders are checking the studs are straight before they are installed. Check that all studs are level from top to bottom with a string line before the sheetrock goes on. "Wall wobble" is very noticeable on finished walls and very unattractive. Wood studs can be leveled with a plane (to lower) or shims (to raise).

Drywall screws hold better than nails and usually look better when filled. Screws should be 6" on center at the edges and 12" on center in the middle of the sheet.

Sheetrock joins will be taped over with paper, cloth or fiberglass tape and plastered over. I prefer fiberglass tape because it is stronger and less likely to crack, but may be hard to find in Thailand.

Other wall types

There are some hi-tech wall products on the market in Thailand; Autoclaved Aerated Concrete http://www.qcon.co.th/indexen.htm and Superblock http://www.superblock.co.th. These lightweight, aerated concrete blocks have several advantages over conventional concrete blocks and bricks. They are lighter, have better sound and heat insulation and fire resistance properties than concrete and brick. They are 2 or 3 times more expensive than concrete blocks and may be hard to find, but may be worthwhile if insulation is a big concern.

Good quality red bricks may be available from http://www.bpkbrick.co.th/

Beware of using low quality red bricks for exterior siding. I have heard they can have problems with mould and need to be painted or varnished regularly.

Window and door frames

In typical Western construction, a rough opening is cut in the wall for windows and doors. After the main structure is complete, the window and door frames are installed in the rough openings and shims (variable thickness wood spacers) are used to control level and squareness of the frames.

In Thailand the walls often are built around the finished window and door frames so the frames must be level and square before the wall is built. After, it's too late!

The major drawbacks of the Thai method are, 1) it is not easy to fix the frame, if in fact it is not level and/or square, 2) you end up with big nail holes in your beautiful wood frames, 3) the frames will be exposed  to sun and rain until the roof goes on, 4) it is very hard to replace the frames.

Check every door frame is the same height using the water tube to check level over long distances. Do not rely on checking height from the rough floor level. The finished floor will likely fix any problems with uneven rough floor height, but if the frames are not all the same height, the doors will not fit well.

Double check frames are vertical and square. I missed one door, on my bedroom, and later when installing the door, had to trip 2cm off one side to compensate for none level top frame.

I recommend you have the builders install rough frames in the walls. The rough frame should be big enough to accommodate your finished frames, with about 1cm of free space all around. This free space will later be used to properly align the window/door frame, using shims. Shims are easy to make on site from scrap wood.

Doing it the "farang" way will take more time and need more wood, but I wish I had thought of it sooner and told the builder to use rough frames. I'm very unhappy about the look of my window frames.

How to install a door or window frame without destroying it

This drawing (below) shows the finished (inner) and rough (outer) frame around a door. The shims are inserted between the inner and outer frames to fine tune the level, squareness, and straightness of the frame.

Connect the inner frame to the outer frame with 3" screws. Pre-drill screw holes in the inner frame and countersink the heads to avoid splitting and hide the screw head with filler later. Place shims and screws under the hinges and lock plate since that is where all the weight of the door will rest.

The inner frame should be installed as late as possible in the building process, ideally after the roof is finished and just before the finish cement wall coat is applied.

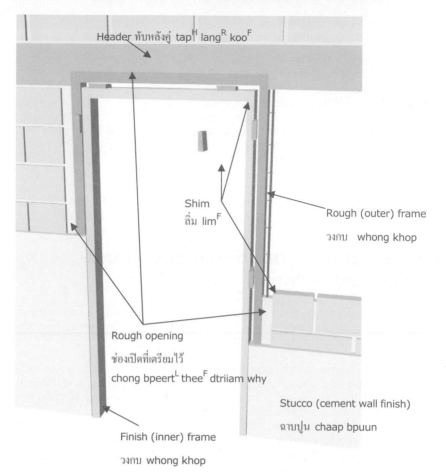

Header ทับหลังคู่ tap^H lang^R koo^F

Shim
ลิ่ม lim^F

Rough (outer) frame

วงกบ whong khop

Rough opening

ช่องเปิดที่เตรียมไว้

chong bpeert^L thee^F dtriiam why

Stucco (cement wall finish)

ฉาบปูน chaap bpuun

Finish (inner) frame

วงกบ whong khop

If the wall is wood, the same principals apply. Install the finish frames just before installing the outer wood wall cladding.

Check all door frames are the same height. The water tube method is the best way to check for level over longer distances. If the door frames are not the same height, you will have problems with fitting the doors after the finish floors go in.

Another pet peeve of mine is the way door and window frames are put together in Thailand. Door and window frames are often bought as pieces and slotted together on site. Then a couple of big nails are hammered into the ends to hold it together. The results often look like this picture on the right.

I suggest your builder pre-drill holes and use 3" screws instead of nails. This will produce a

tighter joint and minimize cracking.

The door frames will likely be installed down to the rough floor level. Cut the frames to the height of the finished floor level just before the finished floor goes in. The wood should stop at or slightly above the finished floor level and not go inside. If the frame goes below the finish floor level, water can seep into the gap and the wood will be sitting in water. This is particularly important on outside doors that will get wet often in the rain. Remember that outside floors will be sloping away from the house so check that the cut in the door frame is sloping also.

Apparently, it is very unusual to cut the door frame above the finish floor level in Thailand. I tried several times to explain why I needed the wood to stop above finished floor level but the builders did not understand, so I showed them how. When the builders saw and understood there would be no water problem this way, it was as if I had invented a cure for cancer!

You should have a small step down from inside to outside floors; about 2cm is enough to keep water out. Place the step under the door so you cannot see it from the inside but water running down the outside of the door does not blow inside in high wind.

Doors and windows

Doors will usually be bought unfinished and about 1cm larger than the specified size, i.e. a 70x200 door will actually be 71x201. This is so it can be cleaned and trimmed to fit the frame. When trimming, keep in mind the door should be about 3-5mm above the finish floor height. Recheck the door frame height and check where your finished floor height will be on each frame so you can determine how much you need to trim vertically. Try to trim about the same amount off the top and bottom of the door to keep the top and bottom rails the same height.

When hanging a door, clean the hinge side first and do a test fit to see where the top of the door lies in relation to the frame. Mark a line parallel to the top frame on the door and trim the door to that line. Next, install the hinges and hang the door, then draw a line on the door following the frame on the other side to the hinges. Trim to this line with a planer or saw, and then do another test fit. Mark the final trim lines and do a final trim to fit. Make a 1-2mm gap between door and frame all around; this is best done with a belt sander but a planer is faster.

The same fitting technique applies to windows.

Make sure the screws on the hinges do not protrude above the hinge plate as this will make closing the door difficult and will stress the hinge joint, eventually causing hinge or screw failure. This can happen if the screws are not put in square (right). If the screws are not square with the hinge plate, take them out, fill the hole with a plug of soft wood, re-drill a pilot hole with a small drill (about 1mm) , and put a new screw in. Do not use old screws, the heads will be damaged and probably weakened.

Also the screws that came with my hinges did not fit very well even when put in square so I used screws with slightly smaller heads and got a better fit. Because this head fit inside the hinge plate a little, I got a much better movement as the door was approaching fully closed.

Even after all this trimming, you may still find pressure stopping the door from closing or friction when the door comes into contact with the frame. There are usually two reasons why doors do not close properly 1) door comes into contract with the frame before fully closed, 2) the screws are protruding above the hinge plate.

Carefully check all the door edges where the door comes into contact with the frame, making sure there are no contact points. You can do this with a piece of cardboard, about 1mm think. Remember to check inside and outside of the door.

If there is contact, or a constriction, you will need to trim the frame or door with a chisel or sander, or take the door off and plane or sand the offending spot down. Remember that when paint or polyurethane is applied, the doors and windows will grow a bit. Also the wood will swell up with rain or high humidity, so check there is 1-2mm space between doors/windows and frames at all points.

The top of the hinge plate should be perfectly level with the surface of the frame or door. If the cutout for the hinge is too deep, you may find the whole hinge side of the door coming into contact with the frame. The easiest way to fix this is remove the hinge and put a small wood or cardboard spacer under the hinge, and then re-attach the hinge.

Also check that hinges are square with door and frame.

If you have protruding screws as described above, take them out and check the door closes without a problem. Then re-attach the screws as described above.

You may find that the door does not lie perfectly parallel to the frame on the opposite side to the hinges. This could be because the door has some twist in it, or the frame is not perfectly vertical on both sides. Check the frame and door for verticalness with a plumb-bob.

If the problem is with the frame and you used rough outer frames as described above, you can make small adjustments by moving the inner (finish) frame. If the inner frame is cemented into the wall, you have a bit of a problem. You can try twisting the door as described below.

If the door has twist in it, or if you need to add twist to correct a frame problem, make a wood frame to put pressure on the door and apply steam and/or boiling water to soften the wood. Gradually apply more pressure over the course of several days or weeks as necessary.

If you have double doors, you will need to use a method to create a water tight seal between the doors. This is usually done with either a strip of wood that is attached on the outside edge of the inactive door (the one that does not have the lock/handle on it) or by using an overlapping join.

If using an overlapping join, cut the overlap with a router for a nice looking join. Ideally, you want the 2 doors to be perfectly parallel all the way from top to bottom, inside and out.

Door and window hanging is tricky and unless you have very experienced carpenters, there is a good chance they will get the first one or two doors slightly wrong and have to patch it. I suggest you have the workers start work on the doors and windows you do not care about so much, such as a back bedroom or bathroom, and leave the important ones, like the main entry door, until last.

Check the hinge and door lock heights are the same on all doors and windows before they cut the holes. While I was away from the house for about one hour, the builders installed my bedroom door lock 4 cm higher than all the other locks, on a custom teak door. When I returned home the builder proudly asked me if the door lock was OK! You can probably guess my reaction. It cost me considerable time and money to get a replacement door.

In any team of builders you are going to get some more talented and careful workers and some that are only dreaming about the next bottle of Chang or the girl they met last night. Use your best carpenters on the important doors and windows and keep the others out of harms way as much as possible. I found the older workers to be more careful and skillful and the younger ones to be careless and hurried. Keep a close eye on the quality of work of each of your builders and try steering them in the right direction or in same cases, tell your builder not to send a worker to your site again.

On this window (left), one young builder managed to make the left upper hinge 10cm below the right upper hinge. Sometimes, you think you've seen everything, but the builders always have more tricks in their bag! Since the builders know I am writing a book, maybe they are trying to create things for me to write about. If so, please don't bother; I have plenty already!

Just remain calm and remind your self that the workers are probably paid less in one day than you used to make back home in 20 minutes.

Door handles should be reasonably easy to install. Handles come with a paper template showing the builders exactly where to drill the holes. However, my builder managed yet again to get most of the handles slightly wrong, resulting in locks that do not open or close correctly.

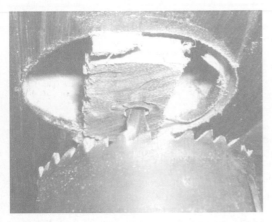

If you are lucky, the builders will have missed the mark on the barrel hole by only a few millimeters. It is possible to re-drill the barrel hole using the following method.

Remove the handle and bolt. Jam a wedge shaped piece of scrap wood in the barrel hole. Hammer it in firmly since this scrap wood will be used as a drill guide to re-drill the hole and should not move while drilling. Insert in line with the grain (as shown in picture, right), not across it, to avoid any possibility of splitting the frame. Using the manufacturers template; mark the correct center of the hole and re-drill as shown in this picture.

Wood doors and windows can look nice if properly made and installed but the Thai climate is hard on wood. Carved wood doors are inexpensive compared to US/Europe and look very nice.

Aluminum and PVC doors and windows are lower maintenance. Good quality uPVC windows are available at http://www.arcaircon.com

Roll down screens

If, like me, you have large open areas in your house (no walls), you may want to install screens to keep rain out. Plastic screens are usually made to fit between the support columns (posts). They are made of clear or colored plastic or canvas and roll up into the roof space when not in use. The steel bar at the bottom of the screen should be heavy enough to stop the plastic from swinging around or bending too much in the wind. In any reasonably strong wind, above 15MPH or so, you will likely have to anchor the bottom of the screen to the floor to stop it blowing up. When the wind catches the screen, the screen will act like a sail; it will balloon and exert a very strong pull in the top and bottom anchor points, so the steel support bars must be attached to the house very firmly.

For large screens, 3 meter or above, the wind pressure in extreme weather could easily destroy the screen, and at the worst possible time, during a raging storm. I had steel eyelets riveted into the left and right edges and I tie the screens to the posts in high wind at several points. I also have a lateral bracing system ready for typhoon conditions.

The company that installed my screens made an absolute disaster of the job. Some of the screens were not long enough to reach the floor, they used the cheapest rollers and rope possible which broke after only a few months. Also, they randomly put the draw strings on the left side on some screens and the right side on others, making it a constant guessing game to find the right draw string for the screen you want to open or close. I was forced to redo the whole thing myself.

An alternative to plastic screens are roll down metal screens which will not have the ballooning up in the wind problem but do not look very nice and are far more expensive than plastic.

Another popular alternative is folding doors. Each door section is usually about 30cm wide and each section is hinged to the next. They usually run on metal tracks installed in the floor and ceiling. This type of folding door system can be a maintenance headache and can easily damaged in strong wind. Install lateral (horizontal) bracing to add structure to the doors for use in strong winds.

English/Thai words and phrases

Wall	ฝาผนัง faa^R pha^L nang
Drywall/sheetrock/wall board	gypsum
Stucco (rendering)	ปูนฉาบ bpuun chaap^L
Door	ประตู bpra^L dtuu
Handle (door)	ด้าม daam^F
Hinge	บานพับ baan phap^H
Lock	กันขโมย gan^M kha^L mooy
Window	หน้าต่าง naa^F dtaang^L
Window pane	กระจกหน้าต่าง gra^L johk^L naa^F dtaang^L
Door or window screen	มุ้งลวด moong^H luaat^F
Shutters for a window	บานเกล็ดหน้าต่าง baan glet^L naa^F dtaang^L
Bolt (of a lock)	กลอน glaawn
Frame (door/window)	กรอบ graawp^L
Header	ทับหลังคู่ tap^H lang^R koo^F
Shim	ลิ่ม lim^F
To spread cement or plaster	โบก bohk^L
Finishing coat of plaster, spackle	ปูนฉาบ bpuun chaap^L
Do not use nails, use screws	ไม่ใช้ตะปู ใช้ตะปูเกลียว mai^F chai^H dta^L bpuu, chai^H dta^L bpuu gliaao
Drill a screw hole first	เจาะรู ก่อน jaw^L ruu gaawn^L

Roof structures and finishes

In my humble opinion, roof styles are the defining feature of Thai architecture. Even this humble sa-laa rim taang (open rest house) has a roof, far more interesting than most American and British houses.

Roof structures can be made of wood or steel. Wood looks nice but steel is faster to build and may be cheaper than wood. Wood can have problems with termites and steel can rust, especially in marine climates. Both wood and steel can have major structural failures in less than 10 years if not properly looked after.

Roof materials

Roof cover can be concrete tile (cpac), ceramic tile, asbestos, galvanized steel or straw/palm leaves, etc. Cpac is relatively inexpensive (about 100-250 baht/m^2) and looks nice but is very heavy, requiring a strong frame. Ceramic tile is very expensive, (about 400-600 baht/m^2) but is lighter than cpac and has a nice glossy finish. Cpac and ceramic tile should last forever and require no maintenance, unless leaks develop or tiles blow off. Asbestos or galvanized steel is cheap but not very attractive. Straw is very cheap, very light, looks nice (if you like rustic) and is a good insulator but does not last long. Wood shingles and composition shingles may also be available in your area. Wood shingles have a nice rustic look but require a lot of maintenance. Composition shingles are very common in America but harder to find in Thailand. Composition shingles are very fast to apply and should last from 15 to 30 years.

A very good website for previewing tile color options and calculating tile quantities is http://www.mahaphant.com. The site has both English and Thai versions and has a very cool tile color simulator. I used the calculator tool on the website to check my builder's estimate of how many tiles I needed:

When buying roof tiles, I recommend you select a type that is commonly available in your area. I bought from a manufacturer that is not readily available. One evening, after several beers and lao-khao, my builders drove their car into a stack of roof tiles. I had to buy more tile to replace the broken ones but could not order 20 tiles. It took me nearly six months to find 20 tiles in the right color!

Cpac roof tiles should be attached with stainless steel screws. You can buy special cpac 2 ¼" screws for the job. Screw every tile to the purlin (horizontal cross members) to avoid the tiles lifting up in high winds.

The underside of Cpac is an ugly grey cement color. If the inside of your roof is visible, painting the inside of the tile before it goes up looks far nicer than natural cement color.

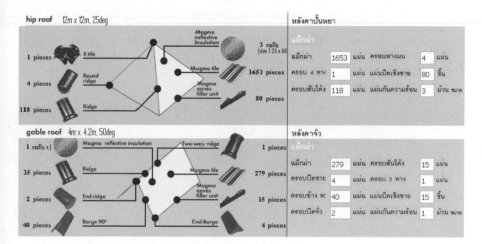

Roof detail

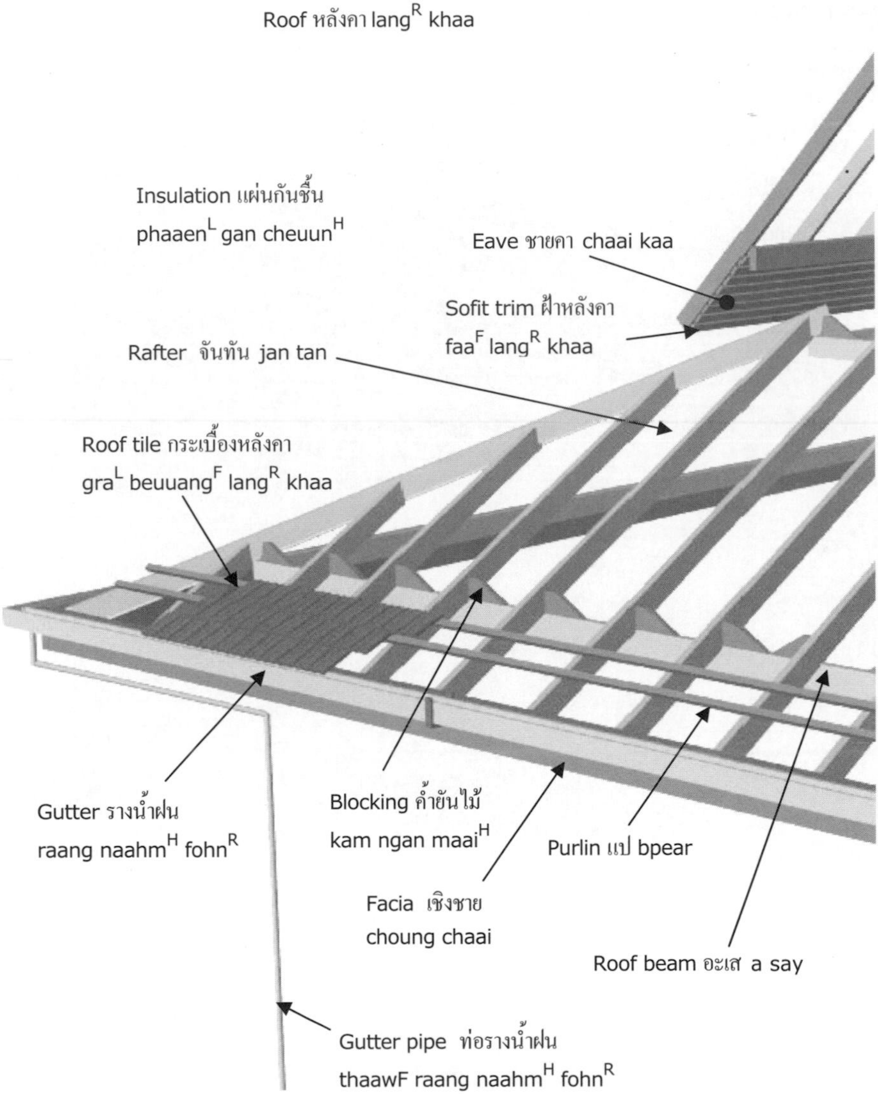

Roof หลังคา lang^R khaa

Insulation แผ่นกันชื้น
phaaen^L gan cheuun^H

Eave ชายคา chaai kaa

Sofit trim ฝ้าหลังคา
faa^F lang^R khaa

Rafter จันทัน jan tan

Roof tile กระเบื้องหลังคา
gra^L beuuang^F lang^R khaa

Gutter รางน้ำฝน
raang naahm^H fohn^R

Blocking ค้ำยันไม้
kam ngan maai^H

Purlin แป bpear

Facia เชิงชาย
choung chaai

Roof beam อะเส a say

Gutter pipe ท่อรางน้ำฝน
thaawF raang naahm^H fohn^R

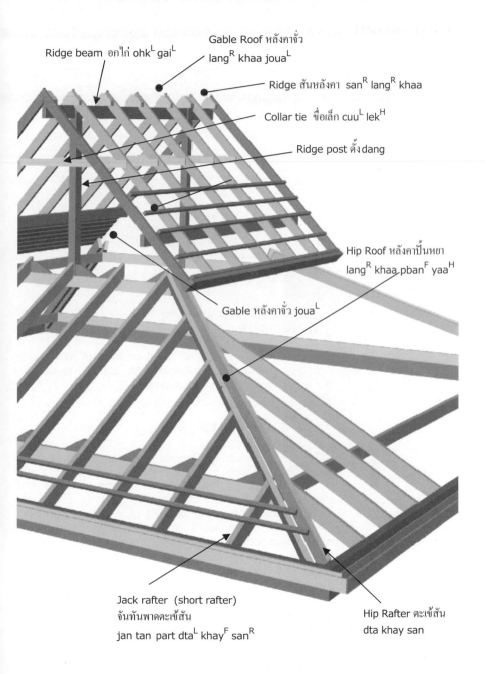

Ridge beam อกไก่ ohk^L gai^L

Gable Roof หลังคาจั่ว
lang^R khaa joua^L

Ridge สันหลังคา san^R lang^R khaa

Collar tie ขื่อเล็ก cuu^L lek^H

Ridge post ดั้ง dang

Hip Roof หลังคาปั้นหยา
lang^R khaa pban^F yaa^H

Gable หลังคาจั่ว joua^L

Jack rafter (short rafter)
จันทันพาดตะเข้สัน
jan tan part dta^L khay^F san^R

Hip Rafter ตะเข้สัน
dta khay san

Ventilation

Attic spaces should be well ventilated to get the heat out of the roof space. Most of the heat entering your house will come from the roof, so unless you like to bake, find as many ways as possible to vent the heat.

This gable end has large ventilation slots. The angled wood slats stop the rain blowing in (at least in theory, it often seems to get in anyway). Use wire mesh behind the wood slats to

stop birds moving in.

You can also add a vent fan behind the opening to add more air flow.

The workers will need scaffolding to work on the roof. They should be able to re-use the wood from the concrete forms.

Gutters

It would be very unusual to build a house in America or Europe without rain gutters, yet rain gutters are not common in Thailand. Catching the rain comming off the roof is very important to the long term health of your foundation. Since a roof catches a huge amount of water and without a gutter, drops it in a small area, the ground close to your house will recieve 10 to 50 times more water than the surrounding soil. This will cause the soil under the footing to harden and soften excessivly in dry and wet seasons, resulting in sinking, cracking and other foundation problems.

Rain gutters will significantly reduce the amout of water soaking into the ground close to your house. It will also help reduce staining of the walls from water runnoff and you can collect the water in tanks to save on your water bills. Also, rain water is better for your garden than public water, which is often heavily clorinated. I only need to use public water one or two months a year, bringing my yearly water costs down to only a few thousand baht.

Gutters should slope towards the drain pipe at a rate of about 6mm per meter. If you are likely to get leaves and debris in the gutters, you can put wire mesh on top to stop blockages.

I have seen many examples of really ugly rain gutter installations in Thailand. Often gutters are not painted to match the house/roof color and the standard gutter hangers only serve to make things worse (left).

I designed my own hangers (below) and had them made at the local steel shop. These hangers support the weight of the gutter from the bottom but leave a nice clean look to the front face of the gutter.

The standard gutter hanger in Thailand puts the gutter very close to the facia board. If making your own gutter hangers, leave about 1-2cm space between the gutter and the facia so if the facia gets wet, there is a big air gap to help it

dry. As with any wood that may be exposed to water, always provide plenty of ventilation so it can dry out quickly.

Gutter hangers should be attached through the facia and into the roof rafters. If they are attached to the facia only, the facia may pull away from the roof if the gutters get heavy with water.

Walls connecting to roofs from above

If a wall joins a roof from above, as is typical in Thai style gable above, hip below roofs, you must ensure rain cannot seep into the joins. This is typically done by using aluminum or galvanized steel flashing as shown below. Note that the flashing starts inside the wall, comes under the outer wall cover and sits on top of the cement mortar which is used to finish the top of the roof tile.

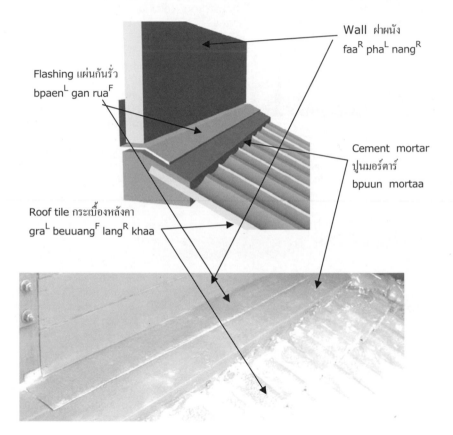

Wall ฝาผนัง
faa^R pha^L nang^R

Flashing แผ่นกันรั่ว
bpaen^L gan rua^F

Cement mortar
ปูนมอร์ตาร์
bpuun mortaa

Roof tile กระเบื้องหลังคา
gra^L beuuang^F lang^R khaa

The photo on the right shows the actual installion on my roof. I painted the cement and the flashing red to match the roof tiles and the wood stain so it's a little hard to see, which is the idea.

English/Thai words and phrases

Roof   หลังคา lang^R khaa

Roof tile   กระเบื้องหลังคา gra^L beuuang^F lang^R khaa

Rafter (sloping beams)   คานค้ำหลังคา kaan kam^R lang^R khaa

Roof beam   อะเส a say

Ridge   สันหลังคา san^R lang^R khaa

Ridge beam   อกไก่ ohk^L gai^L (chicken breast!)

Purline (cross members supporting roof cover)   แป bpear

Eave (overhanging lower edge of roof)   ชายคา chaai kaa

Gable (triangular shaped area at ends of roof)   หลังคาจั่ว joua^L

Gable end   หลังคาจั่ว lang^R khaa joua^L

Ventilation   ระบายอากาศ ra^H baay aa gaat^L

Gutter (rain gutter)   รางน้ำฝน raang naahm^H fohn^R

Gutter pipe, downspout   ท่อรางน้ำฝน thaaw^F raang naahm^H fohn^R

Scaffold (temporary working structure)   นั่งร้าน nang^F raan^H

Leak   รั่ว ruaa^F

Stairs

Staircase บันได ban dai

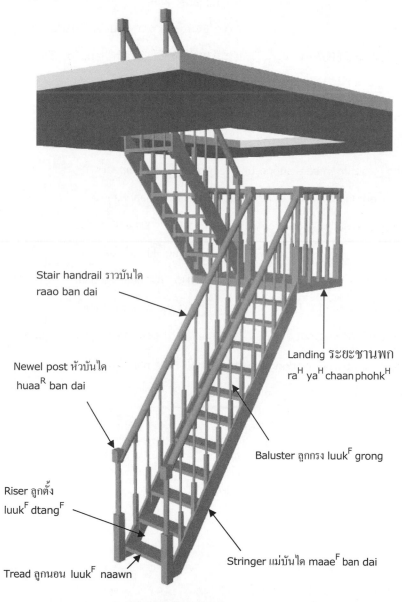

Stair handrail ราวบันได
raao ban dai

Newel post หัวบันได
huaa^R ban dai

Landing ระยะชานพัก
ra^H ya^H chaan phohk^H

Baluster ลูกกรง luuk^F grong

Riser ลูกตั้ง
luuk^F dtang^F

Stringer แม่บันได maae^F ban dai

Tread ลูกนอน luuk^F naawn

American building code specifies that for residential stairs, the maximum rise per tread is 8" (205mm) and minimum tread width is 9" (230mm). The maximum staircase width is 36" (915mm) and handrails should be 34" to 38" (865mm – 965mm) above the front edge (nosing) of the tread. Handrails are generally required on both sides of the stairs and there must be a minimum clearance of 1.5" (38mm) between the handrail and the wall. The gap between balusters must be no more than 4". While Thailand does not require you to follow American building codes, these figures will provide a useful check for the safety and comfort of the stair case design.

Staircase design and building is reasonably complicated and often done badly. It is particularly difficult to get the first and last rise height the same as the middle treads. Architects and/or builders often fail to take into account that the finished floor height is often a few centimeters different from the rough floor height, where the staircase is usually built.

I drew the staircase design on my computer, using Rhino 3D. Then, when the floors were built, I checked the rough floor to floor height, calculated the rise height, and updated my computer model as needed. Then I had a full size mockup of the staircase built in scrap wood (stringer and short treads only) and checked the rise of each tread. Even after measuring, calculating and drawing on

the computer, the first attempt at the mock staircase was still a little off. However, after a few quick tweaks and a perfectly sized model of the stair case was available to use as a pattern for the real thing.

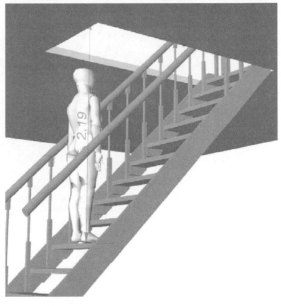

Another thing that was a little perplexing to my builders was making a large enough opening in the floor to accommodate farang head height; even through it was drawn on the plans correctly. Judging from the number of times I have banged my head on hotel/guesthouse stairs in Bangkok, I do not think this is an isolated incident.

I recommend a clearance of 1.9 to 2 meters from the header to tread directly below the header. Check this on the design and the mock staircase.

Stringers should be well secured to the floors at the top and bottom using bolts and 'L' shaped steel brackets as necessary.

On outside stairs, angle the stairs a few degrees so rain water will run off. Also, you can put a roof over the staircase to protect it from sun and rain and check there are sufficient lights. It's a good idea to put a 2 way switch in the outside lights, with one switch at the base of the stairs.

English/Thai words and phrases

Staircase	บันได ban dai
Stringer	แม่บันได maae^F ban dai
Tread	ลูกนอน luuk^F naawn
Riser	ลูกตั้ง luuk^F dtang^F
Stair handrail	ราวบันได raao ban dai
Baluster	ลูกกรง luuk^F grong
Newel post	หัวบันได huaa^R ban dai
Landing	ระยะชานพก ra^H ya^H chaan phohk^H
Straight run staircase	บันไดตรงช่วงเดียว ban dai dtrohng chuaang^F diaao
180° return staircase	บันไดแบบหักกลับ ban dai baaep^L hak^L glap^L
L shaped staircase	บันไดแบบหักฉาก ban dai baaep^L hak^L chaak^L
Spiral staircase	บันไดเวียน ban dai wiian

There must be at least 2 meters above this tread to the opening in the floor

วัดความสูงจากลูกนอนให้ถึงพื้นชั้นที่สอง

ให้ได้สองเมตรกว่า wat^H khwaam suung^R jaak^L luuk^F ban dai hai^F theung^R pheuun^H chan^H thee^F saawng^R hai^F dai^F saawng^R maeht^F gwaa^L

I think that the staircase is too steep ผมคิดว่าบันไดชันเกินไป phohm^R khit^H waa^F ban dai chan geern bpai

Electrical

Electrical wiring

When installing your electrical systems, use grounded electrical cable and grounded outlets (plugs). Thai electricians almost always install 2 wire, ungrounded systems.

This is very dangerous. Use 3 wire grounded cable and provide a good ground connection to the breaker box ground bus (see below).

Three core cable may be quite hard to find, I had to check every hardware shop in Ko Phangan to find this.

The cable above is 2x2.5/1.5, i.e. the live and neutral conductors are 2.5mm^2 and the ground is 1.5mm^2. If you are unable to find 3 core cable, use 2 core and buy a reel of green 1.5mm^2 to run as a ground wire, side-by-side with the power cable. Use 4mm conductors for 30 amp circuits and 2.5mm conductors for 20 amp circuits. 1.5mm conductors may be sufficient for lighting only circuits.

Check that your electricians connect the ground wire in every outlet (plug). Since outlets are typically daisy-chained (several outlets are connected to one feed cable from the breaker box), check that the outgoing as well as the incoming ground cable is connected to the ground connector.

Electricity in Thailand is 240VAC, 50Hz (give or take!). Live is black and neutral is white (or grey) in Thailand, same as America. However, TIT, this is Thailand; always check wires with an electrician's light-up screwdriver, the panel may be wired up wrong.

Usual Thai style electrical wiring is to put the cable on top of the wall where it is visible for the entire world to see. Tell your builder if you want the cables inside the wall. On concrete walls, the electricians will cut a trench for the pipe and install the cable and the outlets. Then the trench will be filled in with mortar as the final coat of cement is rendered on the wall.

Breaker box, grounding and GFCI

Your breaker box instructions will describe how to install a ground post, but typically it is a 2m long copper (or copper plated steel) spike nailed into the ground, at least 60cm deep. Use a minimum 4mm squared cable from breaker box to ground spike connected with a proper cable clamp at the spike and paint the connection with an acrylic paint to avoid oxidization. Some breaker boxes require you connect the main neutral bar to the main earth bar inside the breaker box (an MEN link). Check your breaker box instructions and check with your electricity supplier if this is recommended in your area.

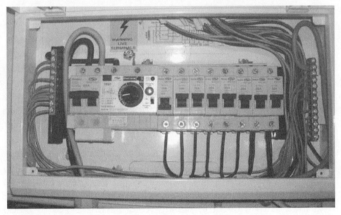 In America, only GFCI (ground fault circuit interrupter) receptacles can be used in bathrooms or outside to reduce the chance of electric shock if wet. I could not find GFCI receptacles in Ko Phangan but my breaker box has a CGFI protector for the whole house (which I know works from personal experience). I recommend using the Safe-T-Cut breaker box (above). The dial on the left side of the breakers is the GFCI unit, sensitively control.

Have the electricians label the breaker so if you need to turn off a circuit without turning off the whole house, it is easy to find.

An average family house will usually need about 6 to 8 breakers. Typically, the circuits are separated like this:

- 20 amp – all bedrooms

- 30 amp – all bathrooms

- 30 amp – kitchen

- 20 amp – living room, study, computer room

- 30 amp - exterior plugs and lights

- 30 amp – air conditioners

- 20 amp – water pumps, utility room

- 30 amp - heavy load items: water heater, clothes dryer, washing machine

There are other methods, such as one circuit for the all the lights and one circuit for all the plugs. Personally I don't like all the lights on lights on one breaker because if that one breaker trips at night, the whole house will be dark, making it hard to get to the breaker box.

Fans and air conditioning

Fans can be either the small blade oscillating type, or the large blade ceiling type. Small blade fans run much faster than large blade fans and make more noise but can cover a larger area than large blade ceiling fans. Ceiling fans are usually quieter than small blade fans and look much nicer, but typically move less air and over a smaller area and can be wobble a lot.

I have 7 ceilings fans in my house and have spent countless hours correcting the wobble. If your fan wobbles, you will need to use weights on the blades to correct the wobble, similar to balancing the wheels on your car when you get a new tire. The fan usually comes with a balancing kit (stick-on weights) and some plastic weight clips. The idea is to move the plastic weight from blade to blade and up and down the blades until you eliminate the wobble. Unlike a tire shop, which has a fancy computerized wheel balancer, you will have to do this by guess work, which is time consuming and quite frustrating if you can't get it to stop wobbling. You may need to use two or even three balance weights and even that may not work. If all else fails, try swapping blades from one side to the other. I was able to fix my fan wobble problems eventually by swapping blades and using several balance weights.

Check ceilings fans are properly secured to a structural member, not the ceiling cover material.

Air conditioner are either single room units or central air. The single room units have two parts, the condenser part is inside the room and the compressor is outside the house. There are Freon and electric cables running between the two units and a water drain pipe which you will probably want to bury in the wall. It is always best to install things in concrete walls before the top coat or stucco (rendering) goes on, since repairing stucco never looks are good as the original.

Central air conditioning uses one big unit for the whole house and pumps cold air around the house in air ducts. Installing central air is a very big job since the air

ducts are large and must be factored into the house design. Room air conditioners can be added after the house is build quite easily. Most central air con units require 3 phase electricity supply.

Air conditioners are rated in BTU (British Thermal Units). 9000BTU is suitable for up to about 10m^2, 16000BTU up to about 16m^2. Air con is a large consumer of electricity so plan your power supply needs based largely on how much air con you plan to use.

Compressors should be located away from rain and sun. On a raised floor house you can hang them from the floor beams.

Lightning protection

Lightning protection is often overlooked until it's too late. My house is on the top of a hill overlooking the sea. It's in the direct path of any storm rolling in from the sea but I didn't quite get around to doing anything to protect the house from lightning strikes, until one day, the house got hit by lightning. The lightning hit the outside lights and ran through the power cables into the breaker box and literally exploded the breaker box. I was standing about 2 meters away at the time; you can probably imagine my reaction!

The next day I researched lightning protection on the internet. The basic principal of lightning protection is that lightning will usually find the lowest resistance path to ground. In my case, it was through the house wiring, into the breaker box and presumably into the ground wire. A lightning protection system will provide a low resistance path to ground without damaging the house electrical systems or causing other damage.

One web site I found useful was http://lightningrod.com. Their recommendation is to have a minimum of 2 ground spikes, at roughly opposite corners of the roof. A heavy gauge electrical cable is run across the roof from ground spike to ground spike. Lightning rods, copper rods approximately 20cm long, are attached to the cable at the highest point of the roof and the corners and should be no more 20′ apart. You may be able to buy lighting rod kits from your local hardware store. I made my own, I doubt lightning can tell the difference.

Conventional wisdom is that lightning rods should have a sharp pointed end and most commercial rods do have a sharp end. An article in USA Today (http://www.usatoday.com/weather/resources/basics/2000-05-15-lightn-rod-tests.htm) says that researchers in New Mexico found that blunt end rods work far better than sharp end rods.

I bonded the cable and rods to the roof tile with car body filler because it is cheap, strong and the right color for my roof. You can probably use roof cement but I do not recommend drilling into the roof tile.

Almost anyone that has lived in Thailand for a long time will have had electrical items such as TVs, computers, etc, destroyed during lightning storms. If lightning hits the power cable anywhere close to your house, you will likely get a high voltage spike which can damage sensitive electronics. The best protection for your electrical items is to unplug them when an electrical storm is approaching. Also, use surge protector power strips and if you are really worried, use an uninterruptible power supply (UPS) which, in theory, totally isolates the load from the electrical supply. I say in theory because in my experience, cheap UPS units are unreliable and are more likely to cause problems than fix them.

Security systems

I use a security system with motion sensors, door and window alarms and a smoke detector. My system cost $290 in the US; I have not seen anything like it in Thailand. It is wireless; easy to install and calls your cell phone with a message if the system is triggered.

Plan for the future

Try to plan for future needs by running additional conduits and cables. Adding later is always a big problem. Think about where you could possibly add a phone or network jack; add another lighting circuit or an air conditioner. It is far easier and relatively inexpensive to add the wires before the walls and ceilings are covered up.

English/Thai words and phrases

Electricity	ไฟ fai
Electrician	ช่างไฟ chang^F fai
Cable	เคเบิ้ล khaeh beern^F
Cable Extension cord	สายไฟ saay^R fai
Electric circuit	วงจร wohng jaawn
Live (positive)	ขั้วบวก khuaa^F buaak^L
Neutral (negative)	ขั้วลบ khuaa^F lohp^H
Ground wire	สายดิน saay^R din
Electric meter	มิเตอร์วัดไฟฟ้า mi^H dtuuhr^M wat^H fai faa^H
Electric poll	เสาไฟฟ้า sao^R fai faa^H
Breaker box (switchboard)	แผงเมนสวิตช์ phaaeng^R main sa^L witch^H
Circuit breaker	อุปกรณ์ตัดกระแสไฟฟ้า oo^L bpa^L gohn dtat^L gra^L saae^R fai faa^H
Transformer	หม้อแปลงไฟ maaw^F bplaaeng fai
Electric current	กระแสไฟฟ้า gra^L saae^R fai^M faa^H
Outlet/plug/receptacle	ปลั๊กไฟ bplak^H fai
2 pin plug	ปลั๊กไฟสองตา bplak^H fai saawng^R dtaa
3 pin plug	ปลั๊กไฟสามตา bplak^H fai saam^R dtaa
Light	ไฟ fai
Light bulb	หลอดไฟฟ้า laawt^L fai faa^H
Light switch (on/off)	สวิตช์ปิดเปิด sa^L witch^H bpit^L bpeert^L

3 way Light switch	สวิตช์ปิดเปิดสามทาง sa^L wit[ch]^H bpit^L bpeert^L saam^R thaang
Fan	พัดลม phat^H lohm^M
Ceiling fan	พัดลมเพดาน phat^H lohm phaeh daan
Table fan	พัดลมตั้งโต๊ะ phat^H lohm^M dtang^F dto^H
Cable clip	คลิปสายไฟ khlip^H saay^R fai
Cool air duct	ท่อส่งความเย็น thaaw^F sohng^L khwaam^M yen^M
Air filter	หม้อกรองอากาศ maaw^F graawng^M aa^M gaat^L
Short circuit	ไฟช็อต fai^M chawt^H
Dishwasher	เครื่องล้างจาน khreuuang^F laang^H jaan
Washing machine	เครื่องซักผ้า khreuuang^F sak^H phaa^F
Cooking stove, oven	เตา dtao
Gas stove, oven, range	เตาแก๊ส dtao gaaet^H
Toaster oven	เตาย่างอาหาร dtao yaang^F aa haan^R
Microwave oven	เตาอบไมโครเวฟ dtao ohp^L mai khr<u>o</u>h wehb^F
Stove hood	เครื่องดูดควัน khreuuang^F duut^L khwan
Refrigerator	ตู้เย็น dtuu^F yen
Freezer	ตู้แช่แข็ง dtuu^F chaae^F khaeng^R
Vacuum cleaner	เครื่องดูดฝุ่น khreuuang^F duut^L foon^L
I want to put the cable inside the wall	ผมต้องการฝัง สายไฟในฝา ผนัง phohm^R dtaawng^F gaan fang^R saay^R fai nai faa^R pha^L nang^R
I want to use 3 pin plugs with a ground wire	ผมต้องการใช้ปลั๊กไฟสามตา กับ สายดิน phohm^R dtaawng^F gaan chai^H bplak^H fai saam^R dtaa gap^L saay^R din

Plumbing, water and septic systems

Sewer (drain) pipes

Many Thai bathrooms smell quite bad. This is because vent pipes and even P-traps (U-bends) are not always used in plumbing in Thailand.

A P-trap (U-bend) is a U shaped section of drain pipe. A little bit of drain water is trapped in the U bend at all times (in theory!). This trap stops gasses from the sewer pipe coming back into the house. (NOTE, western style toilets are made with the U bends inside, so you do not need a U bend in the drain pipe. Thai style squat toilets do need a U bend in the drain pipe). Sinks usually have a u-bend in the

pipe just below the sink drain, so the only u-bend you will likely need to add is for shower and floor drains.

However, sometimes the U bends can empty of water and allow the smell to come into the house. If several fixtures are connected to the same drain pipe, siphoning can occur, usually because a toilet or another drain is flushed. When a sudden gush of water moves down a sewer pipe, it will suck air behind it, like a subway (underground) train leaving a station. This suction can pull the water out of nearby U bends on the same drain pipe, leaving the house open to sewer gasses.

The way to stop this, and the only way you will get a plumbing permit in America, is to install vent pipes in the sewer system. A vent pipe is a plastic pipe, usually the same diameter as the sewer pipe it is venting, going up through the house and poking out of the roof. By using a vent pipe, smells from the sewer system will drift into the breeze, high above the living areas or your house. You can buy a specially designed roof tile

with a rubber boot to accommodate the pipe (left). The rubber boot is cut to fit any size pipe and the left over piece makes a great traditional Thai hat (right).

With a properly installed vent pipe, when a toilet or another drain is flushed, air will be sucked from the vent pipe, not other U bends, so the house will remain smell free.

Remember to install vent pipes through concrete floors before the concrete is poured. I forgot to check, so it was necessary to cut a hole in the floor to add one later.

Drains should slope down from the fixture to the main sewer pipe connection at the rate of about 1-2cm per meter. If too little slope, the solid waste will find a low spot and sit there, constantly blocking the pipe; if too much slope, the water will rush down the pipe too quickly leaving the solid waste behind, also potentially causing a block.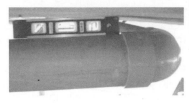

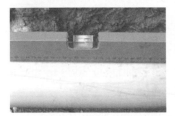 You should check EVERY PART of ALL the drain pipes with a spirit level to ensure adequate slope in the right direction. I found at least 10 places where the builders had no slope or an uphill slope. It is much easier to fix problems before the pipe is glued and the pipes buried so check constantly as the builders are working. You will probably hear the phrase "bpuaat huaa", (headache) many times as well as a few choice terms that I can't translate! Remember to check underground pipes too before they fill the trench (left).

Install a cleanout fitting on the way to the main drain so in the event of a blockage, a pipe snake can be inserted into the pipe to clear the blockage without having to go through the toilet or sink drains. The cleanout (right) is at the end on a chain of pipe connections. Note that this 90 degree turn (left) is two 45 degree turns to be sure a pipe snake will finds its way down the pipe easily. A long radius 90 degree elbow would have done the same job but I could not find one.

In America you can buy a cleanout fitting to put on the end of the pipe. I couldn't 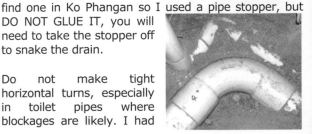 find one in Ko Phangan so I used a pipe stopper, but DO NOT GLUE IT, you will need to take the stopper off to snake the drain.

 Do not make tight horizontal turns, especially in toilet pipes where blockages are likely. I had

the builders change this short radius elbow (above/left) to a long radius (above/right).

Notice that the builders buried the pipe in the sand before I had time to check it so I had it dug out. This is very typical; "out of sight, out of mind"; at least that's what they hoped!

Beware of mystery pipe size changes like this one. For some inexplicable reason, the builder went from a 1 ½" drain pipe to a 1 ¼" pipe and then into the main 2" pipe. The change to a smaller pipe would cause a block. As with all problems, you should replace or fix it.

Check the height of the sink wall drain above the finished floor level. It should match the height of the sink drain pipe. My builders installed the drains at random heights, 10-15cm too high requiring a lot of work to fix.

On a raised house design like mine, ideally, you may not want all these pipes visible from ground level. Using 3D-CAD I was able to plan the ideal positions for the pipe junctions to avoid overlapping pipes. This helps to keep the pipes high up, as close to the floor joists as possible and harder to see when the house is finished. There is a storage room in the center square of my house. All the down pipes are inside this room so the view under the house from ground level is clean and neat.

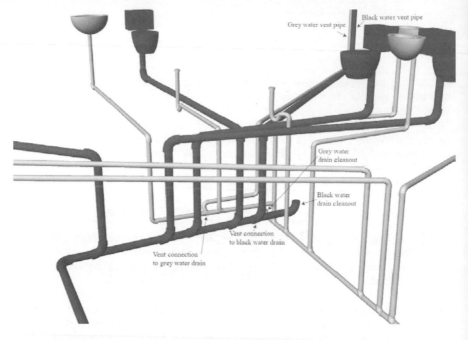

Note the connection of the vent pipes to the sewer (drain) pipes in the detail picture above. The vent pipe should connect at or close to the beginning of the pipe connections (farthest from the tank and most up hill).

Remember that every part of the pipe system must be sloping down from the fixtures to the tanks. Check that there are no sagging sections under the house that will cause a low spot where solids can collect.

Install cleanouts so that if there is a blockage in the main drain, it is possible to snake the pipe without having to go through the toilet or sink. Unblocking drains is no fun!

In America you are required to do a pressure test on your drain system before the inspector will approve it. To do a pressure test, block off the entrances to the tank and all the pipe openings for toilets, sinks, drains, etc. You can buy a special pressure test cap for this. Then fill the pipe with water by putting a hose pipe in the top of the vent pipe. When the vent overflows, the system is full. Carefully check the pipes and joints; you should not see any leaks.

Unfortunately, to do this test you will need to close every drain opening, which in a big house, needs a lot of expensive pressure caps. A shortcut method is to only do the pressure test up to the level of the toilet or sink drain openings. This will check all the joints that will have water in; i.e. up to the bathroom floor level. It will not check the vent pipe for leaks, but that only has air in so you can probably get away with it.

If your house is slab on grade, all the sewer pipes must be installed in the ground before the floor goes in and there is no chance for change later. The raised floor options allows for more flexibility.

Take many photographs for the plumbing system before the walls and floors are covered over. Make notes on the photographs about distances from the walls, etc. so if you ever have need to dig the pipes out, or if you are drilling holes into the wall, you can easily find the pipes from the photos.

In my opinion, there is not one area where Thai builders are more utterly incapable of doing a barely acceptable job than with plumbing. I have seen so many major plumbing disasters that just boggle the mind. Plumbing requires a bit of planning and many different size parts and fittings. Thai builders would rather spend all day heating up a bit of plastic pipe with a cigarette lighter so it can be force fed into another dissimilar size pipe than simply going to the shop and buying the right connector.

I don't have a good solution for avoiding plumbing fiascos other than to do it yourself if you know how.

Septic systems

Unless you live in a town or city, it is likely you will be using a septic system (hole in the ground) for your sewer water. The septic tank is either a concrete lined hole in the ground or a plastic tank that allows leaking of the waste water into the soil.

Concrete rings can be purchased at most building supply shops. Typically the septic tank will be 1 meter diameter and 3 meters deep. A hole is knocked in the side with a hammer to insert the main sewer pipe. The bottom of the hole is left open to the ground so some of the liquid leaches out. Depending on your soils ability to drain water, you may need two or more tanks.

The plastic "apple" style tanks are more sophisticated and may be required by local building departments.

Do not install septic tanks within 30 meters of a well, 15 meters of a stream or 3 meters from a building.

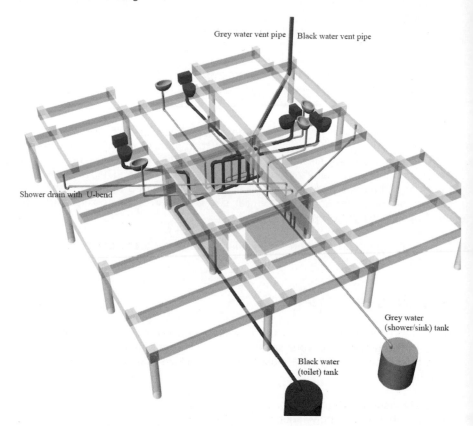

Grey water vent pipe | Black water vent pipe

Shower drain with U-bend

Grey water (shower/sink) tank

Black water (toilet) tank

I use 2 septic tanks one for toilets (black water), another for showers and sinks (grey water). This will eliminate any chance of sewer smells from the toilet tank entering through the shower and sink drains, etc. This does not mean you do not need a vent pipe however; one toilet can still siphon another toilet U bend dry if on the same drain.

Grey water can also be used for watering the garden. Plants seem to do well on the phosphates in the soap and shampoo.

For more information about septic tanks, check this link: http://cecalaveras.ucdavis.edu/realp.htm

Water supply and storage

If you are lucky, you will have water supplied from the public water system. Other sources of water are from a well, from a river, stream or lake, or from collecting rain water.

In any case you will probably need to store large amounts of water for "dry spells". I lived in a bungalow that routinely ran out of water; mai sa-duaak maak maak! Ko Phangan and many other places in Thailand are facing sever water shortage problems because of population growth and lack of rain.

Even if your public water supply is reliable, you may get periods of low pressure when demand from other people on the system is high. Unless you live in a condo, storing water for your house is generally a good idea in Thailand.

I use 4, 2,000 liter fiber glass tanks for a 4 bedroom house with 4 people. You can also use stainless steel or the traditional big earthenware jars which look far more attractive than plastic.

If using multiple tanks, connect water pipes between all the tanks so the water levels will stay equal on all tanks and you will only need one pump for all the tanks. Use flexible pipe, not rigid PVC pipe because the tanks may move a little as the weight changes which would break ridged pipe. If you have a multiple tank configuration, send water into the tanks at the beginning of connector pipe chain and draw the water out of the end of the chain. That way, sediment will settle in tanks other than the one that is feeding the pump.

If you are putting the tanks under ground you may want to build a reinforced concrete room to house the tanks. This will protect the tanks from crushing from the surrounding soil; allow easy access to the tanks and easy replacement if they leak. You should put a submersible sump pump in the room to keep it from flooding in the rainy season which could cause the tanks to float up out of the ground.

If you bury the tanks, you will need to make an access hatch to the surface so you can look inside and clean them out periodically.

I didn't clean my tanks for about 6 months. When I eventually did, I was horrified at the 'khee' that was in the bottom 10cm or so. I recommend draining the tanks every 3 months or so and climbing inside with a bucket and emptying everything out and scrubbing the walls and floor. If you are not able to climb into the tanks, a pump may suffice.

There are typically 2 ways to connect a water tank into your plumbing system, depending on if you plan to run primarily on tank water or mains water. These systems assume your tank is at ground level. If your tank is above roof level, you will not need the pump.

1) Primary water supply from mains with tank as backup:

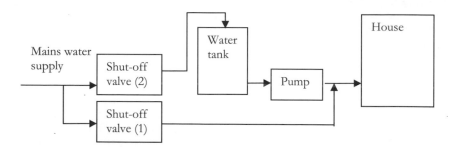

In this configuration, valve 1 is normally open when mains water supply is sufficient. Valve 2 can be opened to fill up the tank if necessary.

When mains water is not available or is too low pressure, close valve 1 (so you don't pump water back into the water main) and turn on the pump to provide water to the house. You may want to open valve 2 to keep the tank topped up but be careful not to over fill and waste water.

The main advantage of this system is you do not need to run the pump unless mains water has stopped. However, it is a good idea to circulate water through the tank every week or so, so it doesn't become stagnant.

2) Primary water supply from tank:

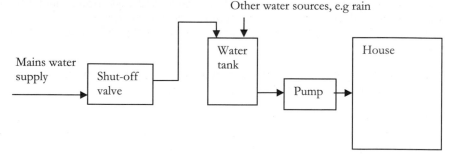

This simpler version of the first system only has one valve, typically the stop tap at the meter. In chapter 4, "Access and services", I mentioned problems with leaking water pipes and big water bills.

This system will increase your electricity bill because the pump will run every time you use water. However, if your supply is unreliable, it may be the only choice you have.

Most people in Thailand seem to turn on and off the main inlet supply to the tank manually. Based on my unscientific observations, I would guess that 10-20% of water and hundreds of thousands of baht is wasted in Ko Phangan because people forget to turn off the water when filling the tank. Everyday I see water tanks overflowing resulting in water bills of thousands of baht.

A better way is to use a float valve to automatically turn on the water supply when the level falls and turn off when the level rises. Float valves such as the one in my tanks (right) are commonly available for a few hundred baht in any good hardware shop.

In the rainy season you may want to switch off the  automatic filler and let the rain do it or you will overflow the tanks every time it rains.

If you are running rain water into the tanks, you will need to install an overflow system to drain excess water to a convenient place. I get about 4000 liters/hours from my 169m^2 roof in a standard tropical downpour, so it's very easy to overflow a storage tank in just a few hours. It is not a good idea to let overflow water simply spill over the side of the tank and into the ground under the tanks since the ground will become very soft at the edges and will cause uneven sinking of the tanks and may break the tank walls.

The first few minutes of rain water will likely be dirty, especially if it has not rained for a while. I have a dump valve on my rain water down pipes which is normally left open. After 5 or 10 minutes of heavy rain, I close the dump valves, sending cleaner water into the tanks.

Mains water inlet pipe (1")

Rain water inlet pipe (2 ½")

2000 liter fibreglass tanks

Overflow pipe (2 ½")

Flexible pipe connecting tanks to equalize the water level

Water pumps

Unless you install your tank on a tower or a high point on your land, you will have to pump the water up to the house. You can pressurize the system using an automatic pressure pump or install a small header tank in the attic space and use a float switch in the tank to control the pump.

If using an automatic pressure pump, a 250W pump is normal unless it is a very small house. Be careful never to let the tank run dry or allow air into the intake pipe since this will cause the pump to run continuously and it could overheat and damage the pump. In my opinion, water pumps should have an automatic thermal cutout switch to prevent overheating but my Mitsubishi doesn't have one.

The pipe connecting the tank and the pump must not have an air trap in it as shown in this diagram below:

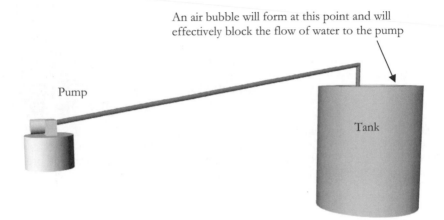

An air bubble will form at this point and will effectively block the flow of water to the pump

Pump

Tank

Avoid an upward facing bend as shown in the diagram above. Air will be trapped in this bend and the pump will have to work very hard to suck water through the air trap. Ideally, redesign the pipe system or move the tank or pump to fix the problem. If you cannot change the pipes, tanks or pump position, you will need to add a system to bleed air from the high point. This can be done by adding a shutoff valve at the high point with a small water reservoir above. When there is air in the system, open the vale and flush out the air with water from the reservoir.

If you have a well, you will need a pump to bring water to the surface. There are two types of water pumps commonly used. Centrifugal pumps have a high speed rotating impellor that moves water by centrifugal force. Centrifugal pumps move a lot of water quickly but have limited suction capacity, typically 9 meters. Piston pumps have an oscillating piston, like a car engine. They produce a lot of suction but are relatively inefficient and do not move big water volumes. However, for any reasonably deep well (10-50m) you will likely need a piston pump.

The well pipe must have a check valve to stop water returning to the well when the pump is switched off. Also, it's a good idea to have a strainer basket on the end of the intake.

All pumps require priming, i.e. the intake pipe must be filled with water since the pump will not pump air. A simple way to allow easy priming of the pump is to use a PVC intake pipe setup like in this photograph (right).

To prime the pump, open the valve at the top and pour water in. When the pipe is full and the water level does not change, close the valve and start the pump. If the water level does not stabilize, you have a leak in the intake pipe or a bad check valve and you will constantly loose prime.

Note that this pump (right) has a reservoir tank and pressure switch which controls the pump automatically when water is used. This whole setup (locally made) costs about 4000 baht. An automatic pressure pump from Mitsubishi, Toshiba, Hitachi or whoever will typically cost about 7000-10000 baht.

Bathroom fixtures

Bathroom fixtures are not cheap in Thailand. I think toilets are actually cheaper in Home Depot in America, which is surprising because they mostly come from Thailand. Perhaps someone can explain this to me! However the choice of bathroom fixtures seems much larger than the selection in American, so you should easily find something to meet your budget and style.

Water heating

For warm water showers, electric water heaters on the bathroom wall are very common in Thailand. Be extremely careful with the wiring of electric water heaters. The unit should be grounded and the electrical supply should use a GFCI circuit breaker. Check the ground wire goes to a good ground post; see your breaker box instructions. Shower fatalities are quite common in Thailand.

I prefer warm water from a tank and a mixer on my showers; it's more comfortable, a lot safer than electric and is almost free to run if using solar heating.

I used solar heating for my hot water. The sun is free and there's plenty of it. In Thailand, your roof will likely get so hot you will not need much of a solar collection system. I use a system by Suntech. It has a 200 liter tank and a 2m x 1.6m solar collector. The whole system including installation and hot water pipes to 4 showers was 42000 baht (although I believe the price has gone up significantly recently). In addition to saving the environment, it feels good to shower in free hot water. It has an electric backup in case there is not enough sun, which I have only needed for about 5 days in the rainy season.

A simple electric or gas heater tank (no solar) will cost about 7000-10000 baht which is clearly cheaper in the short run than solar. Depending on the life expectancy of the solar system and how much hot water you use, it may be cheaper to use solar in the long run.

Water pipes and connections

In America it is required to use copper or steel pipe for water supply inside the house. In Thailand, ¾" and ½" plastic pipe is usually used. Plastic pipe will not hold high water pressure like copper or steel pipe. If you are connected directly to the main water supply, you may have too much pressure for plastic pipe. If the pressure is too high you may blow out the joints and flood the house.

Hot water pipes should be copper or a special white plastic pipe that comes with the water heating system. The white pipe requires a special heater to join at the connections.

Check that your builders are "roughing up" the ends on the pipe and the inside (female) of the connectors with sand paper prior to gluing to ensure a strong, permanent joint.

Each fixture's water supply line should have its own shut off valve so if it is necessary to disconnect the fixture, you will not have to shut off water to the entire house.

My builders ran one water pipe into each bathroom then split the pipe off to the shower, toilet, sink and spray gun on top of the sub floor. When the finished tile floor goes in all the pipe work will be buried in cement. I think this is a bad idea

because if one of those joins develops a leak, it will be impossible to fix without digging up the whole floor and re-tiling. A much better way would be to do the plumbing connections under the floor, not inside the cement, so if there is a problem, it is easy to find and fix.

If the water pipes are to be buried inside the finished floor or wall cover, check there are no leaks before the finish cover is applied. Try to avoid 3 way connections, bring all of the 't' joins into an open area where they can be inspected for leaks. Adding a valve before it goes into the concrete floor will make it even easier to identify problems. I forgot to do this in one of my bathrooms and had a leak under the marble floor. I had to cut out a section of marble floor and dig out the cement to fix the pipe. When I got to the problem I found that the builders had forgotten to glue the pipe. I found four other pipe joints where the builders forgot to glue the pipe. Do not take anything for granted, your builders can and will make significant mistakes.

In retrospect, I should have stopped my builders from doing the plumbing work when I saw how bad a job they were doing and hired a real plumber. It would have saved me considerable time and expense required to fix all the problems later.

English/Thai words and phrases

Plumbing	งานซ่อมท่อ ngaan saawm^F thaaw^F
Plumber	ช่าง ประปา chang^F bpra^L bpaa
Public water system	ประปา bpra^L bpaa
Pipe	ท่อ thaaw^F
PVC pipe	ท่อ PVC thaaw^F PVC
Hot water	น้ำร้อน naahm^H raawn^H
Warm water	น้ำอุ่น naahm^H oon^L
Cold water	น้ำเย็น naahm^H yen
Water pipe	ท่อน้ำประปา thaaw^F naahm^H bpra^L bpaa
Sewer (drain) pipe	ท่อน้ำทิ้ง thaaw^F naahm^H thing^H
Vent pipe	ท่อระบายอากาศ thaaw^F ra^H baay aa gaat^L
Water heater	เครื่องทำความร้อน khreuuang^F thahm khwaam raawn^H
Water tank	ถังเก็บน้ำ thang^R gep^L nahm^H
Septic tank	ท่อส้วม thaaw^F suaam^F
Pump	เครื่องสูบ khreuuang^F suup^L
Water pump	เครื่องสูบน้ำ khreuuang^F suup^L naahm^H
4 inch pipe	ท่อสี่นิ้ว thaaw^F see^L niu^H
2 1/2 inch pipe	ท่อสองนิ้วครึ่ง thaaw^F saawng^R niu^H khreung^F
1 ¼ inch pipe	ท่อหนึ่งเศษหนึ่งส่วนสี่นิ้ว thaaw^F neung^L saeht^L neung^L suaan^L see^L niu^H
Glue	กาว gaao
9	เก้า gao^F

Elbow	ข้องอ khaaw^F ngaaw
2", 90 degree elbow	ข้องอเก้าสิบองศา สองนิ้ว khaaw^F ngaaw gao^F sip^L ohng saa^R, saawng^R niu^H
1 ½", 45 degree elbow	ข้องอสี่สิบห้าองศา หนึ่งนิ้วครึ่ง khaaw^F ngaaw see^L sip^L haa^F ohng saa^R, neung^L niu^H khreung^F
3 way connector	สามทาง saam^R thaang^M
Straight 1" to 1 ½"	ข้อต่อตรงหนึ่งนิ้วทดหนึ่งนิ้วครึ่ง khaaw^F dtaaw^L dtrohng neung^L niu^H thoht^H neung^L niu^H khreung^F
U-bend (trap)	ที่ดักกลิ่น thee^F dak^L glin^L
Clean out	ช่องทำความสะอาดท่อ chaawng^F thahm khwaam sa^L aat^L thaaw^F
Valve	วาว waao
Sanitary ware (bathroom fixtures)	สุขภัณฑ์ sook^H ga pan
Sink (bathroom)	อ่างล้างหน้า aang^L laang^H naa^F
Sink (kitchen)	อ่างล้างชาม aang^L laang^H chaam^M
Toilet (western style)	ชักโครก chak^H khrohk^F
Toilet (Thai style)	ส้วม suaam^F
Shower	อาบน้ำ aap^L naahm^H
Faucet (tap)	ก๊อกน้ำ gaawk^H naahm^H
Pipe hanger	แขวนท่อ khwaaen^R thaaw^F
Slope	สโลฟ slope
Leak	รั่ว ruaa^F
Blocked (pipe, sink, etc)	ตัน dtan
To fix (repair)	ซ่อม saawm^F

There is not enough slope in this pipe · ท่อนี้มีสโลฟไม่พอ thaaw^F nee^H mee slope mai^F phaaw

It should drop 1cm for every meter · มันควรลดลงทุกหนึ่งเมตรต่อ หนึ่งเซ็นติเมตร man khuaan loht^H lohng thook^H neung^L maeht^F dtaaw^L neung^L sen dti^L maeht^F

Use a U-bend (trap) on every shower drain · ใช้ที่ดักกลิ่นทุกท่อน้ำทิ้ง อาบน้ำ chai^H thee^F dak^L glin^L thook^H thaaw^F naahm^H thing^H aap^L naahm^H

I want a vent pipe in the drains · ผมต้องการท่อระบายอากาศที่ท่อน้ำทิ้ง phohm^R dtaawng^F gaan thaaw^F ra^H baay aa gaat^L thee^F thaaw^F naahm^H thing^H

Test for leaks before you cover up the pipes · ควรตรวจท่อน้ำประปาก่อนว่ารั่ว หรือไม่ ก่อนที่จะฝังท่อน้ำ khuaan dtruaat^L thaaw^F naahm^H bpra^L bpaa gaawn^L waa^F ruaa^F reuu^R ,mai^F gaawn^L thee^F ja^L fang^R thaaw^F naahm^H

Chapter 18 Swimming pools

I have recently completed building a swimming pool at my house. What I don't know about building swimming pools can fill a tome! However, I have learned (mostly by trail and error) a few things to be careful of when building and maintaining a pool; this is a collection of my thoughts about pools, it is by no means a definitive reference on swimming pool deign, construction and maintenance.

For great information about swimming pools see: http://en.wikipedia.org/wiki/Swimming_pools

Design and construction

Typically, swimming pools in Thailand are made from reinforced concrete. In the west they are often made with gunnite; a concrete slurry sprayed on to reinforcing steel using special equipment. Reinforced concrete is far more labor intensive than gunite, but in Thailand, labor is cheap.

Most people choose to hire a pool company to design and build their pool. If you do this, I recommend you read this chapter so you can check the design and construction with my observations. If you choose to design and build your own, good luck! And research as much as you can before spending money.

Swimming pool types

Swimming pools basically come in two types, skimmer and overflow. Skimmer pools keep the water level about 10-20cm below the top of the walls. A skimmer is a device built into the wall that allows the surface water to return to the pump/filter so that floating debris is automatically filtered out of the pool.

An overflow pool maintains the water level almost exactly at the top of the wall. When the pump is running, water overflows into collection channels together with floating debris and returns to the pump/filter. An infinity edge pool is the same idea as an overflow pool except that one or more sides are above ground level so water flowing over the side gives the visual effect of extending into infinity. Clearly the top edge of the wall on an overflow pool must be very accurately level for the overflow effect to work smoothly.

On my overflow pool, I have noticed I loose a lot of water over the sides when people jump in the pool; the wave created rolls directly over the overflow return grate. The other problem with overflow pools is the water must be maintained at the full level all the time. This may be a problem if you live in an area where water may be in short supply in the dry season, i.e. Thailand. A skimmer pool allows for about 5-7cm variation in water height so in the dry season (when you loose a lot of water through evaporation) you may be in a better position to go several weeks without topping up.

Overflow pool systems also have a large holding tank to ensure the pump does not run dry. If there is a possibility of several weeks of low water, you should design this tank to hold several thousand liters.

Water flow design

Water in a swimming pool must be circulated through a filter to remove accumulated dirt and debris. Water enters the pool through inlets in the side wall and exits the pool in 3 places:

1) Main drain – the main drain is an opening in the lowest point in the floor. The main drain pipe is usually 2" PVC. Two or more main drain openings are highly recommended because a single drain, if blocked can starve the pump of water and produce dangerous suction that can hold a swimmer to the bottom. Note that the floor of the pool should slope towards the main drain so heavy debris finds its way back to the pump/filter. I have a level floor in the center of my pool which I do not recommend because dirt just sits there. When building the pool, the builder should leave a hole in the soil of at least 10-15cm under and to the sides of the drain opening and the pipe. The PVC pipe should be supported on concrete standoffs with wire ties. This hole will be filled with concrete at the same time the floor is poured to ensure leak free connections.

2) Skimmer or overflow channel – water from the surface of the pool returns to the pump/filter from the skimmer box or the overflow channel.

3) Vacuum port – the vacuum port is a plastic or stainless steel fitting in the side of the wall that connects to a flexible hose. The hose connects to accessories such as a vacuum cleaner head for manually or automatically vacuuming of the bottom of the pool. This pipe is typically 1.5".

Great care should be taken when concreting around all openings in the pool below the water line to avoid leaks. Vibrate the concrete very well and make thicker than usual wall thickness if possible.

Concrete construction

Residential pool floors will typically be about 18-25cm thick and walls 15-20cm thick, reinforced concrete. The concrete mix should be as dry as possible and should be very well vibrated, as described in Chapter 11.

Most pool experts recommend reinforcing steel be made from two layers of 12mm steel (for about 40-80,000 liter pools) in a cross grid, 15-20cm on center. Two layers are necessary to reinforce the steel for both the outward pressure of the water and the inward pressure of the surrounding soil. The two layers must be spaced far enough apart to allow the wet concrete to move freely through the steel structure in the wall as the concrete is poured and vibrated inside the wall. Space the reinforcing steel from the floor and side walls with 5-7cm concrete blocks with embedded wire and space the two layers from each other with 6mm steel rod.

Since it is critical that the concrete be poured without interruption, plan ahead. If you are mixing on site, have enough materials handy to finish the pour. If using a ready mix truck, are you 100% sure the truck will return within an hour or less? Unless you live in a big city, that is unlikely. Perhaps talk to 2 or more cement companies or mix on site to supplement ready mix truck deliveries.

Floor construction

Build a tent over the pool to keep sun off the concrete and keep the concrete from drying too quickly and leave the tent up until tiling is finished (see Chapter 11).

The floor slab should be poured in a single session. Check you have enough materials on hand to finish the pour. Have your workers to stagger their lunch break (very difficult to do in Thailand) so some part of the team can keep the concrete flowing. Try get at least 8 to 12 workers to keep the process moving quickly. If using ready mix from a truck be 100% sure the truck can return within the hour or supplement it with concrete made on site.

Use a concrete vibrator to get air out of concrete to improve strength and water tightness. I recommend having 2 concrete vibrators on site in case one breaks down.

Many pool builders recommend pouring a small section of wall (10-15cm) at the same time as the floor. The theory is, it is easier to waterproof the connection between wall and more wall, than between floor and wall. I can't say I understand the logic in this. My concern is that to build this 10-15cm wall, it is necessary to wait until the floor slab hardens a little before the wall form can be places on top. In the rush to finish the floor, place a wall form and pour some more concrete, it is very easy to make a mistake or let the floor slab harden too much and produce a dry joint. This is especially true if you are hiring your own builders who may never have built a pool before. I built a 10cm wall when pouring my pool floor and in retrospect, I wish I had left it flat, but you may want to seek other advice on this issue.

I think a better way to handle the floor to wall connection is to make the floor flat then form a "key" just on the inside of the steel by sliding a 1½" to 2" wide wood strip, about 1-2" deep into the concrete. Remove the wood strip as soon as the concrete is hard enough to support its own weight, do not let the concrete completely harden or it will be difficult to get the wood out. When the wall concrete goes in, you should achieve a better lock between floor and wall with the key.

Wall construction

Inner wall forms are typically plywood reinforced with 2x3s or 2x4s. 8-12mm plywood should be sufficient if braced every 30-40cm. For curved wall sections it may be easier to use two 5mm sheets overlapped well away from the edges. If you build your pool shortly after building your house, reuse the form wood and save a considerable amount of money. Outer walls are often concrete blocks, backfilled with dirt. If the outer walls are above ground (i.e. unsupported by backfill), beware that they are probably not strong enough to support the weight of 1 meter or so of wet concrete unless they have additional bracing.

Wall reinforcement must be strong enough to support the substantial weight of the wet concrete, especially in the deep end. Breaking or bending of the wood forms is a major disaster during pouring walls so be very sure the forms are strong enough, and have enough wood, nails, tools and especially workers on site to reinforce form work that looks "stressed out" as the concrete is poured and vibrated.

Outer wall forms are typically concrete block. Backfill behind the outer walls to support the concrete blocks when the wet concrete goes in. However, do not backfill to the top of the walls as the dirt will inevitably fall inside the wall forms as the builders work. Leave the grade level about 20-40cm below the top of the outer walls until the wall pour is finished. Reinforce the top 20-40cm with wood if necessary since concrete block walls have very little lateral strength and can bend and break easily under the weight of the wet concrete.

Clean the floor to wall connection extremely well, removing loose concrete and debris, before the wall forms go in. Then clean again just before the concrete goes in and wash with plenty of water (however, do not leave the join submerged) and a joint sealer (see concrete waterproofing below). This is quite difficult to clean since you only have a 15-20cm gap to work in. I used a shop

vac (industrial looking vacuum cleaner) with a 1" PVC pipe to extend the reach of the hose. Shine a very bright light inside and look for loose objects that may have fallen down inside the forms. Also see information below about concrete waterproofing. You should treat the connection between the floor and wall since this is the most likely place for a leak in a concrete pool.

Use ½" rock (not standard ¾" rock) for wall concrete so it flows between the steel better. Pour the concrete evenly around the perimeter and keep moving at a reasonable speed so you can get back to the start point before the concrete starts to harden, usually about 1 hour max. Do not pour one side all at once unless you have some very heavy bracing or it is likely the form work will move or break. This happened to me and the wall on one side is about 35cm thick now. Pour the walls in a single session, same as the floor. I recommend 20 to 25 workers if mixing cement on site. This allows some of the workers to rest while others work so the concrete flow is fast and constant. Also there will be enough people to fix formwork problems should they occur.

Use a concrete vibrator to get air out of the concrete to improve strength and

water tightness. **NOTE THAT THIS WILL MAKE THE CONCRETE VERY HEAVY AND WILL BEND OR BREAK POORLY CONSTRUCTED FORM WORK.** If your builders are unfamiliar with building reinforced concrete walls and using concrete vibrators they will almost certainly build the formwork insufficiently strong, resulting in disaster when the concrete is poured. I can't tell you exactly how to build your form work, but in this pool (right) we used vertical supports every 50cm and horizontal cross beams every meter and we had no problems.

I cannot stress enough the 3 main points of pouring pool walls:

1) Clean the floor in the wall space between inner and outer forms exceeding well and wash and remove all surface water before pouring concrete but do not leave standing water in the low spots.

2) Check that form work is strong and hole free, especially in the deep end where the concrete weight is heaviest. Connect inner and outer formwork with wire ties if possible and be ready to add additional bracing if necessary.

3) Pour concrete continuously in a circular motion around the perimeter adding about 20-30cm at a time and returning within one hour to the start point. Use plasticizer to slow drying and add strength and water tightness by reducing water volume. Vibrate well but be careful not to break formwork. If formwork starts to bulge, stop pouring and vibrating in that area until the formwork is reinforced. If it becomes too "dangerous" to vibrate, pour slowly and carefully and remove air by poking with a steel rod.

When installing plastic conduit for pool lights, remember that the yellow pipe is not pressure pipe and is not watertight. I recommend keeping the pipe for the light cable entirely enclosed in the wall concrete to above the waterline. If that is not practical in your design, use blue PVC water pipe and glue the joins.

Concrete waterproofing

Concrete is porous if untreated. Several, inexpensive, local Thai waterproofing additives and coatings are available in most building stores. Sika Plastercreat is a liquid plasticizer (http://en.wikipedia.org/wiki/Plasticizer) that is added to the concrete during mixing. It allows reduced water content while maintain workability, which as already discussed helps concrete strength and water-tightness. Sika 101a: http://www.sika.co.th/sika/Route/waterproofing?option=W&prdgroup=PG00007 is painted on the surface of the rough concrete or smooth top coat.

Two foreign (and far more expensive) waterproofing compounds are available in Thailand, Xypex (http://xypex.com/) and Contite (http://contite.com/). Xypex and Contite "grow" into minute cracks that develop in the concrete over time. I used Xypex at a cost of 29000 baht for a 5x7m pool. I can't tell you if it was worth the money versus a Thai brand (Sika 101a), you decide. In any case, you should use some waterproofing additive or treatment.

Sika 101a, Xypex and Contite are grey cement like powders that when mixed with water form a thick paste which is brushed onto the surface of the set concrete. You will almost certainly need to render over the concrete to level the surface in preparation for tiling. Apply waterproof coating to the rough outer concrete before rendering so the waterproofing agent acts on both the rough outer concrete and the smooth inner concrete.

Note that if using Xypex or Contite, I believe the manufacturers do not recommend you add plasticizer to the concrete and the concrete surface should be pressure washed before application to open up the pores in the concrete. I think this is a bad idea because plasticizers are useful for slowing initial drying and help workability without excess water content. Please consult the manufactures customer service for complete information.

Finishing

Typically, concrete pools will be tiled. Ceramic tile is most commonly used although I have heard marble looks fantastic under water.

The rough concrete will probably require leveling before tiling. Sika customer support recommends adding Sika Latex with water in a 1:3 ratio when mixing cement for rendering the walls and gluing tile. The Sika Latex will improve adhesion of the tile and improve water tightness.

Pool tile from a pool shop is often 4"x4", quite thick and quite expensive. I use standard 8"x8" wall and floor tile for 190b/m2 and have had no problem with it.

Pool surrounds (decks) can be concrete or wood. I don't recommend wood, I've see too many problems no matter how many times the wood is refinished or re-painted. If you really want the wood look, look at Shera Deck (http://www.mahaphant.com/en/prdct/shrprdct_dtl01.jsp?id=11), an artificial wood look decking made from cement and other materials. It is quite expensive (about 1700baht/m2) but looks like real wood and should last forever with virtually no maintenance.

Concrete desks lasts basically forever with no maintenance. Concrete can be tiled (quick, cheap and easy to keep clean) or sand finish (a little more expensive than tile and harder to keep clean but very non slip). Sand finished concrete should be sealed after application (something I forget to do!) to avoid staining problems.

Pool systems

All pools require a pump and a filter. Most major cities in Thailand have one or more pool shops. Pool pumps and filters are typically imported from China (cheap) or Australia of USA (expensive but generally better quality). Any reputable pool shop will help you choose the size of pump and filter for your pool.

Filters

There are 3 common pool filter types used in Thailand. The following descriptions are from http://poolspa.co.th

Cartridge Filters

Cartridge filters have been around for some time, but they seen to be gaining in popularity in many parts of the country. They consist of a tank that houses three or four cylindrical filtering elements. The filters are actually made of polyester or some other material that can provide a superfine filtering surface. The fabric catches and holds the impurities until you clean or replace the filter.

The cartridge can filter out anything down to about 5-10 microns in size. A grain of table salt is about 90 microns; anything below about 35 microns is invisible to the naked eye. It is important to remember that with any filter, a small amount of dirt actually aids the filtering process. In other words, a filter becomes more efficient the longer it operates. However, there is a point at which the filter is holding onto too much dirt and must be replaced.

In most areas, cartridge filters are less expensive than diatomaceous earth filters are popular because of the minimal maintenance involved. Some families will find it sufficient to simply hose off the cartridge a few times during the swimming season to keep them working properly. Others may need to soak the filters in detergent or replace then. In any case, maintenance takes only a few minutes to keep the filtration system in top shape. Most portable spas contain cartridge filters.

Diatomaceous Earth Filters

Called DE filters, these products can filter our dirt as small as 1-5 microns. If you opened the tank of a DE filter it would look somewhat similar to a cartridge filter. But the grids are packed with diatomaceous earth, a powder made up of billions of fossilized plankton skeletons. It is this powder that actually catches and holds the dirt.

DE filters are usually the most expensive type, and they get the water cleaner than the other filters. But the necessary maintenance can be a drawback for some homeowners. Most manufacturers call for backwashing to clean the filter. In backwashing, the system reverses the flow of water. The clean water cleanses the filter. The dirty water is then drained from the system. To really clean a DE filter, you must remove the grids and clean off the spent DE. This presents the problem of what to do with the old DE.

Sand Filters

These filters use - you guessed it - sand as the filtering medium. Sand filters look like large balls and they can hold hundreds of pounds of pool-grade sand. Basically, water flows into the top of the filter housing and makes its way down through the sand bed where the sharp edges of the sand catch the dirt. On a micron-to-micron comparison, sand filters remove the least amount of dirt - particles as small as about 20 to 25 microns. But again for a time, the dirt left behind contributes to the filtering process. Sand filters certainly are efficient enough to keep just about any pool clean.

To keep a sand filter working, you must clean as often as once a week during swimming season. Maintenance means backwashing where the flow of clean water is reversed back into the filter. The problem with this, however, is that the backwashed water is simply wasted. A typical backwashing session can waste a few hundred gallons of water - water must be replaced in the pool. Sand filters may not be a good idea in area often underwater restrictions. However, waste water can but used for garden irrigation.

Water cleaning and purification

Much has been written about swimming pool maintenance and I will not attempt to repeat it. A couple of good web sites for information are http://poolspa.co.th/pdf/Perfect_Pool_Care_Guide.pdf and http://www.poolindustrysecrets.com/

Adding chlorine has been the standard for pool water purification although in recent years, salt water chlorinators and more recently ozonators have become more popular. Salt water chlorinators create chlorine from salt added to the pool water. Ozonators create ozone gas which sanitizes the water. Both systems remove your reliance on adding chemicals and in theory make swimming pool maintenance easy or even idiot proof, but both systems require an initial outlay of 50-100,000 baht.

One issue that seems to occur often in Thailand (based on my own experience and comments on http://www.thaivisa.com/forum/index.php?showforum=108 is that many people experience problems with metals in the water. I should start out by saying; the absolute best way to fill your pool initially or top it up is with rain water. Rain water is the purest water source you are likely to find. However, it is not usually practical to fill an entire swimming pool with rain water so you may be forced to use government water or well water.

If the water is from an underground source, there is a good chance it will have a high metal or mineral content. When chlorine is added (even chlorine produced by a salt water chlorinator), the metals tend to turn the water dark green or black. A simple, well know by Thai people but seemingly unknown by everyone else way to deal with this, is to add a chemical called Aluminum Ammonium Sulphate, which is commonly know as สารส้ม, saan^R sohm^F ,in Thai. This is usually purchased as big crystal blocks from hardware shops and is used for general water clarification. You can also buy it in granulated form in 50kg bags from pool shops.

Dissolve a few kilograms of saan^R sohm^F in water (or feed it directly into the filter through the vacuum port) and leave the pump running for a few hours to mix it in. (Note that some people recommend raising the ph to 8.2-8.4 first but in my experience this isn't necessary).

Then turn off the pump and let the pool sit (no swimming) for about 24 hours. A layer of grey or brown sludge will settle to the bottom. Vacuum it out with the filter on waste. DO NOT PUT IT BACK IN POOL, the filter will not separate out the sludge and you will be back to square one. Usually you need to wait another 24 hours for more settling and vacuum again and the water will end up crystal clear.

Because pool pumps move so much water, I find the pool level drops 10-20cm in this process which is a lot of waste water. I use a small pump (1/2 hp) and hook up my own vacuum cleaner head using PVC pipe and dump the water on the garden. Then I only waste about 500 liters per cleaning.

Then continue routine pool maintenance using chlorine and algaecide.

Note that chlorine boils at 27 degrees C which is close to the normal water temperate in Thailand. Add chlorine ONLY in the cooler part of the evening or it will simply boil away before doing any good. In most hot countries, bromine is added to stabilize the chlorine but for some inexplicable reason, it seems impossible to buy bromine in Thailand.

For excellent information about how to maintain a swimming pool without being a slave to your local pool shop, I recommend you visit http://www.poolindustrysecrets.com and buy the ebook.

Chapter  Finish work

Wood

Because of the abuse your wood has likely received during the building process (sun, rain, nail holes, etc.), there will likely be a significant need for patching up before the wood is finished. The following applies to wood that will be visible after the house is finished, not wood hidden inside walls, floors, roof spaces, etc.

Wood preparation

Cracks and nail holes will be filled with wood filler. Builders will usually make their own filler using a mixture of clear wood glue, saw dust and various coloring powders. This actually produces better wood filler, if made correctly, than the off-the-shelf wood fillers because you can achieve a much better color match.

The hard wood used in Thailand is very difficult to sand down to a nice finish. You will probably have to start sanding with a course grit paper that you would usually use on softer wood. If your builder does not have a good selection of sanders, such as a belt sander, and some orbital sanders, I suggest you buy them yourself. Sand paper can usually be bought in rolls, by the meter. Sand paper on rolls is dark brown in color and has heavier backing than yellow sand paper and will last longer and cost less. However, for very detailed finish work, yellow sand paper will achieve a better finish.

If using a belt sander, check the builders are sanding along the grain. Sanding across the grain is faster but leaves deep scratch marks which are very hard to remove.

My builders really did not want to sand the door frames, so they tried to convince me that sanding them would make the frames too wide and the doors would not fit! This is ridiculous because only ½ mm or less of wood is actually removed when sanding hard wood and the doors are always made 1cm wider than specified so you can clean off the edges prior to installing.

I have seen many examples in Thailand where almost no preparation has gone into the wood before staining and varnishing. I insisted that my builder sand everything to a perfect finish before staining and varnishing. However, every day I would find ten or more places where stain and even polyurethane had been applied before saw marks, nail holes and cracks had been properly filled and sanded down. I have even found several places where the builders simply stained and  varnished over pencil marks left by the carpenters (right). This resulted in a lot of frustration, wasted time, and expense redoing the work. Stain and polyurethane is expensive, about 1000 baht per gallon. I spent about 60,000 baht on stain and polyurethane on my house. It will save you money and time to have the preparation done properly before you stain and varnish.

I suggest you tell your builder that the workers must check with you or your project manager, every piece of wood, before they apply stain and polyurethane. I told my builder that the workers must check with me before staining and varnishing anything; yet every day I would find wood that was not ready. Unfortunately, Thai builders would rather dig holes in the baking sun than spend 20 minutes sanding wood to a nice finish.

I also found that showing the workers 10 or 20 places that need redoing every day, was totally pointless. I finally resorted to hiding the stain and polyurethane until I checked everything was ready.

I had planned to leave the window and door frames unstained but even after 5 days of sanding, I was still not satisfied with the finish, so I told the workers to use a dark red wood stain. When my builder noticed he said, "If I knew you were going to use color, I would have told them not to do so much sanding". This is an important lesson; always ask for more than you really want, so there is a 50/50 chance you will get what you hoped for in the first place.

The best way to have nicely finished wood in your house is to protect it from the elements and the builders as soon as you buy it and clean it. If you wait until after it has been damaged, it will likely never return to its former glory! Store wood out of the sun and rain or cover it, use rough frames for doors and windows, mask wood that may come into contact with cement, insist that the builders do not put nails in the wood for temporary structures, etc.

When I saw my wood posts being cleaned I was really excited about how beautiful the house would look with these posts varnished and proudly displayed.

However, even with my best attempts to protect them; exposure to the sun and

rain caused cracks in the surface and during building; the builders used them for scaffolding, leaving hundreds of nail holes (below).

The scaffolding could have been secured to the house in other ways without leaving nail holes and I should have wrapped the posts in plastic to protect them from the sun before the roof went on. The nail holes and cracks were filed and we used dark color stain to cover imperfections, but I would have preferred a natural finish. Oh well, next time!

Carefully check all joins, not only to make sure they are structural sound, but also that they look nice. If plywood joins are visible, use wood strips to cover and reinforce the joins.

Stain and top coat

Darker color wood stain is useful because it hides imperfections in the wood. It also protects the wood from sun better than a lighter stain or no stain at all.

Some stains, such as TOA, do not recommend a top coat of polyurethane. I use a stain that can have polyurethane on top, which I prefer because I can use as many coats of polyurethane as I feel is necessary without affecting the color.

Polyurethane should always be used as a top coat. Varnish is cheaper but does not last. Always used exterior grade polyurethane; it is about 100 baht per gallon more expensive than interior grade but will last much longer and protect the wood better. You will need to thin the polyurethane to get a nice finish, especially in the hot Thai climate.

Two coats of polyurethane are usually recommended for inside wood and three for wood that may have exposure to sun and rain. Lightly sand with 200 or higher grit paper after each coat of polyurethane to get a beautiful, deep, smooth finish.

Polyurethane should be lightly sanded and re-applied every 2-3 years or as necessary, for wood exposed to sun and rain.

I found that my builders rarely put tops back on cans of stain and polyurethane or cleaned brushes after use. Complaining did little to improve the situation, so to save money I went around the house every day after the builders finished and did it my self. Some paint products come with money back stickers on or under the lid. Beware; the builders may take the lids to the building shop to get the money back before the can is finished, leaving the paint to dry up. So you waste 500 baht of paint so the builders can get 30 baht for themselves!

Always remove door handles and window and door hardware before paint/polyurethane is applied. It produces a much cleaner finish than trying to paint around the handle, etc. Also, after door handles and hardware have been installed, it's best to take them off and keep them in a safe place, with the keys, screws, etc. so they will not get damaged by the builders.

Remember to paint or polyurethane the tops and bottoms of doors. This will protect the wood from insects, etc. Clearly bottoms must be painted before the door is hung.

Don't forget to keep a few fire extinguishers and smoke alarms in the house. Apparently these are not very common in Thailand, I had to go to Surat Thani to find them!

English/Thai words and phrases

Sand paper	กระดาษทราย gra^L daat^L saay
To sand (verb)	ขัด khat^L
Filler	โป๊ว bpouw^H
To fill	เติม dteerm
Nail hole	รูตะปู ruu^M dta^L bpuu
Paint	สีทา see^R thaa
Primer	รองพื้น raawng^M pheuun^H
Oil paint	สีน้ำมัน see^R nahm^H man
Latex paint	สีทา see^R thaa
Spray paint (can)	สีพ่น see^R phohn^F
Spray paint	สีสเปรย์ see^R sa^L bpraeh
Wood stain	สีทาไม้ stain
Polyurethane	โพรียูรีเทรน poly urathane
Varnish	น้ำมันชักเงา nahm^H man chak^H ngao
Thinner	ทินเนอร์ tin neer
Wood preservative	สารกันแมลง saan^R gan ma^H laaeng
Paint brush	แปรงทา bpraaeng thaa
Roller	ลูกกลิ้งทาสี luuk^F gling^F thaa see^R
Paint tray	กระบะทาสี graL ba^L thaa see^R
To paint	ทาสี thaa see^R
To spray paint	พ่นสี phohn^F see^R

Cupboard	ตู้ถ้วยชาม dtuu^F thuay^F chaam
Safe (for storing valuables)	ตู้เซฟ dtuu^F saehp^H
Wall unit (furniture)	ตู้ติดผนัง dtuu^F dtit^L pha^L nang^R
Wardrobe	ตู้เสื้อผ้า dtuu^F seuua^F phaa^F
Chest of drawers	ตู้มีลิ้นชัก dtuu^F mee lin^H chak^H
Bookcase	ตู้หนังสือ dtuu^F nang^R seuu^R
Bed	เตียงนอน dtiiang naawn
Couch, sofa, armchair	เก้าอี้นวม gao^F ee^F nuaam
Fire extinguisher	เครื่องดับเพลิง khreuuang^F dap^L phleerng
Smoke alarm	เครื่องเตือนไฟไหม้ khreuuang^F dteuuan fai mai^F

Please sand more before you paint/stain/polyurathane ก่อนทาสีกรุณาขัดให้มากกว่านี้ gaawn^L thaa see^R ,ga^L roo^H naa khat^L hai^F maak^F nee^H

Please fill the nail holes before you paint/stain/polyurathane ก่อนทาสีกรุณาเอุดรูตะปูให้ดี gaawn^L thaa see^R, ga^L roo^H naa oot^L ruu^M dta^L bpuu^M hai^F dee

Please tell me before you paint/stain/polyurathane ก่อนทาสีกรุณาบอกผมก่อน gaawn^L thaa see^R, ga^L roo^H naa baawk^L phohm^R gaawn^L

I'm not sure	ไม่แน่ใจ mai^F naae^F jai
(I want to) try/look at it first	ลองดูก่อน laawng duu gaawn^L
That doesn't look good at all	ไม่สวยเลย mai^F suay^R leeuy
Please do it again	กรุณาทำใหม่ ga^L roo^H naa thahm mai^L

Chapter 20 Checklists

These checklists are for you and/or your project manager to take to the job site as the work is happening. With jobs like concrete, which are usually fast paced and impossible (or at least very expensive) to fix later, it is important that you go through the checklist and mark off each item as it happens.

Many of the items in these check lists are things that would have gone wrong with my house construction had I not checked and in some cases did go wrong and I wish I had the checklist myself before building!

Did you already come un-glued because of something that is not in this check list? Please email me your story for the next edition.

Architect /design

☐ Can you communicate well enough with your architect to explain what you want?

☐ Does he have time to design your house and support your builder?

☐ Will he do the structural engineering design himself or use a certified structural engineer? If he is doing the structural design, is he adequately qualified?

☐ What is the payment schedule? Hold off paying as much as possible until the design is finished and the building permit approved.

☐ How will he charge for changes or additions to the design?

☐ Are you planning to follow the advice in this book about using steel plates to join concrete and wood, rough door/window frames etc? If so, is your architect familiar with these techniques, or at least or does he understand the description in this book and why it is important?

☐ Are important design details like clearances between reinforcing steel and side walls of form documented on the design?

☐ Is exterior wood adequately protected from sun and rain?

☐ Is the staircase design convenient and safe?

☐ Check that when the doors and windows open, the will not hit another door, window, post or a wall, unexpectedly.

Builder/contract

☐ What is included in the building contract? Does the builder do the following:

☐ Clear land, rocks, trees, etc?

☐ Water drainage?

☐ Install water supply?

☐ Dig well?

☐ Install electrical supply?

☐ Retaining walls?

☐ Access road?

☐ Parking areas?

✓ Dig footing, main construction, foundation, floors, walls, and roof

☐ Frames, doors and windows including door/window preparation?

☐ Build stairs?

☐ Safety rails?

☐ Plumbing and bathroom fixtures?

☐ Water storage?

☐ Dig hole and install septic tank?

☐ Electrical wiring, lights, outlets, switches, etc?

☐ Fans and Aircon?

☐ Finish floor and wall covering tile/wood?

☐ Paint/decorate?

- ☐ Sand/varnish wood?

- ☐ Kitchen cabinets and fixtures

- ☐ Other furnishings?

- ☐ Clear and clean land when finished?

- ☐ Landscaping?

- ☐ Build outdoor structures (shed, gazebo, etc)?

- ☐ Fence and gate?

- ☐ Pool?

☐ Who is responsible for choosing and buying the following materials:

- ☐ Concrete and steel?

- ☐ Form and structural wood?

- ☐ Roof tile?

- ☐ Frames, doors and windows and door hardware?

- ☐ Stairs and safety rails?

- ☐ Plumbing and bathroom fixtures?

- ☐ Water storage?

- ☐ Electrical wiring, lights, outlets, switches, etc?

- ☐ Fans and Aircon?

- ☐ Finish floor and wall covering tile/wood?

- ☐ Paint, stain, polyurethane?

- ☐ Kitchen cabinets and fixtures?

- ☐ Other furnishings?

- ☐ Landscaping?

☐ Fence and gate?

☐ Pool?

☐ If I want to change the design, how will it change the price?

☐ What guarantee do I have that you will finish on schedule? How will you back up that guarantee (reduced price)?

☐ Do you want to offer a bonus for completing on time? If so, discuss it at the beginning and be clear about the conditions.

☐ How will the builder guarantee the work? What is included in the guarantee and for how long?

☐ Are you only required to make payments up to the value of the materials and services you have received? Be aware that builders often quit in the middle of a job so you should not pay too far ahead of what you have received.

☐ Did you save the contact information of other builders in case your builder quits?

Preparing to build

☐ Mark out the footprint of your planned house with stakes and string and check for obstacles such as large rocks, protected trees, unstable soil and drop-offs, drainage, etc. Also check clearances to neighbors and views?

☐ Remove trees within 3-5 meters of the house location?

☐ Set up temporary water before you plan to start building. It may take longer than you think.

☐ Set up temporary electricity or buy/rent a generator before you plan to start building. It may take longer than you think.

☐ Build a temporary storage shed to store valuable building materials out of the sun/rain.

☐ Check you have a way for heavy delivery trucks to reach your building site. This will make if far easier for heavy items like concrete, concrete floor slabs, wood posts, roof tile, etc.

☐ Plan water drainage to avoid large amounts of rain water running into the house and build a water diversion system if necessary?

☐ If you are raising the level of the lot, check that the new soil/rock/sand is properly leveled and compacted before building.

Foundation and footing

☐ Tell your builder not to start pouring concrete until you or your project manager have checked the footings and form work and given him the go ahead. You must have time to check the footings and forms; once the concrete pour starts, it is too late.

☐ Check string lines are correct size, position and height and that corners are square.

☐ Check the hardness of each footing's floor after compacting. When hit with the same pressure, a test post should sink by same amount, give or take 10%, in each footing. If the test post sinks too much, compact the floor again.

☐ Check the reinforcing steel is at least 5cm away from the side walls of the hole in the ground EVERYWHERE (10cm is better). This is very important. If the steel can come in contact with water after the concrete is poured it will rust out and the concrete will be useless.

☐ Check the bottom of the hole for the footings is clear of loose sand, soil, etc. It should be hard packed sand, clay, soil or rock.

☐ Check the reinforcing steel is tied together with wire.

☐ Check that wood forms are well braced and will not spread apart under the weight of the wet concrete. In the rainy season when the ground is very soft, be especially careful that support structure will not sink under the weight of the concrete. Press hard against the side walls with your foot. If you can move it with your foot, it will move under the weight of the concrete.

☐ If mixing concrete on site, check the mix proportions and consistency (wetness) of the concrete. Thai builders love wet concrete because it's easy to work with. However, concrete strength decreases with wetness.

☐ Check that the concrete is vibrated or poked sufficiently with a steel rod. This is essential for structural concrete. Freshly poured concrete is full of air pockets. Vibrating with a concrete vibrator or poking with a steel rod shakes the air to the surface. If the job is done well, you will see the concrete level fall. If it is done badly, the concrete will be full of air pockets and will not be strong.

☐ Protect concrete from drying too quickly in the hot Thai climate. Concrete gains strength by curing, not by drying. If the moisture evaporates too quickly, it will not have time to cure and will not be strong. Leave wood forms on as long as possible and if they must come off, cover concrete for the first month with plastic and keep it wet if possible.

Concrete floor beams, joists and posts

☐ Check reinforcing steel is raised clear of the bottom of concrete forms. The steel must be well inside the concrete where it will add strength to the concrete and be protected from rust.

☐ Check reinforcing steel is not touching side walls of concrete forms.

☐ If you are using concrete posts, check the steel rods are standing out of the floor for attachment to the concrete posts.

☐ If you are using wood posts on the next level, check the bolts for securing the post base steel plate are standing out of the floor at the correct height. Remember that the finished floor will be at different heights for bathrooms and outside areas.

☐ If you are using wood posts for the next level, check the bolts for securing the post base steel plate are welded to the reinforcing steel.

☐ Check the location of steel rods and bolts standing out of the concrete base to make sure they are in the correct place.

☐ If you are using wood posts, check the bolt threads are taped up so they do not get filled with concrete. (It's also a good idea to put the nuts on but make sure they are above floor level.

☐ Check that wood forms are well braced and will not spread apart under the weight of the wet concrete.

☐ Check there are no holes bigger than ½ cm in the forms or concrete will leak out and leave air pockets. This is particularly important around post bases. Small holes can be filled with wet concrete bags.

☐ Check that the concrete is vibrated or poked sufficiently with a steel rod. This is essential for structural concrete. Freshly poured concrete is full of air pockets. Vibrating with a concrete vibrator or poking with a steel rod shakes the air to the surface. This is particularly important under post bases where the main load from the roof will be transferred to the footings

☐ Protect concrete from drying too quickly in the hot Thai climate. Concrete gains strength by curing, not by drying. If the moisture evaporates too quickly, it will not have time to cure and will not be strong. Leave wood forms on as long as possible and if they must come off, cover concrete for the first week or so with plastic and keep it wet if possible.

☐ Leave supporting structure in place as long as possible. New concrete takes approximately 7 days to reach working strength and 28 days to reach full strength. New concrete beams should not be expected to support the weight of the floor for the first 7-28 days without additional support.

☐ If you are using wood posts on the next level, check the bolts are tightened down to the steel post base before the concrete goes on top.

☐ If you are using wood posts on the next level, check the concrete level under the outside posts is at least 5cm higher than the finished floor level. This is very important because you do not want the base of the wood sitting in a pool of water when it rains. It will decay and be a target for bugs and in time cause the post to collapse.

☐ If using concrete block walls, check there are steel rods standing out of the concrete posts in line with the wall direction. These rods are used to secure the wall to the post.

Concrete floors and rough plumbing

☐ Check outside areas have a step down from the inside floor and that they slope away from the house.

☐ Check 1st floor bathroom drains and water pipes are poking though the floor

☐ Check 2nd and above floor drains and water pipes are through the first floor.

☐ Use vent pipes on your plumbing, and check the vent pipes are through the floor.

☐ Check the distance between the bathroom walls and the toilet drain pipe. A standard toilet is 305mm from FINISHED wall to center of drain pipe. Remember to add the thickness of the wall finishing, concrete, tile etc, usually about 3-5cm.

☐ Check there is some kind of steel attachment point extending above the floor for posts for hand rails and stairs.

☐ If using pre-cast concrete floor slabs as a base for the concrete pour, have the delivery truck place them on top of the floor joists to save the workers having to lift them. But be careful not to put too much weight on one place, it could stress or crack the floor joists. Ask your builder to have lots of workers available to move the concrete slabs as they are being placed on the beams/joists.

☐ Check there are no holes in the floor forms that will let the wet concrete fall through.

☐ Check reinforcing steel mesh is raised above the floor level (can be done as the concrete is poured by pulling up on the steel inside the wet concrete)

☐ Pay special attention to vibrating the concrete below the post bases. This is where the load from the upper floors and roof will transfer to the footings.

☐ After the concrete is leveled, check that bathroom floors slope towards the drain pipe at all points. Hold a long spirit level very carefully resting on the wet concrete. The bubble must be on the opposite side to the drain pipe. Check the whole floor if possible.

☐ After the concrete is leveled, check that outside floors slope away from the house. Hold a long spirit level very carefully resting on the wet concrete. The bubble must be on house side.

☐ After the concrete is leveled, check that there are no mysterious, unplanned, floor level changes.

☐ Protect concrete from drying too quickly in the hot Thai climate. Concrete gains strength by curing, not by drying. If the moisture evaporates too quickly, it will not have time to cure and will not be strong. This is especially true on floors which have a large surface area.

Walls, window and door frames

☐ Check door/window frames are in correct position and open in the correct direction (swing in or swing out)

☐ Check door/window frames are correct size for position (you probably have several different sizes) and oriented the correct way (top/bottom and sides).

☐ Check ALL door/window frames are square and level.

☐ Check door frame height and remember the finished floor level after tiling may be as much as 7cm higher than the concrete sub floor.

☐ Check ALL door frames are the same height with a water tube level, not by measuring distance from the rough floor.

☐ Check builders are making frames by pre-drilling holes and using screws, not by using nails which will split the wood and may separate over time.

☐ If frames are likely to be exposed to sun and rain for a long time (usually because roof is not built yet), apply a protective coat of stain, polyurethane or paint as soon as possible. This will save you countless hours of work later and the door frames will look far nicer.

☐ If temporary supports are attached to the frames to hold them in place while building walls, use screws, not nails, to attach the supports to the frame. Screws leave smaller holes to fill later and will not rust leaving unsightly rust stains in the wood.

☐ Check that when the door swings open, it will not hit another door or a post or a wall, unexpectedly. This should have been taken care of by the architect, but check again.

☐ Headers should be made of reinforced concrete. Do not put concrete block or brick directly on top of the door and window frames, it will cause the frame to sag or even break and cause cracks in the finished concrete lathe.

☐ If you are planning to install electric cable inside the wall, check that "trenches" are made in the wall to accommodate the cables, switch boxes and outlets/plugs.

☐ Install water and drain pipes in bathrooms and check the pipes are the correct position and height for your bathroom fixtures.

☐ If frames are likely to be exposed to sun and rain for a long time (usually because roof is not built yet), apply a protective coat of stain, polyurethane or paint as soon as possible.

Wood floors and floor cover

☐ Clean and sort wood, selecting the straightest pieces with no twists for floor beams and joists. Use curved and twisted wood for blocking or short lengths.

☐ Check floor joists are level with a string line. Check in both directions; inline with and perpendicular to the joists. The difference in height at any place should be less than 2 or 3 millimeters from the average. Plane down or shim up as necessary or your finished floor will not look nice.

☐ If using a plywood sub-floor, are the floor joists on the correct spacing, to match the joins of the plywood, i.e. 4 foot. Plywood must joint on top of the joist.

☐ If perpendicular to the joist plywood joins are not on top of a wall, use a 2"x2" wood block under the joins for extra support and to make it look nicer.

☐ If using T&G (tongue-and-groove) parkea flooring, you should buy the type with the T&G on the ends, not only the sides. This will look nicer at the joins and will not separate as much over time.

☐ If using T&G (tongue-and-groove), you always use a nail gun to nail it to the sub-floor. Using a hammer will damage the wood.

☐ Remember to use wood preservative on all wood, especially structural wood.

Roof structure and roof cover

☐ Clean and sort wood, selecting the straightest pieces with no twists for roof beams and rafters. Use curved and twisted wood for blocking or short lengths.

☐ Check all bolts connecting roof beams and rafters to posts are correct length for joins. There should be 1-2cm of bolt protruding from the nut.

☐ Check every bolt has a washer on the nut end.

☐ Check all joints have enough bolts and that nuts are tightened.

☐ Check rafters are level with a string line in both directions, inline with the rafter and perpendicular to it.

☐ Check purlins are correctly spaced for roof cover material.

☐ For CPAC, check each tile has a stainless steel screw of the correct length to attach firmly to the purlin.

☐ If you are planning to leave the roof structure open and the underside of the tile visible, paint the underside of the tile before it is installed.

☐ Remember to use wood preservative on all wood, especially structural wood.

☐ Check the lower edge of the roof cover is overhanging the roof structure by about 10cm.

☐ Install rain gutters to protect the foundation from water problems and provide a backup water supply. Rain gutter brackets should be attached to roof rafters, not the fascia board.

Windows and doors

☐ Check ALL door handles are the same height.

☐ Check ALL doors and windows open and close properly and locks work smoothly.

☐ Check painters are removing handles before painting/polyurethane, painting around them will not look good.

☐ Check paint/polyurethane and remember to check tops and bottoms of doors. Bottoms must be painted before the door is hung.

Stairs

☐ Check run and rise are comfortable and safe. 11" run and 7" rise are typical.

☐ Check opening in floor above provides sufficient headroom clearance, usually 2 meters.

☐ Check treads are firmly attached to stringer and stringer is firmly attached to floors,

☐ Check hand rails are safe and comfortable and balusters are no more than 4" apart for safety.

☐ For outdoor stairs, check there is a slope for water drainage.

☐ For outdoor stairs, check there is protection from rain and sun, i.e. a roof.

☐ Check there is a light and 2 way light switches at the tops and bottoms of stairs.

Electrical

☐ Check all receptacles (plugs) are 3 pin and that the ground is connected to the breaker box.

☐ Check breaker box ground is connected to ground spike.

☐ Check all receptacles (plugs) that can come into contact with water are GFCI. If GFCI receptacles are not available, use a GFCI breaker box such as Safe-T-Cut.

☐ Check there is a light and 2 way light switches at the tops and bottoms of stairs.

☐ Check ceilings fans are properly secured to a structural member, not the ceiling cover material.

☐ Install a lightning protection system.

Plumbing

☐ Check sewer pipes have sufficient vent pipes and venting is above roof height.

☐ Check all drain pipes slope down from the fixtures to the main drain by about 1cm/m. Check there are no sagging sections and that support brackets are firmly attached.

☐ Check there are no sharp right angle bends in the toilet drains that could cause blockages or be difficult to clean out. Use long radius bends or two 45 degree bends instead on one 90 degree.

☐ Check there is a master water shutoff valve for each room.

☐ Check there are several cleanout ports where drains connect together and into the main drain.

☐ Check all pipes (water and drain) in walls and floors are in correct position and height for your bathroom fixtures.

☐ Check all pipes for leaks before closing up walls and finishing floors. Install stop values in water pipes and turn water on for several days and check for leaks. Block main drain and fill drains with water and look for leaks.

☐ Photograph pipes in walls and floors and mark distances from walls so if you do have to dig them up later you know where to find them.

Swimming pools

☐ Check your builders are using 2 layers for steel or at least 12-16mm thickness on a maximum 20cm grid spaced minimum 5 cm apart.

☐ Check the distance between steel and ground and formwork is at least 5-7cm.

☐ Check pipe works is glues and pressure test before concrete is poured.

☐ Check dirt is excavated around floor drains so concrete will totally enclose the pipe under the floor.

☐ Check main drains ate 2" pipe and inlets and vacuume at least 1 ½".

☐ Check there is sufficient material on site if mixing cement on site.

☐ Check concrete trucks can return within one hour if using ready mix. In reality, this may not happen in any case so be ready to mix on site.

☐ Have a least one concrete vibrator (2 is better) and vibrate concrete well.

☐ Cover the pool site with a temporary roof (plastic sheeting) to keep sun from drying the concrete too fast.

☐ Use plasticizer in concrete to reduce water content, slow hardening, improve water tightness and increase workability.

☐ Make concrete as dry a mix as you can convince your builders to make and check EVERY batch for consistency and dryness.

☐ Keep the concrete pour moving, do not stop for lunch. Have enough people on hand to work through lunch and potential problems.

☐ Build formwork strong enough to support the considerable weight of well made concrete. Be especially careful in the lower sections of the deep end where the weight is greatest.

☐ Install PVC pipe ducting for lights entirely within the concrete structure to above the waterline if possible. If the pipe must exit the concrete structure below the water line, use blue PVC water pipe and glue, do not use yellow electrical pipe which is not watertight.

☐ Clean the area inside the wall forms at the floor connection spotlessly clean using a shop vac then wash with clean water and drain all surface water prior to pouring concrete. Repeat several times and shine a bright light inside to check there is no dirt or loose debris.

☐ Treat the floor to wall join with a bonding agent such as Sika Latex.

☐ Pour wall concrete in a circular path around the pool, adding about 20-30cm of concrete at a time. Return to the start point within one hour.

☐ Vibrate wall concrete very well and do not allow concrete to stick on the upper part of the steelwork. Vibrate the steelwork to shake off sitting concrete.

☐ Constantly monitor the state of the formwork looking for bulging or potential breaks, especially while vibrating which make the concrete very heavy.

☐ Use Sika Latex in cement for rendering walls level prior to tiling.

Finish work

☐ Check wood is sanded and filled before stain and polyurethane is applied. Also check for pencil marks.

☐ For furniture grade items like doors, stairs, handrails, etc. lightly sand polyurethane between each coat.

Final check

☐ Check all bolts and that nuts are tightened. About half of mine were only finger tight!

☐ Check bathroom walls and under house for signs of water leaks.

☐ Check roof for leaks in heavy rain.

☐ Check all doors and windows open, close and lock properly.

Chapter  21
Wrapping it all up

Check-bin, check-bin

Here is the actual cost of my house:

Item		units	no of	cost/unit	cost	
concrete	คอนกรีต					
cement	ปูนซีเมนต์	50kg bag	595	฿115	฿68,384	
sand	ทราย	m3	114	฿500	฿56,835	
stone	หิน	m3	24	฿700	฿16,640	
concrete bricks	อิฐบล็อก	each	4500	฿3	฿14,625	
concrete floor slabs	แผ่นพื้น				฿30,492	
concrete pipe	ท่อปูน				฿2,145	
steel reinforcing bar	เหล็ก				฿81,495	
steel ties	เหล็กยึด				฿20,000	
concrete forms (1x8, 1.5x3, etc)	ไม้แบบ				฿129,352	
Subtotal - concrete structure						**฿ 419,968**
wood	ไม้					
8x8 posts	เสาไม้	m	72	฿880	฿63,232	
other	อื่นๆ				฿345,606	
plywood	ไม้อัด	4x8 sheet	59	฿750	฿44,210	
floor parkea 1x4 T&G	ไม้ปาเก้	m	100	฿650	฿65,000	

balusters	ลูกกรง	each (avg)	650	฿74	฿48,260	
yot naam (roof trim)	หยดน้ำ	m	101	฿100	฿10,120	
Subtotal wood						฿ **576,428**
roof tile	หลังคา	each (avg)	2000	฿19	฿38,245	
marble floor tile	หินอ่อน	m2	150	฿500	฿75,000	
granite counter top	หินแกรนิต	2m piece	3	฿3,500	฿10,500	
doors and windows	ประตู กับ หน้าต่าง				฿169,434	
doors and window hardware	มือจับและ อื่น เกี่ยวกับ ประตู หน้าต่าง				฿16,656	
glass	กระจก				฿11,000	
mirrors	กระจกเงา				฿3,200	
subtotal - doors and windows						฿ **200,290**
paints etc	สีต่างๆ					
wood stain	สีทาไม้	1 gal	35	฿950	฿33,270	
polyurethane	ยูรีเทน	1 gal	40	฿900	฿35,870	
thinner	ทีนเนอร์	1 gal	21	฿380	฿8,000	
paint	สี	1 gal	38	฿400	฿15,220	
glue	กาว				฿18,400 ·	
subtotal paint etc.						฿ **110,760**
tools	อุปกรณ์				฿60,433	

	ไฟฟ้า					
sand paper	กระดาษ ทราย				฿16,295	
screws, bolts, nails, etc	ตะปู ,น็อต, และอื่นๆ				฿23,059	
electrical	ไฟฟ้า				฿68,142	
air conditioners	แอร์	9000 BTU	2	฿19,400	฿38,800	
solar water heater	เครื่องทำ น้ำร้อน	200 ltr	1	฿42,480	฿42,480	
security system	อุปกรณ์ เตือนภัย	each	1	฿40,000	฿40,000	
subtotal electrical						**฿ 189,422**
plumbing, pipes, etc.	ท่อปะปา				฿52,037	
bathroom fixtures	ห้องน้ำ	5 sets			฿56,363	
kitchen fixtures	เครื่องครัว				฿50,000	
water tanks	ถังเก็บน้ำ ฝน	2000 ltr	5	฿8,000	฿40,000	
plastic screens	กันสาด	3m x 2m	12	฿1,892	฿22,700	
rain gutter	รางน้ำฝน	m (avg)	80	฿300	฿24,000	
canvas awning	หลัง คากัสาด	4m x 1.5 m			฿6,500	
safe	ตู้เซป				฿8,000	
delivery	การขนส่ง				฿38,520	

builders	ก่อสร้าง					
general builder	ช่างทั่วไป				฿ 300,000	
electricians	ช่างไฟ				฿28,900	
marble	ช่างหิน อ่อน				฿88,000	
carpenter	ช่างไม้				฿ 141,000	
back hoe, crane, grader, etc	รถแบ็คโคและรถไถ				฿9,500	
subtotal labor						฿ 576,400
TOTAL					฿ 2,585,920	

If I could do it all again

Overall, I think my house building adventure was a success. However, there are several things I would have done different with the benefit of 20/20 hind-sight. This is a list of a few I should have done different/better:

1. Cut down the trees within 3-5 meters of the house before building.

2. Bought a concrete vibrator and made sure the workers used it diligently.

3. Stored and prepared (planed and sanded) all of the wood (posts, beams, joists, window and door frames, etc.) away from the sun and put at least one protective coat of polyurethane on before allowing it to be exposed to the sun.

4. Not allowed my builders to put nails into finish wood to make temporary scaffolding and supports. Where is was absolutely necessary to attach temporary structures to the finished wood work, I should have had the builders use stainless steel screws which leave a smaller holes to fill and do not leave rust stains in the wood.

5. When buying building supplies far from home, buy enough for the whole house plus 10-20% for safety margin for mistakes and damage. Having to go back to Bangkok for a few metal brackets or door hinges is not fun!

6. Hired carpenters earlier in the project to prepare doors and windows and build handrails and balusters, and other detailed carpentry jobs that my general builders could not do. This would have saved months of delay to finishing the house.

My general advice is, as the Thai's say, jai yen yen, take it easy! I am possibly the last person in the world to be giving this advice because I get very excited about new opportunities and tend to jump head first into things, but I sometimes pay the price! Pure good luck has saved me from several potentially very difficult and expensive situations.

Many people, me included, spend years slaving many hours a day on a boring job in your home country, paying mortgage, credit card bills, taxes, braving bitter winters and dreaming of moving to paradise in Thailand and starting over. I made the move and certainly do not regret a thing, but the temptation to set up new roots and leap into property ownership can be very strong. **It really pays to take your time**.

Unless you have a compelling reason to be in a particular area, usually your wife's home town, take the time to explore the country. Are you moving to live in Thailand permanently? If so, stay several months in several parts of Thailand and think about spending the rest of your life, or at least several years there. Get to know the local long term ex-pats and get their advice. Maybe you have found some land with great views or a fantastic price, but is it practical for building a house, shopping, entertainment, health care, accessibility, etc? Sometimes, an opportunity may appear like a once in a lifetime deal that you would be foolish to pass up. In my experience, these once in a lifetime deals pop up every few months if you look hard enough.

Are you living outside of Thailand and buying a place for investment or for future retirement? If it's for an investment, do your home work on the financial planning. How much income can you realistically expect to make from your property? What is the building cost and running cost? What about unexpected problems like flood, fire? Do you really believe you can make money from investment property in Thailand? Almost nobody does! If you are buying for future retirement, how sure are you that in the future you will want to live there? What could happen to your little piece of paradise between now and retirement time? A lady bar on your front door step; a 3 story condo blocking your view? Maybe your money would be better off in a retirement account until you are ready to make the move.

When moving from the west to Thailand, everything seems cheap at first. If you have given up your western job and have to live on savings or a modest income in Thailand, things that once seemed cheap now seem expensive, so take care of your wallet from the beginning, shop around for good deals, don't be afraid to haggle or walk away from a deal if it isn't working out the way you want.

For more general information about living and retiring in Thailand, please read "Retiring in Thailand" by Philip Bryce and Sunisa Wongdee Terlecky.

When the rubber meets the road

When working with your building team, you will quickly find that you will be lucky if you can get half of the things in this book done the way I recommend. Choose your battles! There are some things you should not compromise on, like steel clearances in footings, proper connections for posts to beams, joists, trusses, etc. Some things you will no doubt have to "mai bpen rai" it.

Small scale Thai construction style tends to overbuild to compensate for less than ideal materials and techniques so you will probably be fine if you miss a few small things, and Thais are pretty good at patching up the mistakes.

However, you must be vigilant and **CHECK EVERYTHING** and I really mean **EVERYTHING**. No matter how simple you think something can be, it can still go wrong. It is quite frustrating that for an extra 5% effort, care and attention to detail by the builders, you could get a far better house, but this is Thailand!

Also, **NEVER ASSUME ANYTHING**! Some things seem so obvious that you do not bother explaining how you want it done, like having the door locks all the same height. Yet the builders will somehow find a way to do it different, resulting in unnecessary confusion, expense and frustration. Remember the saying, if you *assume*, you make an *ass* of *u* and *me*!

Beware when you hear "I'll fix it later". This usually translates to "I can't be bothered. You'll fix it later".

All this checking takes time. I spend every day at my site, checking everything, at least 6 hours a day. You or your project manager should be prepared to do the same if you want a high quality house you can be proud of.

If you are away for a few days, either have the builders take a break or find a friend with building experience to watch while you are gone. While I was on a visa run to Malaysia, I came home to fine this piece of wood (right) used as exterior trim on the 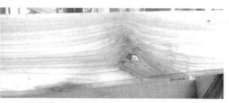 overhanging deck, the most prominent place on the house!

I found my main builders to be proficient at concrete and brick work and acceptable at basic structural wood construction. However, they were clearly incapable of any work that required higher levels of skill and  **patience such as detailed carpentry, door hanging, wood finishing, etc. After numerous frustrations and wasted time and money, I decided it was better to hire specialists for certain jobs, such as the stair cases, handrails, balusters, counters and wood floors**.

The specialty builders I hired for electrical work and the marbles floors did very high quality work at a reasonable price. My bathroom is absolutely spectacular!

I cannot say how typical my case is for builders in Thailand but I suspect my building team was fairly average for Thailand. I expect there are better and I'm sure there are worse builders.

There are two main lessons I have learned: 1) you cannot expect the jack-of-all-trades general builder to do a good job on everything. My recommendation is, check your builder can do a good job, not only the basic construction, but other specialty areas such as plumbing, electrical, floors, detail and finish carpentry. If in any doubt, hire specialists with a good reputation in their field. 2) Thai builders have almost no concept of the aesthetics of the structural part of the building. They will make no attempt to make structural concrete and wood look attractive and when problems are brought to their attention, they always say "we'll fix it later". If the roof doesn't come crashing down, they are satisfied they have done a good job.

If you are a total perfectionist and will settle for nothing less than the highest quality, you probably shouldn't be living in Thailand! That said, I think it is possible to have a very high quality house built, but in my opinion, you could not build it at a fixed price. Any builder, no matter what he says or charges, is always going to want to cut some corners to get the job finished quicker and move on to the next project. If you truly want the highest quality job, I suggest you hire your own team that report directly to you and make it perfectly clear that you will accept nothing less than the highest quality and you are prepared to wait and pay for it, even if it means doing it over and over again.

There were many frustrations and a lot of hard work, but now I have a spectacular house for a building cost of about 2,500,000 baht, $US62,000. Before I moved to Thailand I lived in Palo Alto, California; you couldn't build a garage in Palo Alto for $62,000! I hope you have fun and success with your building project, be diligent, check everything and if things are not working out, don't be afraid to make changes.

Chohk dee, sa wat dee khrap สตีฟ

Index

Estimating the cost, 75

S

security system, 150, 204, 264
selling land, 22, 26, 63
share transfer documents, 14
Sit thi gap gin ta lord shee vit, 16, 17
Site preparation, 86
Slopes and retaining wall, 84
slow sand filter, 56
small land, 29, 45, 64
Sor Kor 1, 33
Sor. Por. Kor 4-01, 34
Squatters rights, 45
steel ties, 128, 132, 262
Storage, 87
structural damage, 84, 87
structural posts, 135
Structures Usage Tax, 68
survey errors, 35
survey methods, 48

T

Taxable value, 21
temporary electricity, 58, 246
Termites, 137
tha-biian baan, 79
Thai people married to foreigners, 20
Thai wife, 10, 30
Thor Tor 3, 29, 65, 66

tones, 3
Tools, 153, 154
transfer tax, 29, 46
transferable title, 28
transferring land, 21
Transferring money, 64, 66
transformer, 58

U

upgrading, 36, 45, 49
Upgrading titles, 49
Usufruct, 16
UV ozone filter, 57

V

village headsman, 33
voting rights, 13

W

Waa, 49
water quality, 56
Well water, 56, 61
when you die, 16
Wood floors, 140, 165, 255
work permit, 14, 50, 66, 81
worker accommodation, 87
Working on your own house, 81

Titles from Paiboon Publishing

Title: **Thai for Beginners**
Author: Benjawan Poomsan Becker ©1995
Description: Designed for either self-study or classroom use. Teaches all four language skills- speaking, listening (when used in conjunction with the cassette tapes), reading and writing. Offers clear, easy, step-by-step instruction building on what has been previously learned. Used by many Thai temples and institutes in America and Thailand. Cassettes & CD available. Paperback. 270 pages. 6" x 8.5"

Book	US$12.95	Stock # 1001B
Two CDs	US$20.00	Stock # 1001CD

Title: **Thai for Travelers** (Pocket Book Version)
Author: Benjawan Poomsan Becker ©2006
Description: The best Thai phrase book you can find. It contains thousands of useful words and phrases for travelers in many situations. The phrases are practical and up-to-date and can be used instantly. The CD that accompanies the book will help you improve your pronunciation and expedite your Thai language learning. You will be able to speak Thai in no time! Full version on mobile phones and PocketPC also available at www.vervata.com.
Book & CD   US$15.00   Stock # 1022BCD

Title: **Thai for Intermediate Learners**
Author: Benjawan Poomsan Becker ©1998
Description: The continuation of Thai for Beginners . Users are expected to be able to read basic Thai language. There is transliteration when new words are introduced. Teaches reading, writing and speaking at a higher level. Keeps students interested with cultural facts about Thailand. Helps expand your Thai vocabulary in a systematic way. Paperback. 220 pages. 6" x 8.5"

Book	US$12.95	Stock # 1002B
Two CDs	US$15.00	Stock # 1002CD

Title: **Thai for Advanced Readers**
Author: Benjawan Poomsan Becker ©2000
Description: A book that helps students practice reading Thai at an advanced level. It contains reading exercises, short essays, newspaper articles, cultural and historical facts about Thailand and miscellaneous information about the Thai language. Students need to be able to read basic Thai. Paperback. 210 pages. 6" x 8.5"

Book	US$12.95	Stock # 1003B
Two CDs	US$15.00	Stock # 1003CD

Title: **Thai-English, English-Thai Dictionary for Non-Thai Speakers**
Author: Benjawan Poomsan Becker ©2002
Description: Designed to help English speakers communicate in Thai. It is equally useful for those who can read the Thai alphabet and those who can't. Most Thai-English dictionaries either use Thai script exclusively for the Thai entries (making them difficult for westerners to use) or use only phonetic transliteration (making it impossible to look up a word in Thai script). This dictionary solves these problems. You will find most of the vocabulary you are likely to need in everyday life, including basic, cultural, political and scientific terms. Paperback. 658 pages. 4.1" x 5.6"
Book   US$15.00 Stock # 1008B

Title: **Improving Your Thai Pronunciation**
Author: Benjawan Poomsan Becker ©2003
Description: Designed to help foreingers maximize their potential in pronouncing Thai words and enhance their Thai listening and speaking skills. Students will find that they have more confidence in speaking the language and can make themselves understood better. The book and the CDs are made to be used in combination. The course is straight forward, easy to follow and compact. Paperback. 48 pages. 5" x 7.5" + One-hour CD
Book & CD   US$15.00 Stock # 1011BCD

Title: **Thai for Lovers**
Author: Nit & Jack Ajee ©1999
Description: An ideal book for lovers. A short cut to romantic communication in Thailand. There are useful sentences with their Thai translations throughout the book. You won't find any Thai language book more fun and user-friendly. Rated R!
Paperback. 190 pages. 6" x 8.5"
Book   US$13.95 Stock #: 1004B
Two CDs   US$17.00 Stock #: 1004CD

Title: **Thai for Gay Tourists**
Author: Saksit Pakdeesiam ©2001
Description: The ultimate language guide for gay and bisexual men visiting Thailand. Lots of gay oriented language, culture, commentaries and other information. Instant sentences for convenient use by gay visitors. Fun and sexy. The best way to communicate with your Thai gay friends and partners! Rated R!
Paperback. 220 pages. 6" x 8.5"
Book   US$13.95 Stock # 1007B
Two Tape Set   US$17.00 Stock # 1007T

Title: **Thailand Fever**
Authors: Chris Pirazzi and Vitida Vasant ©2005
Description: A road map for Thai-Western relationships. The must-have relationship guidebook which lets each of you finally express complex issues of both cultures. Thailand Fever is an astonishing, one-of-a-kind, bilingual expose of the cultural secrets that are the key to a smooth Thai-Western relationship. Paperback. 258 pages. 6" x 8.5"
Book   US$15.95 Stock # 1017B

Title: **Thai-English, English-Thai Software Dictionary for Palm OS PDAs With Search-by-Sound**
Authors: Benjawan Poomsan Becker and Chris Pirazzi ©2003
Description: This software dictionary provides instant access to 21,000 English, Phonetic and Thai Palm OS PDA with large, clear fonts and everyday vocabulary. If you're not familiar with the Thai alphabet, you can also look up Thai words by their sounds. Perfect for the casual traveller or the dedicated Thai learner. Must have a Palm OS PDA and access to the Internet in order to use this product.
Book & CD-ROM US$39.95 Stock # 1013BCD-ROM

Title: **Thai for Beginners Software**
Authors: Benjawan Poomsan Becker and Dominique Mayrand ©2004
Description: Best Thai language software available in the market! Designed especially for non-romanized written Thai to help you to rapidly improve your listening and reading skills! Over 3,000 recordings of both male and female voices. The content is similar to the book Thai for Beginners, but with interactive exercises and much more instantly useful words and phrases. Multiple easy-to-read font styles and sizes. Super-crisp enhanced text with romanized transliteration which can be turned on or off for all items.
Book & CD-ROM US$40.00 Stock # 1016BCD-ROM

Title: **Lao-English, English-Lao Dictionary for Non-Lao Speakers**
Authors: Benjawan Poomsan Becker & Khamphan Mingbuapha ©2003
Description: Designed to help English speakers communicate in Lao. This practical dictionary is useful both in Laos and in Northeast Thailand. Students can use it without having to learn the Lao alphabet. However, there is a comprehensive introduction to the Lao writing system and pronunciation. The transliteration system is the same as that used in Paiboon Publishing's other books. It contains most of the vocabulary used in everyday life, including basic, cultural, political and scientific terms. Paperback. 780 pages. 4.1" x 5.6"
Book   US$15.00 Stock # 1010B

Title: **Lao for Beginners**
Authors: Buasawan Simmala and Benjawan Poomsan Becker ©2003
Description: Designed for either self-study or classroom use. Teaches all four language skills- speaking, listening (when used in conjunction with the audio), reading and writing. Offers clear, easy, step-by-step instruction building on what has been previously learned. Paperback. 292 pages. 6" x 8.5"
Book   US$12.95 Stock # 1012B
Three CDs   US$20.00 Stock # 1012CD

Title: **Cambodian for Beginners**
Authors: Richard K. Gilbert and Sovandy Hang ©2004
Description: Designed for either self-study or classroom use. Teaches all four language skills- speaking, listening (when used in conjunction with the CDs), reading and writing. Offers clear, easy, step-by-step instruction building on what has been previously learned. Paperback. 290 pages. 6" x 8.5"
Book   US$12.95 Stock # 1015B
Three CDs   US$20.00 Stock # 1015CD

Title: **Burmese for Beginners**
Author: Gene Mesher ©2006
Description: Designed for either self-study or classroom use. Teaches all four language skills- speaking, listening (when used in conjunction with the CDs), reading and writing. Offers clear, easy, step-by-step instruction building on what has been previously learned. Paperback. 320 pages. 6" x 8.5"
Book   US$12.95 Stock # 1019B
Three CDs   US$20.00 Stock # 1019CD

Title: **Vietnamese for Beginners**
Authors: Jake Catlett and Huong Nguyen ©2006
Description: Designed for either self-study or classroom use. Teaches all four language skills- speaking, listening (when used in conjunction with the CDs), reading and writing. Offers clear, easy, step-by-step instruction building on what has been previously learned. Paperback. 292 pages. 6" x 8.5"
Book   US$12.95 Stock # 1020B
Three CDs   US$20.00 Stock # 1020CD

Title: **Tai Go No Kiso**
Author: Benjawan Poomsan Becker ©2002
Description: Thai for Japanese speakers. Japanese version of Thai for Beginners. Paperback. 262 pages. 6" x 8.5"
Book   US$12.95 Stock # 1009B
Three Tape Set   US$20.00 Stock # 1009T

Title: **Thai fuer Anfaenger**
Author: Benjawan Poomsan Becker ©2000
Description: Thai for German speakers. German version of Thai for Beginners. Paperback. 245 pages. 6" x 8.5"
Book   US$13.95   Stock # 1005B
Two CDs   US$20.00   Stock # 1005CD

Title: **Practical Thai Conversation DVD Volume 1**
Author: Benjawan Poomsan Becker ©2005
Description: This new media for learning Thai comes with a booklet and a DVD. You will enjoy watching and listening to this program and learn the Thai language in a way you have never done before. Use it on your TV, desktop or laptop. The course is straight forward, easy to follow and compact. A must-have for all Thai learners! DVD and Paperback, 65 pages 4.8" x 7.1"
Book & DVD   US$15.00   Stock # 1018BDVD

Title: **Practical Thai Conversation DVD Volume 2**
Author: Benjawan Poomsan Becker ©2006
Description: Designed for intermediate Thai learners! This new media for learning Thai comes with a booklet and a DVD. You will enjoy watching and listening to this program and learn the Thai language in a way you have never done before. Use it on your TV, desktop or laptop. The course is straight forward, easy to follow and compact. DVD and Paperback, 60 pages 4.8" x 7.1"
Book & DVD   US$15.00   Stock # 1021BDVD

Title: **A Chameleon's Tale - True Stories of a Global Refugee -**
Author: Mohezin Tejani ©2006
Description: A heart touching real life story of Mo Tejani, a global refugee who spends thirty four years searching five continents for a country he could call home. Enjoy the ride through numerous countries in Asia, Africa, North and South America. His adventurous stories are unique – distinctly different from other travelers' tales. Recommended item from Paiboon Publishing for avid readers worldwide. Paperback. 257 pages. 5" x 7.5"
Book   US$19.95   Stock #1024B

Title: **Thai Touch**
Author: Richard Rubacher ©2006
Description: The good and the bad of the Land of Smiles are told with a comic touch. The book focuses on the spiritual and mystical side of the magical kingdom as well as its dark side. The good and the bad are told with a comic touch. The Sex Baron, the Naughty & Nice Massage Parlors, the "Bangkok haircut" and Bar Girls & the Pendulum are contrasted with tales of the Thai Forrest Gump, the Spiritual Banker of Thailand and the 72-year old woman whose breasts spout miracle milk. Paperback. 220 pages. 5" x 7.5"
Book   US$19.95   Stock #1024B

Title: **How to Buy Land and Build a House in Thailand**
Author: Philip Bryce ©2006
Description: This book contains essential information for anyone contemplating buying or leasing land and building a house in Thailand. Subjects covered: land ownership options, land titles, taxes, permits, lawyers, architects and builders. Also includes English/Thai building words and phrases and common Thai building techniques. Learn how to build your dream house in Thailand that is well made, structurally sound and nicely finished. Paperback. 6" x 8.5"

Book   US$19.95   Stock #1025B

Title: **Retiring in Thailand**
Authors: Philip Bryce and Sunisa Wongdee Terlecky ©2006
Description: A very useful guide for those who are interested in retiring in Thailand. It contains critical information for retirees, such as how to get a retirement visa, banking, health care, renting and buying property, everyday life issues and other important retirement factors. It also lists Thailand's top retirement locations. It's a must for anyone considering living the good life in the Land of Smiles. 6" x 8.5"
Book   US$19.95   Stock #1026B

Title: **Speak Like A Thai Volume 1**
           -Contemporary Thai Expressions-
Author: Benjawan Poomsan Becker ©2007
Description: This series of books and CDs is a collection of numerous words and expressions used by modern Thai speakers. It will help you to understand colloquial Thai and to express yourself naturally. You will not find these phases in most textbooks. It's a language course that all Thai learners have been waiting for. Impress your Thai friends with the real spoken Thai. Lots of fun. Good for students of all levels.
Book & CD   US$15.00   Stock # 1028BCD

Title: **Speak Like A Thai Volume 2**
          -Thai Slang and Idioms-
Author: Benjawan Poomsan Becker ©2007
Description: This volume continues the fun of learning the real Thai language. It can be used independently. However, you should be comfortable speaking the Thai phrases from the first volume before you use this one. You will not find these words and phases in any textbooks. It's a language course that all Thai learners have been waiting for. Impress your Thai friends even more. Lots of fun. Good for students of all levels.
Book & CD   US$15.00   Stock # 1029BCD

Title: **Speak Like A Thai Volume 3**
          -Thai Proverbs and Sayings-
Author: Benjawan Poomsan Becker ©2007
Description: The third volume is an excellent supplementary resource for all Thai learners. Common Thai proverbs and sayings listed in the book with the literal translations will help you understand Thai ways of thinking that are differnt from yours. You can listen to these proverbs and sayings over and over on the CD. Sprinkle them here and there in your conversation. Your Thai friend will be surprised and appreciate your insight into Thai culture. Good for intermdiate and advanced students, but beginners can use it for reference.

Title: **How to Establish a Successful Business in Thailand**
Author: Philip Wylie ©2007
Description: This is the perfect book for anyone thinking of starting or buying a business in Thailand. This book will save readers lots of headaches, time and money. This guide is full of information on how to run a business in Thailand including practical tips by successful foreign business people from different trades, such as guest house, bar trade, e-commerce, export and restaurant. This is an essential guide for all foreigners thinking of doing business - or improving their business - in Thailand.